GENDER VIOLENCE, SOCIAL MEDIA, AND ONLINE ENVIRONMENTS

This book examines contexts, practices, and activism on issues of gender violence at the intersections of online and public spaces. Through individual case studies, the volume considers the interplay between the virtual worlds of online spaces including social media, physical spaces and bodies, and the ways in which offline and online dimensions of experience can serve as motivators for, extensions of, or limitations to each other.

Examining both problems and potential solutions, chapters explore the impacts of, and potential resistance to, the intersections of gender violence, social media, and our complex lived environments across national boundaries. Throughout the volume, close attention is paid to the difficult issues highlighted when prior conceptions of basic foundations such as public space, individual rights, and professional responsibility are confronted by new examples that further trouble the boundaries of long-held frameworks of legal, social, professional understanding, and even our comprehension of the "real." Each chapter grapples with a difficult reality related to gender violence, underscores possible ways forward, and highlights limitations, resisting easy answers to complex and persistent questions about rights, personal integrity, and social responsibility.

Offering clear insights into a critical issue, this book will be of interest to scholars and students in the areas of media studies, social media, gender and women's studies, sociology and criminology, digital humanities, and politics.

Lisa M. Cuklanz, PhD, is a Professor of Communication at Boston College. She has published several books and many other publications in the areas of media studies and gender studies. Her research interests center on violence in media.

Routledge Studies in Media, Communication, and Politics

https://www.routledge.com/Routledge-Studies-in-Media-Communication-and-Politics/book-series/RSMCP

GENDER VIOLENCE, SOCIAL MEDIA, AND ONLINE ENVIRONMENTS

When the Virtual Becomes Real

Edited by Lisa M. Cuklanz

R Routledge
Taylor & Francis Group

LONDON AND NEW YORK

Cover image: © Getty Images

First published 2023
by Routledge
4 Park Square, Milton Park, Abingdon, Oxon OX14 4RN

and by Routledge
605 Third Avenue, New York, NY 10158

Routledge is an imprint of the Taylor & Francis Group, an informa business

British Library Cataloguing-in-Publication Data
A catalogue record for this book is available from the British Library

Library of Congress Cataloging-in-Publication Data
Names: Cuklanz, Lisa M., editor.
Title: Gender violence, social media, and online environments : when the virtual becomes real / edited by Lisa M. Cuklanz.
Description: Milton Park, Abingdon, Oxon ; New York, NY : Routledge, 2023. | Includes bibliographical references and index.
Identifiers: LCCN 2022035712 (print) | LCCN 2022035713 (ebook) | ISBN 9781032186450 (hardback) | ISBN 9781032197913 (paperback) | ISBN 9781003260851 (ebook)
Subjects: LCSH: Women's studies. | Women—Violence against. | Violence in mass media. | Women in mass media. | Social media and society.
Classification: LCC HQ1180 .G4657 2023 (print) | LCC HQ1180 (ebook) | DDC 305.4—dc23/eng/20220812
LC record available at https://lccn.loc.gov/2022035712
LC ebook record available at https://lccn.loc.gov/2022035713

ISBN: 978-1-032-18645-0 (hbk)
ISBN: 978-1-032-19791-3 (pbk)
ISBN: 978-1-003-26085-1 (ebk)

DOI: 10.4324/9781003260851

Typeset in Bembo
by codeMantra

CONTENTS

CONTRIBUTORS

Claudia Alvares, PhD, is Associate Professor at the Sociology Department, ISCTE - Lisbon University Institute and researcher at the Centre for Research and Studies in Sociology (CIES) in Portugal. She is elected member of the Academy of Europe since 2020 and former president of ECREA (2012–2016). Her areas of expertise focus on Media and Gender Studies.

Benjamin Brojakowski, PhD, is an Assistant Professor in the Communication and Mass Media Department at Angelo State University. He teaches a variety of undergraduate and graduate courses and conducts research related to sports communication, pop culture & computer-mediated communication.

Victoria Carty, PhD, is a Professor of Sociology at Chapman University. She has written dozens of articles and two books on how new information technologies impact emerging social movements. She has also published three books on immigration on the southern border of the United States.

Gabriel A. Cruz, PhD, Bowling Green State University, is an Assistant Professor of Media Studies at North Carolina Central University in Durham, NC. His research in critical media studies focuses on pop culture and white nationalism. His work has appeared in academic periodicals such as *Howard Journal of Communications*; and the book *Expression in Contested Public Spaces: Free Speech and Civic Engagement*.

Lisa M. Cuklanz, PhD, is a Professor of Communication at Boston College. She has published several books and many other publications in the areas of media studies and gender studies. Her research interests center on violence in media.

Julietta Hua, PhD, is a Professor of Women and Gender Studies at San Francisco State University in the United States. In addition to *Spent Behind the Wheel* (co-authored with Kasturi Ray), she is the author of *Trafficking Women's Human Rights* (Minnesota 2011). She works on migration, labor, and race.

Estibaliz Linares Bahillo, PhD, Faculty of Social & Human Sciences, University of Deusto, Bilbao, Spain served as a Basque Government predoctoral fellow from 2014 to 2017. She combines academic work, teaching, and coeducation workshops. Her research focuses on adolescence, technologies, violence prevention, and coeducation.

Alyssa Glace Maryn, PhD, is a Postdoctoral Associate at the University of Calgary in Canada. She researches sexual consent, masculinities, and gender-based violence prevention. She is also interested in the way that these topics are discussed online on social media, such as among involuntary celibates or Incels.

Gavaza Maluleke, PhD, is a Lecturer in the Department of Political Studies at the University of Cape Town in South Africa. Her research interests are in digital activism, transnational feminisms, migration, gendered violence, masculinities, and media studies in Africa. Her current work focuses on digital activism and gendered violence in Post-Apartheid South Africa.

Dr. Soumen Mukherjee, PhD, is presently an Associate Professor of English at a technological university in South India. His research interests are in subaltern literature, cultural readings, sexuality studies, and strategic communication. He is the recipient of the BESIG-IATEFL Scholarship in 2007, from IATEFL, Kent, UK for his pioneering research on Chronemics.

Paromita Pain, PhD, has published research in refereed journals including *Journalism and Mass Communication Educator, Journalism Studies, Journalism Practice, Media Asia* and *Feminist Media Studies.* As an Assistant Professor of Global Media Studies at the Reynolds School of Journalism, University of Nevada, Reno in the United States, she explores emerging newsroom practices and concerns in a global context.

Candace Parrish, PhD, is an Assistant Professor of Public Relations at Pennsylvania State University. Candace spearheaded the development of the first VR-enhanced SCPR Online Master's Program at Sacred Heart University. She has gained national & international recognition for her research regarding visuals used in public relations and health communication.

Kristin M. Peterson, PhD, is an Assistant Professor in the Communication Department at Boston College in the United States. Her research focuses on religious expression in digital media, and she is the author of *Unruly Souls: The Digital Activism of Muslim and Christian Feminists* (Rutgers University Press, 2022).

Raquel Royo Prieto, PhD, Humanities & Social Sciences Faculty, Univ. of Deusto, Bilbao, Spain is Director of the Master in Intervention in Violence against Women. She teaches courses in the fields of gender studies, sociology, psychology, and community social work and is the author of numerous publications.

Leslie Ramos Salazar, PhD, is Associate and Abdullat Professor at the Paul and Virginia College of Business at West Texas A&M University specializing in interpersonal health communication. She edited the *Handbook of Research on Cyberbullying and Online Harassment in the Workplace* and is the editor-in-chief of *Sage Business Communication Foundations.*

Kasturi Ray, PhD, is an Associate Professor of Women and Gender Studies at San Francisco State University in the United States. She writes on issues of gender and labor. Her most recent publication, coauthored with Julietta Hua, is *Spent Behind the Wheel: Drivers' Labor in the Uber Economy* (Minnesota 2021).

Tremayne Robertson, PhD candidate at Syracuse University, is Director of Diversity, Equity, and Inclusion at the Massey Cancer Center at Virginia Commonwealth University. He has previously served as dean of students at the University of Virginia.

Avina Ross, PhD, has served as the first sexual assault prevention specialist at Mary Washington University, and as Associate Director of the Sexual Harassment, Assault Advising, Resources and Education (SHARE) office at Princeton University.

Maria Silvestre Cabrera, PhD, Faculty of Social and Human Sciences, University of Deusto, Bilbao, Spain, has been Dean of the Faculty of CCPP & Sociology, and Director of the Master in Intervention in Violence against Women. Her research interests and publications focus on political–social values and gender perspectives in the social sciences.

Rowena Briones Winkler, PhD, is a women's authenticity coach, marketing professional, higher education consultant, and instructor who develops and teaches courses in strategic communication and writing.

PART I
Contexts

1

INTRODUCTION

Lisa M. Cuklanz

Gender Violence, Social Media, and Online Environments: When the Virtual Becomes Real takes up a set of critical questions and case studies that highlight the varied relationships between online environments, lived experiences, and forms of abuse in online and social media environments that have been well documented. Multidisciplinary in scope, it draws on scholarship in communication, media studies, gender studies, rhetoric, psychology, computing, sociology, and many other fields to develop several key themes from prior scholarship on the many uses of social media and online environments to both perpetrate and challenge abuse based on gender. This introduction traces key areas of research in a rapidly developing field of study that examines gendered violence in online and other virtual environments, the experiences of those who are targeted by these harmful activities, and the potential of legal and other solutions. This chapter provides an overview of the main areas of study as well as key contributors to this important emergent field.

The field of scholarship focused broadly on gendered violence in online environments can effectively be understood as taking up three main areas of inquiry, with some works including discussions of more than one of these three central themes. The first of these examines issues related to defining and delimiting gender violence within online environments, most often understanding online hate to be expression of the historical phenomenon of misogyny that has been extended and often exacerbated through online platforms, and including abuses that are targeted at individuals for their gender, sexuality, gender identity, or gender expression. From these environments have emerged techniques that employ technologies to engage in various acts of gender violence through a range of increasingly complex means, often utilizing multiple platforms as well as physical threats, and causing psychological, financial, relational, physical, and

DOI: 10.4324/9781003260851-2

other harms to targets. The second major area of scholarship in this area focuses on the ways in which Information and Communication Technologies (ICTs) have been used to create and facilitate challenges to online gender violence, including the use of social media platforms such as Twitter to support the creation or growth of online and hybrid resistance movements. The third key focus of the study has been on efforts at creating legal and policy remedies to the issues presented by online gender violence. Much of this work has necessarily focused on the limitations and failures of such approaches to mitigate harms or to provide justice to victims and targets. The chapters that follow in this volume take up many of the key foci of work in these three main areas, providing discussions of contexts for understanding broad issues faced in examining gender violence in social media and online environments, and providing case studies of individual instances of online gender abuse, experiences of and resistances to it, and limitations of current frameworks for understanding and preventing it. These chapters point to the varied and complex ways in which online and offline environments interact and share increasingly blurred boundaries regarding the commission of abuse, a target's experience of it, and policies and programs designed to combat it.

This volume aims to provide detailed considerations of the ways in which online gender abuses are influencing our understanding of basic elements of life such as our sense of public and private, the common good, reasonable work expectations, and even concepts of self-determination, autonomy, and identity. Through case studies based in a range of platforms, national and geographic locations, and modes of communication, the studies in this volume explore a range of abuses as well as approaches to combatting related harms. A number of extant works point to the trend of blurred boundaries between online behaviors and lived, embodied experiences of harmful targeting of individuals on the basis of gender, often in relation to multiple aspects of subjectivity including sexual identity, race or ethnicity, or political affiliation. As Poland notes, "[t]he continued and rapid erasure of the lines between online and offline activities makes it impossible to fully separate online and offline harassment" (3). In their volume *Online Othering: Exploring Digital Violence and Discrimination on the Web*, Lumsden and Harmer take a broad view of the various forms of hate, noting in their first chapter that some of their analyses emphasize ways in which online environments can contribute to intensified experiences of crimes that can also be perpetrated offline (2019). Lumsden and Harmer emphasize the need to move beyond the old dichotomies between "real" world and "virtual" world, and instead "acknowledge the interconnected and fluid nature of our use of ICTs" (22). Their analyses also treat motivations and effects of online abuse on its targets. The concept of continuity is also employed to focus on similarities and differences between targeted behaviors taking place across virtual and real-world contexts. The chapters that follow in *Gender Violence, Social Media, and Online Environments* provide further evidence of this fluid and connected interplay in which any sense of two different realms of virtual and real is increasingly difficult to sustain. The subtitle of this volume, *When the Virtual Becomes Real*, underscores an emphasis on the multifaceted interplay among environments that have become increasingly difficult to delineate.

Overview of Literature

As noted, the field of scholarship on gender violence in social media and online environments is rapidly developing, and has so far focused on three primary areas of research. Several important recent works take up the central notion of gendered violence online as simply the expression of the very familiar cultural phenomenon of misogyny, expanded in virtual environments with enhanced proliferation facilitated by social media and online platforms. These works show how, while the means of expression may be new, the harmful gender-based content is not. Ging and Siapera (2019) show how online expressions of gender hate and abuse are best understood as extensions of misogyny already existing in the wider historical culture. They offer a useful analysis of the convergence and interplay between misogyny and anti-feminism as well, and argue that we are at a crisis point in terms of the proliferation of the use of these forms of abuse that requires immediate attention. Works focusing on the concept of extending misogyny use a range of terminology to label and define various forms of gender hate in online environments, often noting that forms of abuse based on gender, gender identity, and gender expression have been persistent, vitriolic, and widespread. Often, these works also warn that the diffusion of misogyny online will most likely continue to worsen rather than responding meaningfully to what so far seem to be quite insufficient efforts at mitigation.

Misogyny is a useful concept for understanding the pervasiveness and particular intensity of online gender abuse. Mantilla's *Gendertrolling: How Misogyny Went Viral* (2015) provides an important explication of specific distinctions between generic trolling and what she labels as "gendertrolling." Mantilla offers a clear explanation of the difference in character between trolling and this phenomenon she calls "gendertrolling," noting that while trolls are usually not particularly engaged with the beliefs they espouse and can often be understood as engaging in a form of entertainment through the act of trolling, "gendertrolling is exponentially more vicious, virulent, aggressive, threatening, pervasive, and enduring" than generic trolling (p. 11). This is in part because gendertrolls often persuade others to participate in the abuse, enlisting the help of many to sexualize and objectify the target, typically across multiple platforms. Poland (2016) emphasizes that many of these abusive behaviors are aimed at delimiting who can participate as a legitimate member of an online community or space, often with the goal of driving the target offline. Thus, another familiar aspect of gender bias, hostility toward women's engagement in the public sphere, is also effectively carried over into online environments. The goal of these concerted efforts is to silence the target or drive them out of the conversation entirely. There are numerous well-publicized examples of successful efforts of this type, perhaps most notably the campaign to push Lindy West off of Twitter in 2017 (see Vickery & Everbach, 2018).

The gender hatred so frequently expressed in online environments has made these spaces inhospitable to women, even as participation in them can often be a professional requirement, as in the case of journalists. Female journalists in many countries have been targeted with misogynist abuse in the normal course of online engagement with their readers, and have had to develop strategies to combat the abuse (Masullo Chen et al., 2020). Masullo Chen et al. found that "harassment disrupts the routinized practice of reciprocal journalism" (p. 877). Members of marginalized groups including women of color have been targeted with particularly vitriolic and persistent forms of online abuse that reiterate negative stereotypes (Francisco & Felmlee, 2022). Noble and Tynes (2016) more generally argue the need for an intersectional approach to the study of online culture.

Gender-based abuses including cyberstalking, the "relentless pursuit of a targeted person online" (Mantilla p. 13), cyberharassment, cyberbullying, revenge porn (online publication of intimate images of the target taken and/or distributed without their consent), doxxing (distributing personal information and/or documents online, inviting others to use the information against the target), and gendertrolling. As Mantilla notes, motives for these abusive and violent behaviors usually include "revenge against, anger at, or obsession with the target" (p. 13). For Poland, "cybersexism often has a goal of creating, enforcing, and normalizing male dominance in online spaces" (3). "Cybersexism refers to bullying, doxxing, and other behaviors that make online spaces uncomfortable, unpleasant, and unsafe for women" (3). While these terms target specific types of online abuses, some authors have proposed a range of terminology aimed at capturing a multiplicity of abusive online behaviors. Powell and Henry (2017) suggest the phrase "technology-facilitated sexual violence" (4) as an umbrella concept to encompass all of these diverse forms, while in *Misogyny Online: A Short (and British) History*, Emma A. Jane coins the term "e-bile" as a general label for verbal hatred expressed online (2017). Powell and Henry also suggest the term "harms" to capture physical, social, psychological, financial, or other consequences to targets/victims. This concept is helpful in pointing to the varied ways in which targets can experience negative consequences from online or "technology-facilitated" abuse. Gender violence has importantly been understood as targeting individuals for their gender, gender expression, and/or sexual or gender identity. For instance, Powell and Henry emphasize that gender violence refers not only to violence against women and girls, but more generally to patterns of abuse that may be gendered in a number of ways, such as the targeting of gay men or transgender individuals based on reactions to their gender expression.

Although researchers have demonstrated that gender violence has thrived in rapidly proliferated and intensified form in social media and online environments, these platforms have also provided opportunities for healing through the sharing of personal narratives, and for resistance movements to raise awareness of issues related to gender violence in efforts to combat both online and offline abuse. Thus, the second area of research focus in recent works points in the direction of how resistance movements, individuals, and groups have deployed some of the same technologies and platforms in which abusive behaviors have become problematic, in order to push back, resist, and call out problematic actions and words. Several authors have examined the use of Twitter to resist and challenge both online and offline gender abuse (see Masullo Chen et al., 2018; Mendes et al., 2018; Mendes et al., 2019). In their studies of #BeenRapedNeverReported and other hashtags, Mendes, Ringrose, and Keller document through interviews the flood of "carefully produced testimonials that were scaffolded after sleepless nights" (2018, p. 3). Their work documents the important role played by Twitter in the sharing of personal narratives about sexual abuse and "the significant support… received from tweeting about their assaults" (2018, p. 4). Twitter and other online spaces offer a way for victims and survivors to share their own stories and receive support from others who have had similar experiences. Bailey's (2021) work examines a range of strategies used by Black women and allies to combat what she calls the "misogynoir," or specifically racist misogyny, through the use of digital platforms including Youtube and Tumblr to create alternative discourses, form networking alliances, and critique mainstream practices of racist and sexist attacks.

While digital platforms have served as spaces for the effective "coming out" as victims and survivors of sexual assault (Regehr & Ringrose, 2018, p. 255), such platforms have further offered opportunities for the development of movements against various forms of hate including misogyny. Sarah Jackson, Moia Bailey, and Brooke Foucault Welles examine the potential of Twitter to serve as a platform for the development of movements against hate in their book *#HashtagActivism: Networks of Race and Gender Justice*. Their chapter "Women Tweet on Violence: From #YesAllWomen to #MeToo," examines specific hashtag movements that "highlight women's experiences with interpersonal and institutionally enabled violence… precipitated by high-profile events involving male perpetrators" (2020, p. 1). The authors emphasize how their case studies "illustrate how storytelling on Twitter raises consciousness, creates solidarity, promulgates new cultural narratives, and articulates demands for change" (p. 27). Hashtag feminism has become an important form of social organizing around issues of gender justice (Dixon, 2014) and has also been the focus of research specifically about Black women's resistance to racist violence (Williams, 2015). While hashtag activism is perhaps the form of digital activism with the most widespread reputation for success, scholars have focused on many other forms of resistance in online environments. Vickery and Everbach offer a collection of case studies focusing on "Feminist Resistance," including the use of personal narratives and the important example of the anti-street harassment movement. Other examples include Brightwells examination of the use of Tinder to respond to online harassment (2019), and Lokot's study of resistance on Russian internet (RuNet).

Solutions to diminish these behaviors, mitigate the harms to targets, and provide sanctions to perpetrators lag far behind the proliferation of online gender-based abuse. Thus, a third central area of research focuses on the limitations to legal and other solutions, particularly those based on the idea of hate speech, as largely ineffective in addressing the question of harms or effects on those at the receiving end of the abusive behavior. Poland analyzes a range of available approaches to mitigating online abuses within specific platforms and environments, such as blocking specific individuals, reporting abusive behavior, and pursuing legal action under existing laws (2016). She emphasizes the importance of both individual and collective action. Although her work offers some hope that legal approaches can be effective in limited instances, several other recent works highlight the limitations of current laws. Citron's *Hate Crimes in Cyberspace* (2014) is an important early contributor to this conversation, raising questions about free speech, harassment legislation and its impacts on online culture, and highlighting some of the blind spots in legal approaches to providing justice for victims. Citron highlights the multifaceted challenges of regulating online abuses, and emphasizes the need to provide justice to targets and possibilities for holding not only harassers but also social networking sites and internet service providers accountable for harassing behavior they facilitate.

Numerous works provide case studies as well as general discussions of the ineffectiveness of legal remedies to online abuse. Barker and Jurasz (2019) examine limitations of a hate speech approach when dealing with abusive textual behaviors on Twitter. Similarly, Powell and Henry (2017) argue that legal approaches in general, are not well-suited to address the aspect of harms suffered by targets of abuse and they consider possibilities for informal forms of justice to supplement legal efforts. Amundsen examines UK legal approaches to revenge porn, arguing that the law is ineffective due to an emphasis on individual intent rather than on "social attitudes towards depictions of female sexuality and bodies" (2019, p. 144). Jane (2017) also argues that hate speech approaches are largely ineffective in providing relief and justice to targets of online abuse, since they focus on punishment rather than prevention. In general, legal and policy remedies come as "too little, too late" when harms to targets have already been done and when breaches of privacy can no longer be undone.

Historical Origins in Mainstream Media and Culture

Several aspects of our cultural history and contemporary social environment provide the elements that foster the spread of gender hate online. The roots of this phenomenon reach back far earlier than the advent of online communication, and include a tendency to doubt women's word regarding their own experiences. Victims and survivors of abuse have similarly sought means of making their voices heard as they have described their experiences of sexual assault in the public sphere. As early as the 1960s, victim advocate groups were organizing speak-outs at which victims of rape and other sexual abuse could tell their stories and denounce cultural ambivalence to their experiences of harm and trauma. One of the first discoveries of these early second-wave events, along with the related consciousness-raising groups started during the same period, was the similarity in experiences among victims of sexual assault. These survivors reported that they had been generally disbelieved all along the way as they told their story of assault to police, attorneys, family members, and others. Importantly, cultural and legal bias against rape claimants meant that victims were often treated with skepticism and their cases were not pursued. Special jury instructions, based in British common law and retained in the US judicial system until the 1960s, cautioned jurors that claimants of rape tended to be untruthful (Cuklanz, 1996). In the early 1970s, in order to address the inadequacy of state responses to sexual assault, an organized rape law reform movement successfully advocated for legal changes that would aim toward improving conviction rates by providing for the possibility (if still not the expectation) of truthfulness on the part of the claimant. Both the tendency to discount women's experiences and the victim's effort to be heard are elements carried forward from the past into the contemporary social media and online environments.

The pervasive distrust of women's word is taken up in Leigh Gilmore's *Tainted Witness: Why we Doubt What Women Say About Their Lives* (2017). Gilmore examines what she sees as a pervasive distrust of women's words as a form of misogyny. Gilmore and many others have also pointed out the costs that often accrue to women who speak up about their experiences of sexual abuse. Women who come forward with accusations of sexual abuse are often placed under further scrutiny rather than understood as survivors of trauma. A notable historical example is the victim of the Big Dan's rape case, which became the subject of the film *The Accused*. The real-life victim was targeted with death threats and forced to flee her home state. The experience of meeting with skepticism, doubt, and disbelief is taken up in the recent Netflix miniseries *Unbelievable*, based on the true story of a rape victim who herself became the target of a police investigation after reporting her rape, while her rapist escaped detection. These high-profile media treatments provide well-known illustrative examples of the phenomenon of disbelief of rape claimants.

The phenomenon of disbelief has been understood as so common that it has fostered the notion of a "second rape" of victims who come forward to tell about their experiences and are met with sufficient doubt to effectively force them to re-live their trauma through repeated hostile interrogation. While certain media genres, notably detective fiction, have emphasized the importance of victims coming forward and pressing charges, a pattern of painful re-traumatization and even additional bullying and harassment has historically served to silence many who have experienced sexual abuse. Rape and assault prevention programs have typically focused on behaviors that women and girls can develop in order to avoid being victimized. Such programs have come under criticism for their focus on changing behaviors of potential targets of abuse rather than trying to create a culture that focuses on perpetrators and is less tolerant of rape, sexual assault and sexual harassment. Recent scholarship illustrates how the same tendency to disbelieve and blame victims and place the burden of prevention on them has carried over into the realm of cybercrimes (Black et al., 2019). This pattern, when repeated in online environments, can have devastating effects on those who try to speak out against abuse. The speed and magnitude of online efforts to intimidate and drive individuals offline exacerbate a set of problems already well-established.

The failure to grant credibility to victim's word is just one aspect of rape culture that has helped to foster an environment in which online abuses proliferate easily and rapidly. Patterns of media representations of sexual assault and other forms of gendered violence have been established long before the advent of online forms of communication, and these patterns also serve to construct understandings of these behaviors that we see reproduced in online platforms. Not only have mainstream entertainment media including film and television tended to portray gendered violence in specific ways, but even news coverage of instances of criminal conduct evinces problematic patterns that tend to doubt and blame victims, exonerate perpetrators, limit attention to the harms that result from these crimes, and minimize the voices of victims and survivors (Benedict, 1992). Accompanying the tendency to doubt the claims of those who speak about traumatic sexual abuse and harassment is the notion that those targeted for abuse are somehow to blame for their own victimization. In general, our social environment is one in which many victims are held accountable or blamed for their own abuse, and victims have routinely been asked what they were wearing, whether they were drinking or partying, or what sort of reputation they have in terms of sexual relationships. The familiar idea that engaging in a range of behaviors such as wearing a certain style of clothing, consuming alcohol, or doing drugs means that someone is "asking for" abuse has been pervasive in our mainstream culture for many decades (Grubb & Turner, 2012). Not surprisingly, these biases are also found in online environments (Stubbs-Richardson et al., 2018). Similarly, certain categories of person are considered less sympathetic victims than others. Sex workers, persons of color, and women who have had many sexual partners have been seen as lesser individuals in terms of legal protections against sexual abuse. Differential rates of conviction based on the race of the perpetrator and race of victim have been demonstrated in LaFree's important work (1980), which showed that conviction rates and sentences were highest for Black perpetrators with white victims, and lowest for white perpetrators assaulting Black victims. Clearly, many of these elements have carried forward into contemporary social media and online environments, where Black women are often labeled with terms emphasizing promiscuity (Francisco & Felmlee, 2022).

One of the correlated elements of a belief system in which victims of sexual crimes can be told that their own clothing or choice to frequent a bar at night were responsible for the crime committed against them has been the tendency to focus on the identity and reputation of the accused. While rape was long considered a particularly heinous crime, there was an accompanying and persistent belief that only the most marginal, mentally ill, or violent of individuals would commit such a crime. In spite of this belief in the horrible nature of the crime, conviction rates for rape remained abysmally low. The death penalty was allowed in cases of rape in the United States until the Supreme Court eliminated this sentencing option in Coker v. Georgia (1977). Feminists, along with many others, supported the elimination of the death penalty, arguing that the possibility of such a severe penalty contributed to a pattern of jury reluctance to convict in cases of rape. Other efforts focused on rape law reform throughout the 1970s resulted in a graduated understanding of offenses, the removal of special instructions to the jury, and the elimination of evidence related to the alleged victim's sexual history. These changes took place at the state level, with many states also adopting reformed laws on marital rape by the late 1970s (Goldberg-Ambrose, 1992). Rape law reform measures have been advanced in many nations. Frank et al. examined reform laws in 40 countries taking place between 1945 and 2005 (2009).

As ideas about the crime of rape shifted, with the elimination of the death penalty for rape, and the introduction of graded sexual assault crimes, the idea that seemingly normal persons could also commit rape gained attention, although this shift took pace much more gradually and slowly, experiencing significant public resistance. Having once been understood as one of the most heinous crimes that could be perpetrated only by deranged or marginalized individuals, rape and sexual assault continue to carry a stigma that the public found difficult to attach to seemingly normal citizens. This tendency is particularly pronounced in celebrity cases, where the potential loss of reputation and income to the accused becomes a principal topic of discussion. Perpetrators such as Harvey Weinstein, Matt Lauer, and Bill Cosby were able to successfully shield themselves from prosecution for some time, often for decades, before a sufficient number of their victims emerged to establish a pattern of repeated abuse of multiple individuals. We are now in a position to take the long view back in history in an effort to comprehend how serial perpetrators such as Larry Nassar and Jerry Sandusky were able to abuse dozens of victims. It is clear that a tendency to disbelieve victims and protect perpetrators from negative effects of seeing the truth about their actions have been supporting elements in this structure of belief. Some shifts in these persistent patterns of understanding sexual assault have been noted, particularly since the advent of #MeToo movements. Fileborn and Loney-Howes address the importance of #MeToo in its ability to reframe dominant understandings of sexual assault, at least to some degree, and place this accomplishment in the context of feminist history (2019). The diffusion of the #MeToo movement has been studied across national borders and in nations including China (Lin & Yang, 2019), South Africa (Shefer & Hussen, 2020), and numerous others (Chandra & Erlingsdóttir, 2020). In spite of these advances, other work emphasizes the ongoing need for further development in our understanding of, and reporting on, powerful people who engage in sexual abuse and harassment (Cuklanz, 2020). Boyle's recent book on this subject assesses media narratives about #MeToo movements, critiquing their tendency to protect and defend the accused, particularly those who are celebrities (2019). This pattern of focusing on harms to the accused rather than to targets, victims, and survivors has persisted into the contemporary realms of social media and online communications, and contributes to an international context of ineffective laws and weak institutional responses to online abuses. Harms that accrue primarily to women can too easily be understood as individual in nature rather than as part of a pattern of cultural biases and values, and can even lead to speculation that the target is in some way to blame.

Chapter Previews

Gender Violence, Social Media, and Online Environments: When the Virtual Becomes Real is informed by the rapidly expanding field of study examining gender abuses online and in social media. It takes up the well-established challenges of cultural misogyny in relation to ideas about gender, sexual assault and harassment as they intersect with, and are augmented through online environments. The chapters in this book take up difficult questions about the ways in which online and other technology-based systems of communication and representation interact with the embodied experiences of those who are the targets of gendered violence. The volume is organized into three thematic sections, with each section taking up a complex nexus of themes related to consent, marginalization, globalization, gender, race, religion, class, and national context.

The first section, "Contexts," starting with this introduction, provides discussions of significant loci of debate around topics of online gender abuses. Chapter 2, "From street to screen: on the right to public space in the age of algorithms," by Claudia Alvares examines a highly publicized case in Portuguese media in 2017. Taking place during *Queima das Fitas*, or Ribbon Burning, celebrated by graduating university students, a nonconsensual video of the sexual assault of a young woman was disseminated on social media and later also through the mainstream media outlet *Correio da Manhã*. The chapter shows how current Portuguese law did not provide adequate privacy protection for the victim, who decided not to make a formal complaint because of her fear that this would only make the case more well-known and the video more highly circulated and attached to her name, thus ultimately further invading her privacy. Alvares argues that *Correio da Manhã*'s claim about the importance of the public's right to know and be outraged against the crime must be weighed against the victim's right to privacy. The chapter highlights several contexts of the shifting definitions of public and private spheres, as well as the limitations of Portuguese media and law as seen through the lens of the case. Chapter 3, "Scrutinizing sexual persecution in digital communication through the field of haptics," by Soumen Mukherjee and Leslie Ramos Salazar examines sexual harassment through haptic communication, considering a broad range of harassing and abusive behaviors that encompass physical touch and virtual touch across virtual and physical contexts of social interaction. The chapter considers examples and effects on targets of this unwanted behavior, as well as strategies for resistance and ideas for future research in this rapidly evolving area of study. The chapter highlights the blurred boundaries and multifaceted interplay between physical and virtual environments and experiences.

The volume's second section, *Practices*, includes case studies illustrating the practice of gender abuse through communication technologies as well as a range of harms associated with them. Chapter 4, "Female corporealities of blame & invasion in cases of sexual & sexist cyberbullying in the Basque region," by Estibaliz Linares Bahillo, Maria Silvestre Cabrera, and Raquel Royo Prieto assesses experiences and impacts of cyberbullying and harassment on teen girls. The authors conducted focus groups with teenage girls and their mothers in the Basque region of Spain. Examining the experiences and beliefs of the girls and their mothers, the authors find that, while cyberbullying is quite common among the participant teens, only a few mothers and girls hold bullies more responsible than the targeted girls themselves, particularly if girls can be understood as participants who initially sent explicit photos to a boy. The authors also explore the many embodied effects of bullying on the girls in their study. The chapter places the discussion of the focus group findings in the context of patriarchal cultural beliefs that create asymmetrical power relationships for teen girls in online spaces and provide limited means of resistance on the part of girls and their mothers. While Chapter 4 assesses cyberbullying and its effects on teen girls, Chapter 5, "Busting trolls: examining the hate campaign against actress Leslie Jones," by Benjamin Brojakowski and Gabriel Cruz employs Critical Discourse Analysis to assess a specific case study of the campaign of hate directed against a celebrity on Twitter. Although she also had supporters on the platform, Jones was driven off of Twitter by the campaign of hate against her. Brojakowski and Cruz examine tweets that criticized Jones as well as those that supported her, finding that both critics and supporters shared some important characteristics facilitated by social media environments. In particular, both supporters and critics displayed a sense of familiarity with Jones that was expressed through expressions of equality and superiority in relation to her. Brojakowski and Cruz highlight the significance of the intersectionality of race and gender in the case, documenting the use of racism and misogyny as well as justifications of such abuse in the hate campaign against Jones. In Chapters 4 and 5, the authors make clear how the broader cultural environment contributes to the perpetration of online abuse, as well as how such abuse results in specific harms experienced by those targeted.

Chapter 6, "Drivers against the machine: reproductive labor and reproductive justice in a phantom public," by Kasturi Ray and Julietta Hua takes a very different approach to the physical experiences of gender violence facilitated by communication technologies, exploring the boundaries of conceptualizations of reproductive labor and gender violence. The chapter examines the embodied experiences of ride hail drivers, the majority of whom are male, as they perform what Ray and Hua understand as the reproductive labor of gig driving.

Ray and Hua show how, in this case, gendered violence against the mostly-male drivers is masked by the ride-hail companies' efforts to construe their services as safe for female riders. By focusing on the protection of the supposed feminine vulnerability of riders as their mission, these companies are able to hide the abuse of drivers that they commit through wage theft, unfair labor practices, and refusal to treat drivers as employees. Ray and Hua argue that examining this situation through a feminist lens requires an understanding of the physical depletion of the drivers through reliance on gender stereotypes wielded by corporate power interests. Chapter 7, "'Suddenly we were the story': women journalists, the #MeToo movement, and online misogyny in India," by Paromita Pain also assesses the abuse of workers in the course of performing duties related to their employment. The chapter provides a study of harassment and resistance of women journalists in India, and the general failure of employers to shield or defend the journalists against harm. Pain analyzes interviews with women journalists who covered the #MeToo movement in India, documenting online abuse experienced by these journalists, and focusing particularly on the role played by the requirement of online presence as an integral expectation of doing journalism in India. The chapter documents several strategies employed by the women journalists interviewed as they struggle to combat the abuse in institutional contexts where their experiences are not taken seriously and there is little institutional response. Ultimately, online abuse had measurable impacts on the way the journalists performed their jobs, as some of the journalists noted that their experience of online abuse affected their choice of which stories to post in online environments. Nonetheless, the journalists remained committed to the idea of their professional responsibility to engage with the public.

The final section, Activism, includes four chapters focused on efforts to combat, challenge, and resist online and offline abuse through the use of social media and online tools. Similar to Ray and Hua's analysis, Chapter 8, "#RhodesWar: contesting institutional silencing in the struggle against rape in post-apartheid South Africa," by Gavaza Maluleke examines the exercise of power by an institution over individuals, in the case of Rhodes University's expulsion of students who protested the school's weak response to rape on campus. However, in this case, the individuals were able to prevail to some degree over the institution, in part thanks to the use of Twitter to resist the university's account of events. The chapter provides an analysis of #RhodesWar following protests against unfair treatment of women who had been protesting the lenient treatment of rape at Rhodes University. Maluleke emphasizes elements of history and context in post-Apartheid South Africa, arguing that the hashtag prevented the university from controlling the narrative in its dispute with, and expulsion of, feminist anti-rape activists. The chapter shows how the politics of respectability intersects with the representation of Black feminist activists in this case, and illustrates the importance of writing in combination with rioting in this context. The case analysis illustrates how the acceptable parameters of public rape narratives in South Africa have shifted away from victims asking to be believed, and can now be presented as a matter of fact, and offers an example of the effectiveness of combining street action (rioting) with social media visibility.

The use of social media to provide a public voice and create counter-narratives is also a focus of Kristin M. Peterson's Chapter 9, "Rectifying gender violence within religious communities through hashtag activism." Peterson examines the #MosqueMeToo and #ChurchToo Twitter hashtags, showing how members of specific religious communities have been able to express their own experiences as well as provide a critique of sexism and victim-blaming attitudes within these Evangelical and Muslim communities. More importantly, Peterson's chapter shows that through these hashtags, individuals who have experienced gendered violence within these religious communities also call out the ways in which religious texts and teachings have been used to further shield perpetrators within these religious organizations, often further placing blame on victims. The hashtags have enabled these individuals to respond meaningfully by speaking about their own experiences and even at times by utilizing religious teachings to provide the grounds of further critique against perpetrators and those who have shielded and supported them. Peterson's chapter shows how these hashtags have been used to reject the idea that victims should feel shame and to provide a voice for those targeted within religious communities. The chapter also examines the intersections of racism and sexism in its analysis of anti-Muslim use of the #MosqueMeToo hashtag.

Rather than extended case studies, the final two chapters offer more general considerations of the potential of social media to push back on gender abuse by facilitating education, activism, and investigation. Chapter 10, "'You can start a movement with a hashtag': an exploration of student-led social media activism," by Candace Parrish, Lorena Briones Winkler, Avina Ross, Tremayne Robertson, and Alyssa Glace Maryn presents findings of focus groups the authors conducted with university students. The study was designed to assess attitudes and perceptions of the students in relation to the use of social media as means to disseminate awareness and education aimed at the prevention of intimate partner violence and sexual assault (IPV/SA). Students agreed that social media offered potential in these areas, although they noted the need to include measures to mitigate social media's tendency to provide information that does not necessarily inspire action. Students were hopeful that programs could overcome the tendency toward "slacktivism" to develop prevention campaigns that would reach the campus audience and create a changed campus environment around these issues. Chapter 11, "Using social media tools to contribute to and challenge gendered violence," by Victoria Carty considers several well-known case studies that took place between 2012 and 2017, highlighting several important dynamics at play. While online environments serve as platforms for the perpetration of abuse, Carty also shows how, in some cases, digital traces from social media communications have been instrumental in the detection of these crimes. The chapter also illustrates the effectiveness of hybrid forms of activism in which online protest spill over into street protests. Tracing some of the most highly publicized early cases of the use of social media to distribute video evidence of sexual abuse and to provide a platform for bullying and harassment, the chapter provides these glimmers of hope in the form of resistance potentials that can at least be facilitated through the same technologies that foster and exacerbate abuse.

These chapters provide critical insights into the operations of power within and across platforms and embodied experiences. They take up central themes such as constructions of the public and private sphere; the cultural tendency to blame the victim; intersectionalities of gender, race, religion, and nation; the inadequacy of existing laws and the harmful influence of weak institutional responses; the potentials of social media and online environments to facilitate not only harms but also solutions; and the limitations of viewing online abuses as individual rather than as structural problems. Together the chapters in this volume show important linkages between broader social, cultural, and historical contexts, and the instances of abuse and resistance in social media and online environments.

References

Amundsen, R. (2019). Cruel intentions and social conventions: Locating the shame in revenge porn. In D. Ging & E. Siapera (Eds.), *Gender hate online: Understanding the new anti-feminism* (pp. 131–148). Palgrave.

Bailey, M. (2021). *Misogynoir transformed: Black women's digital resistance*. New York University Press.

Barker, K., & Jurasz, O. (2019). *Online misogyny as a hate crime: A challenge for legal regulation*. Routledge.

Benedict, H. (1992). *Virgin or vamp: How the press covers sex crimes*. Oxford University Press.

Black, A., Lumsden, K., & Hadlington, L. (2019). 'Why don't you block them?' Police officers' constructions of the ideal victim when responding to reports of interpersonal cybercrime. In K. Lumsden & R. Harmer (Eds.), *Online othering: Exploring digital violence and discrimination on the web* (pp. 355–378). Palgrave. DOI:10.1007/978-3-030-12633-9_15

Boyle, K. (2019). *#MeToo, Weinstein & feminism*. Springer International Publishing.

Brightwell, L. (2019). Feminist tinder: Young women talk back to harassment online. In D. Ging & E. Siapera (Eds.), *Gender hate online: Understanding the new anti-feminism* (pp. 233–252). Palgrave.

Chandra, G., & Erlingsdóttir, I. (2020). *Routledge handbook of the politics of the #MeToo movement*. Routledge.

Citron, D.K. (2016). *Hate crimes in cyberspace*. Harvard University Press.

Cuklanz, L. (1996). *Rape on trial: How the mass media construct legal reform and social change*. University of Pennsylvania Press.

Cuklanz, L. (2020). Problematic news framing of #MeToo. *The Communication Review* 23(4), 251–272.

Dixon, K. (2014). Feminist online identity: Analyzing the presence of hashtag feminism. *Journal of Arts and Humanities, 3*(7), 34–39.

Fileborn, B., & Loney-Howes, R. (Eds.) (2019). *#MeToo and the politics of social change*. Palgrave McMillan.

Francisco, S. C., & Felmlee, D. H. (2022). What did you call me? An analysis of online harassment towards black and Latinx women. *Race and Social Problems 14*(1), 1–13.

Frank, T. J., Hardinge, T., & Wosick-Correa, K. (2009). The global dimensions of rape law reform: A cross-national study of policy outcomes. *American Sociological Review 74*(2), 272–290.

Gilmore, L. (2017). *Tainted witness: Why we doubt what women say about their lives.* Columbia University of Press.

Ging, D., & Siapera, E. (Eds.) (2019). *Gender hate online: Understanding the new anti-feminism.* Palgrave.

Goldberg-Ambrose, C. (1992). Unfinished business in rape law reform. *Journal of Social Issues 48*(1), 173–185.

Grant, S. (Showrunner) (2019). *Unbelievable* [TV miniseries]. Netflix.

Grubb, A., & Turner, E. (2012). Attribution of blame in rape cases: A review of the impact of rape myth acceptance, gender role conformity, and substance abuse on victim blaming. *Aggression and Violent Behavior 17*(5), 443–452.

Jackson, S. J., Bailey, M., & Welles, B. F. (2020). *#HashtagActivism.* MIT Press. https://direct.mit.edu/books/book/4597/HashtagActivismNetworks-of-Race-and-Gender-Justice

Jane, E. (2017). *Misogyny online: A Short (and British) history.* Sage.

Kaplan, J. (Director) (1988). *Accused, The* [Film]. Paramount Pictures.

LaFree, G. (1980). Variables affecting guilty pleas and convictions in rape cases: Toward a social theory of rape processing. *Social Forces 58*(3), 833–850.

Lin, Z., & Yang, L. (2019). Individual and collective empowerment: Women's voices in the #MeToo movement in China. *Asian Journal of Women's Studies 25*(1), 117–131.

Lokot, T. (2019). Affective resistance against online misogyny and homophobia on RuNet. In D. Ging & E. Siapera (Eds.), *Gender hate online: Understanding the new anti-feminism* (pp. 213–232). Palgrave.

Lumsden, K., & Harmer, R. (2019). *Online othering: Exploring digital violence and discrimination on the web.* Palgrave Studies in Cybercrime and Cybersecurity.

Mantilla, K. (2015). *Gendertrolling: How misogyny went viral.* Praeger.

Masullo Chen, G., Pain, P., & Chen, V. (2020). 'You really have to have a thick skin: A cross-cultural perspective on how online harassment influences female journalists. *Journalism 21*(7), 877–895.

Masullo Chen, G., Pain, P., & Zhang, J. (2018). #NastyWomen: Reclaiming the Twitterverse from misogyny. In J. R. Vickery & T. Everbach (Eds.), *Mediating misogyny: Gender, technology, and harassment* (pp. 371–388). Palgrave.

Mendes, K., Ringrose, J., & Keller, J. (2018). #MeToo and the promise and pitfalls of challenging rape culture through feminist digital activism. *European Journal of Women's Studies 25*(2), 236–246.

Mendes, K., Ringrose, J., & Keller, J. (2019). *Digital feminist activism: Girls and women fight back against rape culture.* Oxford University Press.

Noble, & Tynes, B. M. (Eds.) (2016). *The intersectional internet: Race, sex, class, and culture online.* Peter Lang Publishing.

Poland, B. (2016). *Haters: Harassment, abuse, and violence online.* Potomac Books (University of Nebraska).

Powell, A., & Henry, N. (2017). *Sexual violence in a digital age.* Palgrave.

Regehr, K., & Ringrose, J. (2018). Celebrity victims and wimpy snowflakes: Using personal narratives to challenge digitally mediated rape culture. In J. R. Vickery & T. Everbach (Eds.), *Mediating misogyny: Gender, technology, and harassment* (pp. 353–370). Palgrave.

Shefer, T., & Hussen, T. S. (2020). Critical reflections on #MeToo in contemporary South Africa through an American feminist lens. In G. Chandra & I. Erlingdóttir (Eds.), *Routledge handbook of the politics of the #MeToo movement* (pp. 397–409). Routledge.

Stubbs-Richardson, M., Rader, N. E., & Cosby, A. G. (2018). Tweeting rape culture: Examining portrayals of victim blaming in discussions of sexual assault cases on Twitter. *Feminism & Psychology 28*(1), 90–108.

Vickery, J. R., & Everbach, T. (Eds.) (2018). *Mediating misogyny: Gender, technology, and harassment*. Palgrave.

Williams, S. (2015). Digital defense: Black feminists resist violence with hashtag activism. *Feminist Media Studies 15*(2), 341–344.

2

FROM STREET TO SCREEN

On the Right to Public Space in the Age of Algorithms

Claudia Alvares

Introduction: Nonconsensual Images *Online*

Modern masculinity has traditionally been associated with public space, while femininity has tended to be relegated to the realm of the private sphere. Feminist history and philosophy of law describe how binary models that pit public life against privacy have historically functioned to keep the abuse of women and children within the "private" domestic sphere (Marsh et al., 2015; Miles, 2015). By declaring that the personal was political in the 1970s, the feminist movement celebrated the possibility of including issues such as domestic violence and sexual abuse within the public realms of law and governance (Landes in Miles, 2015, p. 280).

Today, however, society has changed significantly with respect to issues of privacy, much because of the impact of new technologies on individual control over personal information (Hoven et al., 2019). In an age of big data, the rapid evolution of new technologies has increasingly facilitated possibilities for surveillance and control of Internet users through datafication. Datafication refers to processes of collection, storage, and perusal of large quantities of digitized personal data acquired through the monitoring of online behavior and consumption habits (Van Dijck, 2014). These novel big data practices depend on the commodification and monetization of people's online data (Holloway, 2019) in what has been termed as "surveillance capitalism" (Zuboff, 2015), a process that converts human experiences into resources which are put to use for surveillance purposes (Chan & Kwok, 2021). By predicting or modifying the behavior of the very persons from whom data was extracted, big tech companies can maximize profit and control (Zuboff, 2015), thus raising concerns over the linkage between surveillance capitalism and platform power, personal data-centered business models and their impact on the public interest and public values (Chan & Kwok, 2021; Van Dijck, Nieborg & Poell, 2019).

DOI: 10.4324/9781003260851-3

As Hoven et al. (2019) argue, the conjugation of the increasing clout of new technology and the growing ambiguity of the limits of privacy induce new difficulties in the realm of law, policy, and ethics. These difficulties should be discussed in light of the General Data Protection Regulation (GDPR), implemented in European Union member states on May 25, 2018, with the objective of giving citizens, across Europe, more control over their personal data in a context of rapid advances in computational technology. Among the calls to the reinforcement of the right to privacy looms the right to personal identity as a sphere of individual autonomy to be protected against unsolicited intrusion, defended as such by Article 8 of the European Convention on Human Rights. The GDPR understands data protection within the framework which links privacy to the right to personal identity, as indicated by Article 7, subordinate to the topic "Informational Self-Determination." This was already visible in a Report drawn up by the European Commission in 2012 (104), which drew attention to the fact that "individuals are often neither aware nor in control of what happens to their personal data and therefore fail to exercise their rights effectively." The right to Informational Self-Determination, articulated by the GDPR, thus upholds consent as fundamental in the grounding of limitations on the right to privacy. This idea of consent is based on a theory of free will as a precondition for the moral responsibility involved in the capacity to take (informed) decisions (Zürcher et al., 2019) free from "undue influence" (Stannard, 2015, p. 424).

The view that privileges autonomy and the free will in discourses on privacy is mirrored, as Miles (2015, p. 283) notes, in prevalent perceptions of "our self-image as our property," that is, "something to be owned and a fragment of our very individuality that must be protected." A correlation may thus be drawn between current understandings of privacy and a culture of individualism visible in the rights of publicity, according to which the individual alone, as owner of her own self-image, has the right to disseminate that image as personal property (Miles, 2015). In the online sphere of social media, the management of self-image has become an increasingly important tool to influence reputations, often acting to reinforce the normative dimensions of social belonging (Draper, 2020) within a particular community. Self-image management online becomes akin to brand marketing, a potential source of social and economic capital, even when it is the individual alone who is responsible for the commodification of her own image. The ease with which digital communication technologies can be used to widely circulate contents beyond their original context of authorship (Murthy, 2012) enhances the potential impact of negative risks inherent in online visibility. This has contributed to growing consciousness of the need to update legislation so as to aid individuals in confronting novel challenges to reputation management online (Draper, 2020).

The ubiquity and popularity of social networks, such as Facebook, Instagram, Snapchat, YouTube, and Twitter, have contributed to the staging of new practices of representation and interaction, with strong implications in terms of the generation of sensitive data and possibilities of identity theft (Feher, 2021).

The unauthorized or nonconsenting distribution of selfies, photos, videos, or other content on social media platforms of a sexual nature exacerbates the problem insofar as one tends to find legal and/or public policy formulation responses that are decontextualized from the development of new technologies, as well as the behaviors they propitiate. This situation risks causing further harm to the individuals involved, namely the victims who tend to be morally condemned along with those responsible for the nonconsenting dissemination of sexual or sexualized images (Henry & Powell, 2015b, p. 766). Characterized by indirect contact between perpetrator and victim, online abuse can involve the publication on social media of derogatory, private, or false information, in the form of comments, dissemination of documents, images, videos, etc. about individuals on online forums, social media, or websites (Vakhitova et al., 2018, p. 349), affecting women's right to sexual autonomy (Albury, 2017).

New digital contexts may thus facilitate misogynistic behaviors online, often conflated, in mainstream public discourse with cyberbullying. Although the two types of abuse may overlap, discourses on cyberbullying tend to revolve around the dangers concerning a lack of online literacy in the young. Although online literacy is also an important theme when discussing reputation management online, online misogyny against adult women, often including behaviors such as the nonconsensual production and distribution of sexually charged images through the Net, involves a specific gendered violence-centered perspective (Henry & Powell, 2015a, p. 105), crucial to feminist studies, that tends to be somewhat downplayed in debates on cyberbullying among the young.

The right to Informational Self-Determination, as foreseen by the GDPR, draws attention to the importance of individual awareness concerning the loss of control over personal data online, positing that individuals give their consent to limitations on the right to privacy. As such, the GDPR grounds informational autonomy on consent, implying that the individual in question is able to freely choose among distinct courses of action. While the young are juridically considered to not yet have the full competence to take decisions autonomously, adult women are juridically considered to have full competence to decide for themselves over the limits of their own privacy online and the subsequent taking of legal action to defend these limits. However, juridical recognition for their capacity to autonomously press charges to defend their right to privacy is somewhat compromised by their legitimate fears of being further victimized upon filing a claim, due to concerns about their privacy not being preserved throughout the legal process.

This chapter analyzes one such situation, within the Portuguese context, that led to a lack of effective responses to the harms experienced by adult women, deriving from technology-facilitated sexual violence (Henry & Powell, 2016). Because crimes of this nature fall within the categories of sexual coercion or rape in the Portuguese Penal Code, they depend on the filing of a complaint on the part of the victim. Here, as we shall see, the victim relinquished the possibility of taking legal action so as to protect her own privacy.

The case under consideration occurred in Portugal during the traditional academic festivities (*Queima das Fitas*, or Ribbon Burning) of graduating university students in May 2017, involving an alleged nonconsensual video recording, disseminated on social media, in which a young male student genitally manipulates a young female student, apparently unconscious due to excess drink, in public transport especially chartered for the event, while a multitude of students watched, laughed, and clapped, simultaneously filming and photographing the scene (*Expresso*, 17.05.2017; *Jornal i*, 17.05.2017; *Sol*, 17.05.2017). The fact that the victim chose not to take any formal legal action in order to protect her own privacy is a compelling aspect of the case under scrutiny. However, more than revealing any lack of competence or understanding of consent, I would argue that the victim's choice to remain silent results from her perception of the inadequacy of the legal framework for Internet privacy to ensure protection against further risks to reputation management online.

My aim will be to understand how the Internet, as an integral part of expanding public space, plays an increasingly important role in redefining the boundaries that delimit public and private realms. While feminists of the 70s fought to make the private public, drawing attention to private issues that remained cast away from the public eye due to being confined to the domestic sphere, there now appears to be a contrasting trend which is that of attempting to bring publicized intimacy back into the sphere of privacy. Considered within this chapter are the contexts within which collective understandings of sexual rights (within the frame of the concept of privacy) are being visibly challenged and redefined in light of digital publics (Albury, 2017) and publicity. I intend to argue that the concepts of public space, public, and publicity are intertwined with each other, impacting on regulatory practices of both the legitimation of sexualized gender performances as well as the mechanisms of the intersection of informal and formal justice.

Public Space, Publicity, and Digital Publics

A pure definition of public space would be that of a universalistic space accessible to the entire population, with few restrictions on participation (Cornwell, 1973; Goodsell, 2003). According to this perspective, public space would be conceived as a domain of contact and exchange between strangers, where they reciprocally observe each other (Hatuka & Toch, 2017). Open to any individual, even those who belong to categories considered "deviant," individuals only pose a threat to public space when they display antisocial behavior in that space (Cornwell, 1973). By the term "antisocial," we mean the manifestation of activities that break certain tacit rules regarding respect for the rights of others in public places, requiring recourse either to moderating instances or to legal sanctions so as to re-establish the public nature of public space (Goodsell, 2003). In a Habermasian sense, the prevention of unacceptable behavior in public space is based on genuinely deliberative discourse, in which participants focus on a common problem and exchange views, being open to changing perspectives in the course of conversation.

If we attend to the physical space where public sociability takes place (Terzi & Tonnelat, 2017, p. 521), we can define it as referring to (1) public places where people who tend not to know each other gather, such as a street, pavement, square, or park; (2) circulation networks that enhance mobility between these places, such as roads, public transport lines, and pavements; and (3) the public transport which circulates between the various points of that geographic space. All these outdoor spaces are intended to be used by the public, allowing for the formation of social bonds, the establishment of connections to a common past, and the creation of group identity (Goodsell, 2003, p. 367).

The Portuguese case that this chapter analyzes took place in a public bus; however, it had been especially chartered for the event. Moreover, the event—the traditional academic festivities of graduating university students known as *Queima das Fitas*—is frequently characterized by successive moments of "carnivalesque displays" that aim to "challenge the status quo" (Weeks, 1999, p. 37) through transgression of normative behavioral boundaries under the public eye. This transgressive moment potentiates a sense of inclusion and connection between group members, who, in this particular case, were physically present within a range of direct audibility and visibility, with face-to-face contact. For Goodsell (2003), this type of rooting of public space in a physical place is the most effective in achieving true connection and interaction between participants, thus enhancing group identity. And this is precisely the context in which the scene between the two young people takes place, transcending the boundaries of the strictly personal sphere to integrate the intragroup domain. The transgressive moment thus becomes, in the first instance, a "practice of intimacy" (Jamieson, 2011, p. 154) through which individuals forge a sense of closeness in the relationship between group members.

According to Németh (2012), the universalism of public space is challenged by the existence of various social, cultural, and legal practices that serve to control how public space is used and by whom. A perspective which focuses on the tensions inherent in conflicting rights within public space tends to consider the latter as shaped by a regulatory regime of socially constructed norms that govern behaviors and bodies, displacing those that are deviant from public view (Cook & Whowell, 2011) through the allocation of access codes and mechanisms of exclusion and inclusion (Blomley, 2003). Following from this line of reflection, it is important to ask how a regulatory regime moulds the publicness of public space (and consequently the privacy of private space) (Ruppert, 2006). For the latter author, interactions in public space are crucial for the formation and redefinition of social identities, as these result from a constant renegotiation of what "public" means and who belongs to this category.

Hatuka and Toch (2017) note that the personal use of technological devices is influencing individuals' relationship with public space, and visibility should now be considered the key concept of public life, extending far beyond the concrete physical space where one observes and is observed to encompass an entire practice related to exposure through digital media. For these authors, physical space no longer dictates social interactions in our age, with the digital leading to an alteration in our spatiotemporal perception while blurring the distinction between the real and the virtual. Moreover, surveillance practices associated with new technologies generate situations of "asymmetric visibility" (2016, p. 5), with significant implications at the level of the redefinition of public space, as well as the autonomy of individuals in managing their visibility.

The Case and its Legal Context

Regarding the case under analysis, the judicial investigation was closed early regarding the possible occurrence of a crime against sexual self-determination, due to the fact that, according to Articles 163 (sexual coercion) and 164 (rape) of the Portuguese Penal Code, crimes of this nature, contemplating "any means … used for the practice of a relevant sexual act against the conscious will of the victim," depend on the lodging of a complaint on the part of the victim (Article 178, paragraph 1) so that the respective criminal proceedings can be initiated. Exceptions to this requirement, which characterizes crimes of a semi-public nature, are allowed should the crime be committed against a minor or result in the suicide of death of the victim (Article 178, paragraph 1). In Portuguese law, semi-public crimes are those in which promotion of the criminal procedure, at the hands of the Public Prosecutor, depends on a complaint from the victim or another party (cf. Article 49 of the Portuguese Penal Code), contrary to public crimes, in which the Public Prosecutor can initiate criminal proceedings (cf. Article 48 of the Portuguese Penal Code), and private crimes, in which the victim, or her representative, can file a private accusation (cf. Article 50 of the Portuguese Penal Code) (cf. Simões, 2012, p. 12–13 (nn 17,18,19)).

The semi-public nature of crimes against sexual self-determination has been a contentious issue of late in the Portuguese media, with growing recognition, among law specialists, that while this status may protect the privacy of the victim, it simultaneously contributes to facilitate the evasion of prosecution by the accused (cf. Lopes, 2021). However, what is particularly important regarding this case concerns the crimes of illegal recording and invasion of private life, given the online circulation of a video registering the occurrence. According to Article 192, paragraph 1, of the Portuguese Penal Code, it is illegal to "capture, photograph, film, record or disclose images of people or intimate objects or spaces," without the consent of those involved, other than for the purpose of acting in the "legitimate and relevant public interest" (Article 192, paragraph 2). The Portuguese Penal Code contemplates sanctions for those who produce and distribute illegal recordings and photographs (Article 199), where illegality is not so much connoted with the unlawfulness of the content itself but rather with the form through which it was obtained, namely without the consent of those whose image is disseminated.

Article 79 of the Civil Code, in turn, further expounds on the right to the image, defining various restrictions in the case of exhibition, reproduction and dissemination of images for commercial purposes without consent, particularly in the case of images that may cause reputational damage, "unless that reproduction is framed within public places, or within facts of public interest or that have taken place in public" (Article 79, paragraph 2). It should here be noted that "the right to the image thus encompasses two autonomous rights: the right not to be photographed and the right not to have one's photograph disclosed" (Pereira et al., 2017, p. 2).

Despite relevant legislation regarding the right to the image, the right to privacy and the right to data protection, Portuguese law does not specifically refer to the online context, implying that this theme has been juridically broached in practice rather than in theory. One important court decision in this regard dates from 26 May 2015, when a Court of Appeal in the city of Évora ruled on the circulation of images of minors on social media, stating that parents should abstain from disclosing photographs or information identifying their children on social networks so as to safeguard the right to privacy, the protection of personal data, and the safety of the security of minors in the digital sphere, in light of the right to freedom of expression and the prohibition of State interference in the private lives of citizens (cf. Judgment of the Court of Appeal of Évora, 2015).

Despite the absence of legislation focusing specifically on the Internet, Pereira, Alves and Ferreira (2017, p. 5) note that,

> In the absence of consent to the publication of photos online, the injured party may appeal directly to the entity that posted his or her image or contact the competent regulatory authority (ANACOM, in the case of electronic communications) so that it may order the removal of the image.

In the case in point, the latter possibility is contradictory with the semi-public status of the crime against sexual self-determination, which, as mentioned above, is evoked so as to protect the victim's privacy. If the injured party were either to appeal to the entity that posted the video that came to circulate online or to ANACOM, so as to enforce removal from the Internet of this video, it is likely that her privacy would not be preserved. As such, this case demonstrates possible incompatibility between the need to safeguard privacy on the one hand, especially as regards crimes of a semi-public nature, and the right to image proprietorship in an "increasingly connected and complex digital society" (Pew Research Centre, 2017, p. 14), in which it is ever more difficult to control the repercussions of image dissemination due to the instantaneity of online communication, potential anonymity of the author of posts, and the comprehensive scope of the virtual audience (cf. Alvares, 2018).

The images of the scene inside the bus at Queima das Fitas in Porto were first posted online on the website IMASOLDIER, which aims to share sexually explicit content on Facebook. Open only to male members over the age of 18, the material made available is characterized by having been "captured without the knowledge of the participants" (*Observador*, 18.05.2017), in line with the increasing expansion of an online market for the consumption of nonconsensual sexual images, frequently obtained in a disguised manner (Powell, 2010). The situation became even more intricate when the video was disseminated by the popular Portuguese newspaper *Correio da Manhã* both in its online version and on its television channel.

Although the media outlet had attempted to distort the image of the alleged victim, the release of the video was strongly criticized by several quarters of Portuguese society. The Commission for Citizenship and Gender Equality (CIG) filed a complaint against the dissemination of the video by *Correio da Manhã* to the Directorate of Investigation and Criminal Action (DIAP) and the Ethics Council of the Journalists' Union also went public to condemn the release of the video as "going against all the rules of journalism" (*Lusa*, 2017). The Portuguese Regulatory Authority for the Media (ERC) also opened a case against the *Correio da Manhã* television channel, following the receipt, in a single day, of more than 500 complaints against the video (*Sol*, 2017).

ERC (Resolution 2021/95, p. 46) sentenced the Defendant to pay a fine of 75,000.00 euros on the grounds of being a national generalist pay-per-view broadcaster with unconditional access and thus nonexempt, according to the Portuguese Law on Television and On-Demand Audiovisual Services, from including "an appropriate visual warning" identifying contents "susceptible of having negative influence on the formation of the personality of children and adolescents" (Article 27, paragraph 4) as well as "a set of signs identifying the different age brackets, according to the contents presented, and that respects… the parameters of the show classification commission" (Article 27, paragraph 7).

It is interesting to note that the crimes against the right to sexual self-determination, the right to privacy, and the right to the image were not invoked as the basis for taking legal action in this case. The reason for this resides in the fact that such crimes depend on a previous complaint, but in this case, there was no such complaint lodged either against the person who could have been accused of infringing on sexual self-determination, or the person/s responsible for collecting or circulating the image. Indeed, that complaint would in all likelihood have implied that the victim's privacy would not be preserved. Instead, it was the Portuguese Regulatory Authority for the Media (ERC) that sued the *Correio da Manhã* TV Channel for successive exhibitions of the video on its news service, subsequently to having received various complaints from shocked viewers. However, worthy of note is the fact that rather than suing the channel for exhibiting a video with potentially criminal content, or that was obtained in an illicit manner, the grounds invoked for penalizing the channel were rather those concerning not having appropriately identified content in accordance with age classification for audiovisual programs.

On Technology-Facilitated Sexual Harassment

The ambivalence of the case was emphasized in the public debate generated around the dissemination of images, because in the latter it was not perceptible whether or not the girl in question had consented to sexual interaction, given her state of apparent drunkenness. It may be relevant here to bring to mind Weeks' (1999, p. 37) concept of sexual citizenship as involving public calls for attention through the staging of moments that transcend the limits of the personal sphere so as to claim sexual legitimation in the public space. An important barrier separates such interventions from the acceptability of the dissemination of private situations in a public context. Indeed, the type of sexual citizenship that Weeks mentions implies a conscious choice over the conversion of that which is normatively designated as belonging to the private domain into something which is publicly shared. In the present case analyzed, the girl reveals herself as an objectified body, void of will, which becomes public through the will of others, first within the scope of a restricted community of students and then within the scope of a wider public, due to the diffusion of online images.

Salter (2016, p. 2725) observes that the circulation online of digital images of bodies amplifies gender inequalities because "the public feminine body is narrowly conflated with pornography," automatically connoting sexual promiscuity. By going beyond the limits of the student group, the filmed scene of this particular case reached a widened and diffuse audience through online circulation. As such, the message of transgressive intimacy that could circulate within a more or less restricted group gained proportions of another order. Indeed, the message of online intimacy that is passed on to the public matches signifiers of femininity to signifiers of passivity, absence of consciousness and of self-will. Self-conscious sexual subjectification (Gill, 2003) is hence omitted from these images, with the reduction of the girl filmed to the status of an object to which something is done, before the gaze, not only of students who shout "how disgusting," between giggles, on the bus but also before a wide-ranging and anonymous gaze, similar to that of the Foucauldian panopticon, the latter serving as a metaphor for societal surveillance.

Among cyberbullying narratives of technology-facilitated sexual violence (Henry and Powell, 2016), three North-American cases stand out as references in the academic literature on sexual assaults that were the first to be documented on social media (Gjika, 2020). The first occurred in January 2012, when a 14-year-old girl, accompanied by her friend, joined a group of boys at a house party in Maryville, Missouri, and was assaulted by one of these young men while his friend filmed the abuse on his cell phone. The circulation of these images online led to her becoming a victim of social media harassment and shaming. The second case, known as the Steubenville High School rape case, occurred in August 2012 in Ohio, and involved the sharing of photos and videos on social media of the assault of an unnamed 16-year-old girl at the hands of two of the School's star football players, with the victim in the incident being the target of extensive comments through text messages. In September 2012, a 15-year-old girl from Saratoga, California, was also assaulted at a party by three young men and committed suicide after photos of the abuse were circulated among classmates at School.

These cases share in common the fact that they involved peer sexual assault, the intoxication of victims during the abuse and the lack of memory of the victims regarding the events themselves. Of particular importance is the fact that social media was used as technological evidence of the assault (Pennington & Birthisel, 2016), having served to perpetuate and propagate the abuse beyond the original spatiotemporal context of occurrence, thus seriously worsening the reputational and emotional damage inflicted upon the victims (cf. Gjika, 2020). As Dodge states, the documentary evidence produced by the image "reiterates the event, extends the event and is an act of sexual violence in and of itself as it humiliates, violates and invites more and more viewers to join in on the violation" (2015, p. 70). In effect, technological witnessing of the abuse provides justification for judgment of the victim's character as well as her social and family background, constituting a very real threat to her public standing.

Back in 1993, Thompson (315–316) had observed that women's entry into public space was often accompanied by stares, scrutiny and verbal comment by anonymous males. In other words, street harassment would serve to corroborate the genuinely public status of a world where people did not know each other. The absence of familiarity would enhance the exercise of harassment, insofar as it facilitated the objectification of women. In the digital age, harassment in public space is often filtered through new media, sometimes being practiced by someone with whom the victim has had a close relationship. Both the architecture of networks and the business models that underlie the latter are geared towards maximizing content sharing and interaction between users (Salter, 2016). This implies that themes with a higher degree of popularity due to their sexually explicit content end up reaching a larger number of social media users, according to the logics of an algorithmic culture that privileges the highest number of views and interactions on social networks (Alvares, 2018). This situation is allied to the apparently incorporeal nature of the online environment, which provides a certain degree of anonymity, favorable to disinhibition and absence of civility (Papacharissi, 2004). Moreover, the extension of the audience promotes the intensification of voyeuristic capacity and increased opportunities for viral message dissemination, thus reinforcing chastisement for perceived deviance from the norm.

Nadim and Fladmoe (2021, p. 246) emphasize the continuity between offline and online worlds, by pointing to online gendered harassment as "off-line misogyny moved to a new arena." However, these authors simultaneously recognize the specificity of the challenges that confront the domain of the Internet, deriving from potential anonymity and the long duration of the material posted online, due to difficulty in controlling its dissemination through the links that constitute Internet architecture. By amplifying possibilities for the haunting and hounding of victims beyond the circumstances of physical aggression, the abuse of women online aims to stabilize gendered social roles, restoring "both women and men to 'their place'" (Nadim & Fladmoe, 2021, p. 246), while contributing to silence women in the context of a prevalently patriarchal online culture (Fuchs & Schäfer, 2021; Megarry, 2014).

By continuously producing and reproducing the scene referred to in this case study in ways that are "out of place" (Fanghanel & Lim, 2017, p. 3), or "out of context," the circulation of such images works toward the disciplining of female behavior, at the same time that it demonstrates the widening of public space by virtue of an increasingly deterritorialized virtual context. The punishment exerted on supposedly bad female behavior is visible in the shame of public exposure that online exhibition represents for those involved in these situations, as attested to by the fact that the female student involved preferred to abstain from taking legal action so as to protect her right to privacy.

Public Interest, Social Morality, and the Interest of the Public

There are some recurrent characteristics in these types of cases that derive from the specificity of new media. On the one hand, new technologies, with their algorithmic logic, serve to accentuate "rape culture" by prolonging the experience of power based on the intimidation, harassment, and humiliation of victims through the nonconsensual dissemination of images. On the other hand, these same technologies fulfill an important role as witness to the abuse itself, providing evidence of the crime and contributing to mobilizing wider society against the crime committed (Pennington & Birthisel, 2016).

The director of *Correio da Manhã* newspaper and television channel, Octávio Ribeiro, added fuel to fire by justifying his decision to disseminate the video on the channel's TV news service so as to disclose "a relevant and controversial fact" because "without news, there is no reflection" (*Lusa*, 17.05.2017). Simultaneously, he emphasized that the TV channel had protected the identity of those involved by blurring their image (*Lusa*, 17.05.2017). According to Henry and Powell (2016), in this type of case, some legal systems require effective proof that the accused have distributed images with the precise intention of causing moral damage. If we attend to the intentionality of *Correio da Manhã* in disseminating the images, the idea of alleged defense of the public interest then arises. This situation poses a challenge to legislators, insofar as it is unclear whether entities which are not involved in the original nonconsented dissemination of the image, but subsequently distribute it—in this case on the grounds of protecting the so-called public interest— should be punished. As Citron (2014, p. 15) argues: "the 'reposting' of photos in which a stranger appears nude should not constitute a criminal act, as long as there is no idea that that person intended to keep the photos private." Moreover, as we have previously seen, Article 79°, paragraph 2, of the Portuguese Civil Code allows the reproduction of images, even those images which may constitute a risk to reputation, as long as these are "framed within public places, or within facts of public interest or … have taken place in public."

Public interest reveals itself here as an inherently conflicted concept, as it is divided between two poles that are often antagonistic to each other: the right to privacy on the one hand and the right to be informed on the other. Since the public interest is notoriously difficult to define, it only becomes visible through the values defended by a given society. It thus emerges as inseparable from a certain moral sense, representative of a sense of social solidarity that preserves the bonds of community (Morrison & Svennevig, 2007). The defense of the public interest is thus claimed by *Correio da Manhã* as a motive for the publication of the video, since it would serve the purpose of mobilizing society around a cause, namely that of collective indignation against a scene of possible sexual abuse.

The fact that a theme of public interest may have been considered as having news value, due to its ability to arouse the interest of the public (Morrison & Svennevig, 2002), does not remove the relevance of public discussion on the theme. However hypocritical it may seem, *Correio da Manhã* effectively managed to achieve this, as the topic of sexual abuse momentarily entered the public debate, with the video exhibited by *Correio da Manhã*, on various news slots, accounting for 15,889 shares (Câncio, 22.05.2017). If the video had kept circulating on the IMASOLDIER website, it is likely that its subject matter would have escaped the mainstream public eye. However, subsequently to *Correio da Manhã*'s disclosure of the video, the issues related either to the invasion of privacy, facilitated by new technologies, or to the existence of possible sexual abuse were quickly colonized by collective fury against the media group for having infringed upon "almost all journalistic rules" (Câncio, 22.05.2017). However, if we take into account the defense of the alleged public interest invoked by *Correio da Manhã*, described above, it remains unclear that the dissemination of the video constitutes a criminal act. Indeed, rather than criminal, the act could be considered immoral, due to the publication of images of a private nature, captured by third parties, with the presumable objective of protecting the public interest. Indeed, the public interest here is understood as akin to preserving social morality, by drawing the public's attention to something potentially immoral—and punishable—that took place within the public space.

In effect, despite all the hype and complaints concerning *Correio da Manhã*'s hypocrisy in invoking the public interest as a justification for disclosing the video, the fine imposed by the Portuguese Regulatory Authority for the Media (ERC) was substantiated on the basis of the TV channel not having included adequate age classification visual warnings on the content exhibited. As such, any potential violation of public interest on the part of *Correio da Manhã* was not summoned by ERC as grounds for penalization.

Conclusion: The Specificity of Gendered Dynamics

Mobilizing society through digital technologies can be regarded as community-inclined action, signalling a new trend in justice, where informal social practices of justice increasingly tend to intersect with formal criminal justice processes (Powell, 2015). Indeed, as Powell (2015, p. 13) states, digital technologies are "facilitating new meanings and practices of informal justice in techno-social subaltern counter-publics." A potentially negative aspect of this situation is that new technologies can facilitate the taking of justice into one's own hands, which corresponds to a kind of "digital vigilantism," defined by Trottier (2020, p. 598) as "digitally mediated denunciation and shaming." In effect, by entering into a logic of crescendo that is based on the reinforcement of opinions through the largest number of shares or views on social networks, digital media contribute to stir up emotions within public space. If, on the one hand, the fact that citizens can make their voices heard through informal social practices of justice testifies in favor of the democratization of institutions under the rule of law, at the same time the pressure of majority opinion, frequently expressed within online discursive cocoons, leaves little room for opposing opinions and dissent.

This chapter raised the question concerning how a regulatory regime, corresponding to the disciplinary society in which we live, shapes the publicity of the public space and consequently the privacy of the private space (Ruppert, 2006). In the online domain, this regulatory regime often punishes female behavior that is deemed transgressive of social norms of modesty by publicizing and policing these perceived transgressions before a virtual audience, which is increasingly extensive in reach. Emotions of fear deriving from the potential risk of public exposure can lead to possibilities of "identity theft" (Feher, 2021) that leaves the victim in a vulnerable situation, causing her to refrain from exercising her legal rights in public space. Technology-facilitated sexual violence (Henry & Powell, 2018), which in the case-study analyzed takes the form of dissemination of a video of nonconsensual sexual violence without the victim's consent, reveals itself as an increasingly recurrent form of exercise of control over the presence of nonacceptable female behavior in public space. By continuously producing and reproducing gendered sexualized signifiers as "out of place" (Fanghanel & Lim, 2017, p. 3), the intimacy-violating images posted online act as a technology of discipline on female behavior, converting the female body into an object (cf. Sadowski, 2016). Decontextualization and displacement function, through public exhibition, in such a way as to transgress both the boundaries of the body as well as the prevalent consensual norms of femininity, paving the way for the reinforcement of gendered power relations in everyday life. The ultimate goal is that of threatening the misogynist object of discourse with a potential loss of control over the situation, a loss that has precisely to do with "loss of context" (Butler, 1997, p. 4).

However, as witnessed above, it is difficult to demonstrate that the dissemination of images that violate privacy—and that lead to loss of context for the woman filmed—by a TV channel, which did not capture them in the first place, is constitutive of a crime. Indeed, on the basis of existing legislation, the media outlet can legitimately invoke the defense of the public interest in reproducing images that may be damaging to reputation, due to these having occurred in public, involving facts of public interest. Indeed, had it not been for the frequent dissemination of the video by *Correio da Manhã* TV, it would have been unlikely that this case would have come to be discussed in the public sphere. Subsequently to this case, in the following years, time and again, the academic festivities of *Queima das Fitas* would come to receive media attention due to the occurrence of cases of misogyny and sexual violence against female students. Sex games in exchange for alcoholic drinks given to young girls, with the videos running on social media, half-naked girls who have presumably been victims of abuse in the venues where the festivities occur, and sexualized names and imagery—often alluding to the female body—that are chosen to identify the booths of the venues have come to surface in the media. The focus on such incidents during this celebration period led the Student Association of the University of Oporto to collaborate with feminist activists and psychologists, carrying out awareness-raising campaigns against sexual violence by putting up posters in buses chartered for the event and distributing flyers with the objective of alerting students to various situations of sexual abuse. A 'Lilac Point' was also set up within the venue of the 2019 *Queima das Fitas*, consisting in a room where a team of feminist activists gave support to those who sought out help, registering complaints against sexual assault, general sexist attitudes or misogynous behaviors deemed unacceptable such as the unauthorized capture and dissemination of images and videos of a sexual or sexualized nature (*JPN*, 10.05.2019; *Público*, 09.05.2019; *Público*, 26.04.2019).

The media outlet that reproduced such images, on the condition that it did not film them, may thus effectively uphold the defense of the public interest as a motive for dissemination. In effect, what this case shows is that existing Portuguese legislation does not sufficiently protect either the victim's right to privacy or her right to the image in the context of rapidly evolving digital technology, in which the gendered violence that occurs in offline environments is increasingly migrating online. As Henry and Powell (2018, p. 204) note, although this phenomenon is not strictly novel, "the reach, nature, and duration of these harms, as well as the current gaps in legal redress available to victims, makes them both insidious and difficult to respond to." The possibility of recognizing the specificity of gender-based dynamics within technology-facilitated sexual violence may be a way forward to combat this phenomenon in juridical, regulatory, and pedagogical terms.

References

Albury, K. (2017). Just because it's public doesn't mean it's any of your business: Adults' and children's sexual rights in digitally mediated spaces. *New Media and Society, 19*(5), 713–725.

Alvares, C. (2018). Online staging of femininity: Disciplining through public exposure in Brazilian social media. *Feminist Media Studies, 18*(4), 657–674.

Blomley, N. (2003). Law, property, and the geography of violence: The frontier, the survey, and the grid. *Annals of the Association of American Geographers, 93*(1), 121–141.

Butler, J. (1997). *Excitable speech: A politics of the performative*. London: Routledge.

Câncio, F. (2017, 25 May). Op-Ed: O Correio da manhã ou o jornalismo como álibi do crime. *Diário de Notícias*. https://www.dn.pt/opiniao/opiniao-dn/fernanda-cancio/interior/o-correio-da-manha-ou-o-jornalismo-como-alibi-do-crime-8494392.html (accessed 22 December 2021).

Chan N. K., & Kwok, C. (2021). The politics of platform power in surveillance capitalism: A comparative case study of ride-hailing platforms in China and the United States. *Global Media and China*, September.

Citron, D. K. (2014). *Hate crimes in cyberspace*. Cambridge: Harvard University Press.

Cook, I. R., & Whowell, M. (2011). Visibility and the policing of public space. *Geography Compass, 5*, 610–622.

Cornwell, D. (1973). The management of tensions between conflicting usages of a public place. *Sociological Review, 21*, 197–210.

Dodge, A. (2015). Digitizing rape culture: Online sexual violence and the power of the digital photograph. *Crime, Media, Culture, 12*(1), 65–82.

Draper, N. A. (2020). Metaphors of visibility: Rhetorical practices in the normalization of individual online image management. *American Behavioral Scientist, 64*(11), 1627–1645.

ERC. (2021, 24 March). Resolution 2021/95 (CONTJOR-PC) Processo contraordenacional N.º 500.30.01/2018/1 em que é arguida a Cofina Media, S.A., titular do serviço de programas. *Correio da Manhã* TV (CMTV). https://www.erc.pt/download/YToyOntzOjg6ImZpY2hlaXJvIjtzOjM5OiJtZWRpYS9kZWNpc29lcy9vYmplY3RvX29mZmxpbmUvODEwWOS5wZGYiO3M6NjNjoidGl0dWxvIjtzOjMyOiJkZWxpYmVyYWVYWNhby1lcmMyMDIxOTUtY29udGpvci1wYyI7fQ==/deliberacao-erc202195-contjor-pc (accessed 28 December 2021).

European Commission. (2012). *Proposal for a regulation of the European parliament and of the council on the protection of individuals with regard to the processing of personal data and on the free movement of such data (General Data Protection Regulation)*. https://eurlex.europa.eu/LexUriServ/LexUriServ.do?uri=COM:2012:0011:FIN:EN:PDF (accessed 2 January 2022).

European Convention on Human Rights. https://www.echr.coe.int/documents/convention_eng.pdf (accessed 10 December 2021).

Expresso. (2017, 17 May). *PSP do Porto averigua caso de rapariga alegadamente vítima de abusos em autocarro*. https://expresso.sapo.pt/sociedade/2017-05-17-PSP-do-Porto-averigua-caso-de-rapariga-alegadamente-vitima-de-abusos-em-autocarro#gs.AoLAFuA (accessed 15 December 2021)

Fanghanel, A., & Lim, J. (2017). Of 'sluts' and 'arseholes': Antagonistic desire and the production of sexual vigilance. *Feminist Criminology, 12*(4), 341–360.

Feher, K. (2021). Digital identity and the online self: Footprint strategies – an exploratory and comparative research study. *Journal of Information Science, 47*(2), 192–205.

Fuchs, T., & Schäfer, F. (2021). Normalizing misogyny: Hate speech and verbal abuse of female politicians on Japanese Twitter. *Japan Forum, 33*(4), 553–579.

General Data Protection Regulation (GDPR). Chapter 2. https://gdpr-info.eu/art-7-gdpr/ (accessed 18 December 2021).

Gill, R. (2003). From sexual objectification to sexual subjectification: The resexualisation of women's bodies in the media. *Feminist Media Studies, 3*(1), 100–106.

Gjika, A. (2020). New media, old paradigms: News representations of technology in adolescent sexual assault. *Crime, Media, Culture, 16*(3), 415–430.

Goodsell, C. T. (2003). The concept of public space and its democratic manifestations. *American Review of Public Administration, 33*(4), 361–383.

Hatuka, T., & Toch, E. (2017). Being visible in public space: The normalisation of asymmetrical visibility. *Urban Studies, 54*(4), 984–998.

Henry, N., & Powell, A. (2015a). Beyond the 'sext': Technology-facilitated sexual violence and harassment against adult women. *Australian and New Zealand Journal of Criminology, 48*(1), 104–118.

Henry, N., & Powell, A. (2015b). Embodied harms: Gender, shame, and technology-facilitated sexual violence. *Violence Against Women, 21*(6), 758–779.

Henry, N., & Powell, A. (2016). Sexual violence in the digital age: The scope and limits of criminal law. *Social and Legal Studies, 25*(4), 397–418.

Henry, N., & Powell, A. (2018). Technology-facilitated sexual violence: A literature review of empirical research. *Trauma, Violence and Abuse, 19*(2), 195–208.

Hoven, J. van den, Blaauw, M., Wolter, P., & Warnier, M. (2019). Privacy and information technology. In *Stanford Encyclopedia of Philosophy*. https://plato.stanford.edu/entries/it-privacy/ (accessed 1 January 2022).

Holloway, D. (2019). Surveillance capitalism and children's data: The internet of toys and things for children. *Media International Australia, 170*(1), 27–36.

Jamieson, L. (2011). Intimacy as a concept: Explaining social change in the context of globalisation or another form of ethnocentrism? *Sociological Research Online, 16*(4), 151–163

Jornal i. (2017, 17 May). *Jovem filmada a ser abusada em autocarro no Porto perante colegas que nada fazem.* https://ionline.sapo.pt/563656

JPN. (2019, 10 May). *Enterro da Gata vai ter rondas para identificar práticas sexistas.* https://www.jpn.up.pt/2019/05/10/enterro-da-gata-vai-ter-rondas-para-identificar-praticas-sexistas/ (accessed 5 March 2022).

Judgment of the Court of Appeal of Évora. (2015). *Proc.º N.º 789/13.7TMSTB-B.E1.* http://www.dgsi.pt/jtre.nsf/134973db04f39bf2802579bf005f080b/7c52769f1dfab 8be80257e830052d374 (accessed 27 December 2021).

Lopes, A. M. (2021, 31 March). Crime de violação: que caminho trilhar do semi ao público? *Observatório Almeida: De Especialistas Para Especialistas.* https://observatorio. almedina.net/index.php/2021/03/31/crime-de-violacao-que-caminho-trilhar-do-semi-ao-publico/ (accessed 5 January 2021)

Lusa. (2017, 17 May). Conselho deontológico dos jornalistas condena vídeo de alegado abuso sexual no Porto. *Público.* https://www.publico.pt/2017/05/17/sociedade/noticia/conselho-deontologico-dos-jornalistas-condena-video-de-alegado-abuso-sexual-no-porto-1772544

Marsh, A., Miles, M., & Palmer, D. (2015). *The culture of photography in public space.* Bristol: Intellect.

Megarry, J. (2014). Online incivility or sexual harassment? Conceptualising women's experiences in the digital age. *Women's Studies International Forum, 47*(A), 46–55.

Miles, M. (2015). Photography, privacy and the public. *Law, Culture and the Humanities, 11*(2), 270–293.

Observador. (2017, 18 May). *IMASOLDIER. O grupo secreto do Facebook que publicou o vídeo da jovem alegadamente abusada.* https://observador.pt/2017/05/18/imasoldier-o-grupo-secreto-do-facebook-que-publicou-o-video-da-jovem-alegadamente-abusada/

Papacharissi, Z. (2004). Democracy online: Civility, politeness, and the democratic potential of online political discussion groups. *New Media and Society, 6*(2), 259–283.

Pennington, R., & Birthisel, J. (2016). When new media make news: Framing technology and sexual assault in the Steubenville rape case. *New Media and Society, 18*(11), 2435–2451.

Pereira, D. S., Alves, C. P., & Ferreira, T. (2017). O direito à imagem: Toda a imagem tem o seu preço. *Carlos Pinto de Abreu e Associados Publications.* https://carlospintodeabreu.com/wp-content/uploads/2018/10/35_societario_direito_imagem.pdf (accessed 5 January 2022).

Pew Research Centre. (2017, 19 October). *The future of truth and misinformation online.* https://www.pewresearch.org/internet/2017/10/19/the-future-of-truth-and-misinformation-online/ (accessed 27 December 2021).

Portuguese Civil Code. *Updated according to decree-law* n.º 72/2021, of 12 November. https://www.pgdlisboa.pt/leis/lei_mostra_articulado.php?nid=775andtabela=leis (Accessed 10 December 2021).

Portuguese Law on Television and On-Demand Audiovisual Services. *Updated according to decree-law* nº 74/2020, of 19 November. http://www.pgdlisboa.pt/leis/lei_mostra_articulado.php?nid=923andtabela=leis

Portuguese Penal Code. *Updated according to decree-law* n.º 79/2021, of 24 November. https://www.codigopenal.pt/#:~:text=de%2006%2F09-, Lei%20n.%C2%BA%2040%2F2020%2C%20de%2018%2F08,%2F2021%2C%20de%2024%2F11 (Accessed 10 December 2021).

Powell, A. (2010). Configuring consent: Emerging technologies, unauthorized sexual images and sexual assault. *Australian & New Zealand Journal of Criminology, 43*(1), 76–90.

Powell, A. (2015). Seeking rape justice: Formal and informal responses to sexual violence through technosocial counter-publics. *Theoretical Criminology, 19*(4), 571–588.

Público. (2019, 26 April). *A queima das fitas do Porto vai ter um ponto lilás para prevenir violência sexual.* https://www.publico.pt/2019/04/26/p3/noticia/a-queima-das-fitas-do-porto-vai-ter-um-ponto-lilas-para-prevenir-violencia-sexual-1870390 (accessed 7 January 2022).

Público. (2019, 9 May). *Nudez ou beijos por shots? Na Queima do Porto, fecharam-se barracas que promoviam comportamentos 'indignos'.* https://www.publico.pt/2019/05/09/p3/noticia/queima-fitas-porto-1872014 (accessed 7 January 2022).

Ruppert, E. S. (2006). Rights to public space: Regulatory reconfigurations of liberty. *Urban Geography, 27*(3), 271–292.

Sadowski, H. (2016). *Digital intimacies: Doing digital media differently.* Linköping, Sweden: Linköping University.

Salter, M. (2016). Privates in the online public: Sex(ting) and reputation on social media. *New Media and Society, 18*(11), 2723–2739.

Simões, A. V. (2012). Tese de mestrado em direito processual penal – A vítima em processo penal. *Universidade Católica Portuguesa Repository.* https://repositorio.ucp.pt/bitstream/10400.14/8944/1/TESE%20DE%20MESTRADO%20A%20V%C3%8DTIMA%20EM%20PROCESSO%20PENAL.pdf

Sol. (2017, 17 May). *Polícia está a investigar caso de rapariga vítima de abuso em autocarro.* https://sol.sapo.pt/artigo/563652/policia-esta-a-investigar-caso-de-rapariga-vitima-de-abuso-em-autocarro

Sol. (2017, 18 May). *Mais de 500 queixas à ERC após divulgação de vídeo de alegado abuso sexual no Porto.* https://sol.sapo.pt/artigo/563756/mais-de-500-queixas-a-erc-apos-divulgacao-de-video-de-alegado-abuso-sexual-no-porto-

Stannard, J. E. (2015). The emotional dynamics of consent. *The Journal of Criminal Law, 79*(6), 422–436.

Terzi, C., & Tonnelat, S. (2017). The publicisation of public space. *Environment and Planning A, 49*(3), 519–536.

Thompson, D. M. (1993). The woman in the street: Reclaiming the public space from sexual harassment. *Yale Journal of Law and Feminism, 6*(2), 313–348.

Trottier, D. (2020). Confronting the digital mob: Press coverage of online justice seeking. *European Journal of Communication, 35*(6), 597–612.

Vakhitova, Z., Webster, J., Alston-Knox, C., Reynald, D., & Townsley, M. (2018). Offender-victim relationship and offender motivation in the context of indirect cyber abuse: A mixed-method exploratory analysis. *International Review of Victimology, 24*(3), 347–366.

Van Dijck, J. (2014). Datafication, dataism and dataveillance: Big Data between scientific paradigm and ideology. *Surveillance and Society, 12*(2), 197–208.

Van Dijck, Nieborg, J. D., & Poell, T. (2019). Reframing platform power. *Internet Policy Review, 8*(2), 1–18.

Weeks, J. (1999). The sexual citizen. *Theory, Culture and Society, 15*(3–4), 35–52.

Zuboff, S. (2015). Big other: Surveillance capitalism and the prospects of an information civilization. *Journal of Information Technology, 30*(1), 75–89.

Zürcher, T., Elger, B., & Trachsel, M. (2019). The notion of free will and its ethical relevance for decision-making capacity. *BMC Medical Ethics, 20* (1), 1–31.

3

SCRUTINIZING SEXUAL PERSECUTION IN DIGITAL COMMUNICATION THROUGH THE FIELD OF HAPTICS

Soumen Mukherjee and Leslie Ramos Salazar

Introduction

Sexual harassment, the "unwelcome sexual advances, requests for sexual favors, and other verbal or physical conduct [behaviors] of a sexual nature," often occurs through haptics or touch communication (U.S. Equal Employment Opportunity Commission [UEEOC], 2016). According to Hornstein (1984), "sexual harassment refers to repeated demands or continuing behavior of supervisors or co-workers that add a discriminating condition or term of employment or create a harmful work environment for women" (p. 233). Interestingly, in modern times, sexual harassment of men is also on the rise. Stockdale, Visio, and Batra (1999) believe that even women at times become the aggressor and in the process of sexually harassing the men, they help in instituting an antagonistic work environment. Traditional sexual harassment often results from *haptic communication*, or communication through physical touch such as touching body parts that are off-limits to others, except one's romantic partner (Andersen, 1999). Sexual harassment in the context of haptics includes giving an intimate massage, touching a person's physical body, and kissing (UEEOC, 2016).

However, haptic communication has intensified in relationships by relying on communication technology to initiate and maintain social bonds. Haptic communication in online environments is called *virtual haptic communication*, or virtual touch, defined as "a tactile feedback technology that takes advantage of users' sense of touch by applying force, vibrations, or motion to the user" (Brewster, 2001, p. 1). Technological devices such as cellular phones, tablets, and laptops enhance users' vulnerability to online sexual harassment. These technological developments have created a new realm of sexually harassing behaviors such as coercing a person to share self-touching pornographic pictures or videos through text messages and inappropriately touching another's avatar.

DOI: 10.4324/9781003260851-4

A newspaper publication came out with the shocking revelation that four out of five people in India have faced some or the other form of online harassment (2017). Approximately 62% of Americans state that online sexual harassment is a major social problem that leads to negative effects such as powerlessness, lack of sleep, lowered self-esteem, and online apprehension (Duggan, 2017).

Virtual haptic communication ranges from nonintrusive to more intrusive sexual harassment behaviors. Examples of less intrusive virtual touch behaviors include flirtatious behaviors such as 'poking,' 'loving' someone's Tweet message, or touching a screen using a sexualized 'selfie' image. Other intrusive forms of sexual harassment through haptic communication include touching an *avatar* or a virtual representation of a person with a joystick. Since haptic communication evolved in digital environments, online sexual harassment has become more prevalent. *Online sexual harassment* is defined as sexual harassment that occurs via technological devices such as a computer or a mobile device across Internet mediums such as chats, forums, social networking sites, email, or instant messaging (Sexual Harassment on the Internet, 2010). Computer-mediated communication has enabled strangers to rapidly interact using virtual touch to express intimacy (psychological and physical closeness) with sexual desires and to send frequent messages to their targets. Also, virtual haptic harassment experiences increase when ex-partners press for continued activities like cybersex. Thus, virtual haptic harassment incidents in online environments seem likely to increase in frequency.

Yee and Bailenson (2007) expounded on *virtual interpersonal touch* or virtual haptic devices that permit person-to-person touch. Adopting virtual haptic devices to sexually stimulate others using computers may lead to short-term or long-term relationships with strangers or ex-partners. Individuals in committed face-to-face relationships may explore their sexuality online using virtual haptic devices, which can lead to *online infidelity*, or performing cybersex outside of a committed relationship (Vossler, 2016). Also, exploring virtual haptic devices to touch others in chat rooms or video games in a flirtatious manner can lead to online sexual harassment, especially when website hosts lack civility policies/ norms, which can produce ethical harm in virtual realms (Vanacker & Heider, 2012). Consensual users in long-distance romantic relationships may agree to use *teledildonics* or cybersex toys to engage in mutually satisfying tactile sexual sensations with a mobile device via text and a webcam. However, when a user coerces another person to use teledildonics without their consent, then this behavior becomes haptic harassment.

One reason for the frequent use of virtual haptics to attain sexual gratification may be due to an increasing interpersonal problem called *touch deprivation*, or the need for affectionate touch (Punyanunt-Cart, 2009). Touch deprivation has been a problem in America within the last decade, and 72% of Americans experience loneliness from being touch-deprived from close relationships (Floyd, 2014). Lonely individuals may use technology without others' consent to achieve "virtual interpersonal touch" as a substitute to traditional touch (Saadatian et al., 2014). Affectionate touch deprivation is often experienced by lonely and depressed individuals who lack the competence to fulfill their touch desires through face-to-face relationships (Floyd, 2014). Deprived individuals are motivated to seek affectionate virtual touch from others in online environments because they are less intimidating and it enables individuals to remain anonymous and express secret desires without feeling rejected by others in person or without fears of being caught for engaging in abusive behavior (Wolak et al., 2008). Deprived individuals can become physically stimulated by giving or receiving virtual touch, using tactile technologies to engage in virtual kissing (Saadatian et al., 2014), virtual hugs (Tsetserukou, 2010), and intimate cyber sexual activities (Solon, 2005). If deprived individuals are not able to receive virtual touch with consent, individuals can use coercion to receive affectionate virtual touch from others using manipulation techniques to sexually abuse others online (Wolak et al., 2008). Deprived individuals can coerce others by requesting intimate virtual touch favors in exchange of gifts or money through video chat technologies such as *Kissenger* to exchange realistic kisses.[1] Victims of coercion may feel pressured to engage in intimate activities out of fear of being shamed; however, they can choose to document the experience and report it to chat organizers.

Nonconsensual sexual harassment touch behaviors can occur in online multiplayer video games using virtual avatars as well. For instance, a Second Life teen victim reported virtual haptic sexual harassment when a male avatar took her avatar to a nude beach and asked her to go skinny-dipping with him (Allendale, 2007). Before she realized it, she noticed that the penis of the avatar appeared and it started to have sexual intercourse with her nude avatar (Allendale, 2007). With feelings of disgust and betrayal, she felt that those sexual behaviors were not consensual and asked him to stop multiple times using the text feature of the game (Allendale, 2007). When he finally stopped, she got dressed again and left him isolated at the beach. She realized how naïve she was to trust another virtual user that quickly and how easily one can be manipulated into having nonconsensual cybersex in Second Life (Allendale, 2007). This experience highlights how quickly and unexpectedly virtual haptic sexual harassment can occur in simulated video game environments. Unfortunately, users in virtual games continue to be at risk for virtual haptic sexual harassment; however, no studies have investigated the prevalence of incidents of haptic sexual harassment. Second Life's Linden Lab has developed policies to prevent sexual harassment offenses by promoting mutual respect among the avatars and offering one- to three-day suspensions to predators that get reported by the avatar victims (Bugeja, 2010).

Despite the likelihood of high prevalence, virtual haptic harassment as a subset of sexual harassment is a new area of research, and few studies have dealt with this issue. To guide future research, this chapter will offer a conceptualization of virtual haptic sexual harassment in hybrid settings and the use of technology to identify and cope with this problem. This chapter will also explore questions including: what are the prevalence risks of virtual haptic sexual harassment? What are the different types of virtual haptic sexual harassment? What are the effects of virtual haptic sexual harassment on women as well as men? The purpose of this chapter is to review the prevalence of online sexual harassment literature through haptics in gendered communication, conceptualize haptic communication and sexual harassment in hybrid and digital settings, review the effects of online sexual harassment, and discuss future research directions.

Literature Review of Online Sexual Harassment and Gender

Prior to discussing the prevalence of online sexual harassment against men and women across different types of virtual abuse via haptics, we will distinguish the difference between virtual and traditional haptic sexual harassment.

Virtual Haptic vs. Traditional Haptic Sexual Harassment

Virtual haptic sexual harassment ranges from mild to severe forms of unwanted virtual touch. Mild forms can include excessive 'poking' of someone's picture or video, moderate forms can include sending self-touching sexual pictures (Biber et al., 2002), and severe forms can include virtually touching the private parts of someone's avatar or engaging in cybersex. Also, virtual haptic harassment includes *nonphysical* and *physical virtual haptic harassment.* Nonphysical virtual haptic harassment occurs when a person's avatar is being touched inappropriately through virtual reality technologies by another person's avatar. However, coercive physical virtual haptic harassment occurs when a person engages in unwanted self-touching behavior of their own physical body witnessed by others. Moderate forms of virtual haptic harassment include requesting self-touching nude pictures. It can also include the exchange of self-touching photos and videos. And, severe forms include coercive cyber-sexual activity using self-touching of one's genitals or breasts using cybersex toys with a webcam. For example, Mitchell et al. (2007) collected national data, representing 1,500 youth aging 10–17 who use the Internet, and found that 4% reported receiving unwanted sexual requests to send pictures of themselves touching their private parts or displaying nudity to strangers or others whom they met online, which represents a *moderate* and *physical* form of haptic harassment.

Another sample of 2,051 adolescents as part of the National Survey of Children's Exposure to Violence found 96% aged between 10 to 17 reported being harassed online through websites or social networking sites, or through unwanted online sexual solicitations via email or instant messages. In addition, 9% of online youth reported being sexually offended online for several years through being flashed through webcams or through rated-R pictures of physical bodies (Mitchell et al., 2011). Another study found that 6–8% of youth have reported being coerced into engaging in unwanted sexual haptic activities such as sharing self-touching pornographic videos and images of their physical bodies *(moderate harassment)* and engaging in cybersex through their webcams *(severe harassment)* (Kopecky, 2017). For this reason, both young women and men continue to be at risk for virtual haptic sexual harassment via their physical bodies.

Adults also often report being cyberstalked in today's modern era. Cyber-stalking is nothing but a consistent and recurrent attempt by an individual to disturb the tranquility of the victim in the virtual world. It is frequently done by surreptitiously following the victim's activities in social networking sites or by sending an array of throwaway emails and is designed to emotionally harm the target. Studies have examined the perpetration rates of online gender harassment. Since predators may have easy access to victims through the use of social media and mobile devices and they believe they are less likely to get tracked for their misconduct, it has become easier for offenders to sexually victimize individuals (Chawki & Shazly, 2013). The outcome of cyber-stalking on the health of the victim can be disastrous too (Frommholz et al., 2016).

Several offenders reported engaging in haptic sexual harassment by sending threatening emails and messages on Facebook, extorting nude photos, and self-masturbating videos to engage in cybersex with women in several states (Chawki & Shazly, 2013). For example, Asapxcecilia, a female user, received nude images of a male friend via Facebook messenger (Cuen, 2016). However, after sending his own images, he then coerced her to provide self-touching revealing photos of herself through Facebook instant messenger, and she sent him revealing pictures because she felt threatened. Afterward, the predator warned her that if she did not have cybersex with him using a webcam, he would smear her reputation by posting her private photos to the public Facebook community (Cuen, 2016). Although she attempted to block him, he continued to contact her using different Facebook accounts using the same threats (Cuen, 2016). While developed countries like the United States, the UK, Canada, and Australia have enacted stringent anti-cyber stalking laws, enforcement has proven difficult, and developing countries like India are later in legal measures to address the problem (Joshi, 2013).

A 2010 study found that 18% of online sexual harassment offenses occur in chat rooms, and these offenses are tailored to young individuals (Chawki & Shazly, 2013). Also, about 82% of offenders who adopt the use of social networking sites such as Facebook use them to investigate a victim's page (Chawki & Shazly, 2013). Studies have reported that online offenders use the Internet to harass up to 75% of girls and 25% of boys aged 13 to 15 years of age (Chawki & Shazly, 2013). As far as gender is concerned, a few studies suggest that mid-adolescent boys (ages 13 to 18) are more likely to engage in online gender sexual harassment in comparison to girls (Raskauskas & Stolz, 2007). Other studies report mixed findings suggesting that both males and females perpetrate at proportional levels (Li, 2006; Wolak et al., 2007).

Online Gender Harassment Victimization

A Pew Research Center study found that 19% of participants witnessed others being sexually harassed online and 18% reported being cyber-stalked by another person (Duggan, 2014). For the most part, young women between the ages of

18 and 24 were more likely to be sexually harassed or stalked on the Internet through social media. Approximately 25% of the young women reported experiencing sexual harassment online (Duggan, 2014). Generally, men are slightly more likely than women to experience at least one of the behaviors of online harassment, 44% vs. 37% (Duggan, 2014; 2017). Additionally, males regardless of age were more likely to experience online sexual harassment when playing online games than with other online activities such as using social networking sites, websites, or instant message applications (Duggan, 2014). In *Second Life*, 38% of women and 13% of men reported receiving unwanted sexual advances to engage in cybersex through their avatar (Behm-Morawitz & Schipper, 2015). Also, female avatars are more likely to experience online gender sexual harassment in *Second Life* than male avatars do (Behm-Morawitz & Schipper, 2015). More specifically, female avatars that use provocative clothing and appear physically fit with enlarged breasts are more likely to experience sexual harassment in comparison with 'nonsexual' female avatars that use conservative clothing, appear overweight, or appear physically unattractive (Behm-Morawitz & Schipper, 2015). Therefore, choosing a male or an unattractive female avatar may reduce the risk of haptic harassment for women users. Physically attractive avatars in Second Life, however, are at risk of experiencing haptic harassment because players can use sexual features enabling intimate virtual touch activities, such as cuddling, kissing, fondling, and displaying different types of sexual positions using multilove poses (Kidd, 2007).

Users can also use digital sex toys on other avatars and can type 'sexual scripts' to direct their avatar's touch behavior on others using an instant message (IM) feature (Kidd, 2007). Thus, websites, online games, email accounts, discussion sites (e.g., Reddit), and online dating websites/apps have emerged as virtual spaces where women as well as men continue to report online haptic harassment. Additionally, a study by Priebe and Svedin (2012) found that sexual minorities, especially gay boys, had four times increased odds of being sexually harassed using mobile devices through text messages and six times increased odds of being exposed to sexual pictures or videos in comparison to straight men (Priebe & Svedin, 2012).

Online Workplace Harassment

Not only are youth being sexually victimized online, but the prevalence of working adults' online sexual harassment is also notable. In a study of heterosexual women in the workplace, 41% reported being sexually harassed through the Internet through unsolicited pornographic videos or images (Griffiths, 2000). Another study found that 17% of women reported being sexually harassed at work by colleagues or supervisors through email messages with explicit visual photographs and 49% reported receiving offensive emails with sexual connotations about their sexual identity (Whitty, 2004). Online workplace harassment of either gender can also occur outside of employees' regular work schedule.

Individuals may receive sexually explicit or suggestive images, videos, or text messages from a colleague or a supervisor after work (Ricotta & Marks, 2017). As far as haptics are concerned, individuals may report being coerced into engaging in cybersex during or after work or exchanging self-touching sexual photographs or videos using a mobile device via texting and instant messaging (Cooper et al., 2002). To address this issue, Guerin advises organizations to make it clear that the rules of conduct at work should extend to email and instant messages (Society of Human Resource Management, 2009). Interestingly, workplace predators report harassing their colleagues at work using online platforms due to mental illness, sexual addiction (Cooper et al., 2002), and broken romantic relationships (Mainiero & Jones, 2013) or even marriage troubles.

In addition, victims can be sexually abused via haptics in both physical and mediated settings due to the physical proximity with predators from broken romantic relationships at work (Mainiero & Jones, 2013). For instance, a victim may receive physical touches on the thigh from an ex-partner at work and also request to engage in cybersex using virtual touch to stimulate the predator's sexual desires outside of work hours. A victim may initially refuse or decline the request; however, if the predator holds power over the victim, the predator may coerce the victim to engage in cyber-sexual activities by threatening the victim with a loss of credibility or even loss of employment. Given this situation, victims may feel coerced to unwillingly engage in unwanted cybersex behaviors. Receiving both physical and online haptic sexual harassment from ex-partners can be emotionally devastating and uncomfortable for the victims (Mainiero & Jones, 2013). To reduce online sexual victimization, victims and bystanders need to become aware of their organization's policies regarding online sexual harassment and report these behaviors to human resources or their direct supervisors (Barak, 2005). Individuals may also sign 'love contracts,' or contracts signed by both partners after a workplace romantic relationship has ended that prohibits unethical conduct regarding digital abuse, which can help provide for recourse against online haptic sexual harassment at work (Tyler, 2008). The dismissal of the CEO of American Red Cross, Mark Everson, occurred because his subordinate partner filed a complaint of online sexual harassment after their romantic relationship ended. If a 'love contract' is signed with a partner during their romantic relationship, after the breakup, the subordinate victim has a legal document that enables them to file a lawsuit against the predator.

Sexual Harassment Laws Can Include Virtual Sexual Harassment Cases Too

As virtual sexual harassment is emerging in society, the traditional sexual harassment laws are slowly including cases of virtual sexual harassment. The Equal Employment Opportunity Commission (2016) defines sexual harassment as the "unwelcome sexual advances, requests for sexual favors, and other verbal or physical conduct of a sexual nature." As sexual harassment cases have been reported in online environments, online sexual harassment is defined as any "unwanted sexual conduct on any digital platform" such as email, social media, websites, and blogs (Project deShame, 2019). Legally speaking, in the United States, Title VII of the Civil Rights Act of 1964 is the only national-level law that protects individuals from both physical and virtual sexual harassment in work-related settings (EEOC, 2016). Also, the Title IX of the Education Amendments of 1972 law protects students and employees from sexual harassment in federally funded education programs and institutions (EPA, 2017). While these laws have traditionally been implemented to address face-to-face sexual harassment, lawyers have been using them to protect victims of virtual sexual harassment by emphasizing the 'sex discrimination' component of these laws, due to the lack of a specific federal online sexual harassment law. For instance, when five students at the University of Mary Washington in Virginia were virtually sexually harassed using the Yik Yak app, lawyers used Title IX's section that protects victims from sexually condescending harassment (Wheeler, 2020). Additionally, some states have developed their own laws to protect employees and employers from sexual harassment in online environments.

In India, the Prevention of Sexual Harassment (POSH) Act of 2013 is being used to combat sexual harassment that occurs not only face-to-face, but also in online environments, and it describes harassment that is unwelcome and sexual and not only physical, but also as being both nonverbal and verbal (Varma, 2020). It has been enacted for the prevention and reparation of complaints of sexual harassment and for issues related to the atrocious offense against women at work. Recently, as a step towards gender-neutral Prevention of Sexual Harassment (POSH) Policy, some forward-thinking organizations in India have started accepting grievances from all. Here, men have the 'right' to register a case of sexual harassment against women. Again, in order to protect men from being sexually harassed and coerced by women at the office, section 377 of Indian Penal Code had been introduced, which penalizes the offender if proven guilty. In Canada, the Section 10 of The Canada Labour Code protects individuals of both the genders from sexual harassment, and it is defined as "engaging in a course of vexatious comment or conduct that is known or ought to be known to be unwelcome" (Ontario Human Rights Commission [OHRC], 2020). This may include online sexual harassment acts such as sharing pornographic and sexual pictures via text message, displaying graphical sexual jokes via email, and requesting virtual sexual favors (OHRC, 2020). Also, because sexual harassment cases are occurring in online environments, it is important to understand digital sexual harassment as an extension of traditional sexual harassment.

Outlining Virtual Haptic Sexual Harassment

Haptic sexual harassment includes quid pro- quo harassment and hostile working environment. *Quid pro-quo harassment* or 'this for that' refers to threatening a person to engage in unwelcome virtual sexual behavior to obtain or retain employment or receive bonuses. For instance, a boss can request a self-touching nude photo of an employee or request cyber-sexual touch during work hours, and if the individual declines this request, the boss may threaten to terminate the employee. *Hostile working environment*, conversely, is unwelcome sexual behavior that occurs at work, which affects employees' ability to function properly. For example, employees may post sexually provocative photos in private electronic exchanges and intimidate colleagues with unwanted, ambiguous, or overly friendly touches or rubs, which means that employees can receive both physical and virtual forms of haptic harassment. Virtually speaking, a hostile working environment is created when employees share self-touching pornographic images, videos, or websites using a mobile device or a computer at work or during breaks, which cultivate distress and embarrassment in colleagues that witness this unwelcome behavior. Working in a hostile working environment could lead to feeling negative emotions such as anxiety, embarrassment, guilt, shame, disgust, and stress (Spector, 2017).

Sexual discrimination can also be defined given the abuse of power via quid pro quo harassment. An individual in a position of power, such as a manager in an organization, may hold certain authority over others and may abuse their power by using quid pro quo harassment through haptic communication. Recently, a store manager at the Dollar General sexually harassed a female employee by sending her unwelcome textual messages and threatened to fire her if she did not provide sexualized nude images. After she filed a lawsuit using Title VII of the Civil Rights Act of 1964 against Dollar General, the manager was suspended and fired for his conduct (EEOC, 2017a). Additionally, a United Airlines pilot posted sexually explicit pictures to different public websites of his ex-girlfriend, who continued to be a flight attendant, by providing her name and using a tagline 'Fly the Friendly Skies' to humiliate her in front of her colleagues (Kilgore, 2018). However, despite her complaints, United Airlines failed to discipline the pilot's behavior, and as a result, she sued the airline with a violation of Title VII of the Civil Rights Act of 1964 (Kilgore, 2018).

Additionally, *gender-based discriminatory harassment* occurs when one harasses a person due to expressing their femininity or masculinity. Gender-based discrimination occurs with the use of virtual haptics in same-sex or cross-sex relationships at work, or in other settings. For example, Steven was coerced into undressing and engaging in self-masturbation via video chat (Stop Online Abuse [SOA], 2018). An LGBTQ member demanded more sexual images, and he eventually posted them on Facebook and Twitter. Steven contacted the police and the video-chat website for his IP address, and the offender was convicted with blackmail and sentenced to one year in prison (SOA, 2018). Also, Loretta, a transgender individual, shared sexual self-touching videos with a man through FaceTime and Skype (SOA, 2018). As time went on, the man became demanding and requested more frequent sexual videos, threatening that if she didn't comply, he would publicize her transgender identity and the sexual photos and videos (SOA, 2018). When Loretta ended contact with him, he retaliated and posted a sexual video of her on Facebook and the video went viral. Facebook officials removed the video from Facebook, and then the police charged the man with this offense (SOA, 2018). Of course, as noted elsewhere in this volume and in many other sources, this sort of after-the-fact removal of abusive or nonconsensual content does not remove the harm to the target (Barker & Jurasz, 2019; Powell & Henry, 2017).

Unexamined challenges exist when identifying virtual haptic sexual harassment in hybrid settings for targets and employers. First, targets might be hesitant to report haptic sexual harassment due to embarrassment or fear. Second, if targets do not save the evidence of haptic sexual harassment, it becomes difficult to punish virtual offenders. Third, if individuals accuse the offender of virtual haptic sexual harassment in a workplace environment, the human resource department might not know how to handle this type of abuse. From employers' perspective, having a policy in a written handbook may not be sufficient. Employers need to take an active stance to require supervisors and employees to be trained about how to identify, cope with, and report virtual haptic sexual harassment.

Defining Virtual Haptic Sexual Harassment Using Technology

Human–computer interaction (HCI) permits end users to recognize the textures and contours of remote objects using virtual touch. HCI helps express desires, build trust, and perform behaviors such as engaging in interactions using audiovisual technology, navigating 3D environments, and using tactile emoticons with the Braille system using raised dots to enable vision-impaired individuals to facilitate interaction. *Reverse-electro-vibration* or virtual touch can initiate virtual haptic sexual harassment, which may lead to cyber-rape. Virtual haptics are manifested with virtual reality (VR) and augmented reality (AR) technology.

VR space has social gaming apps where people can log in to interact and socialize, such as *Rec Room,* where one can team up with others to complete quests or competitions. Also, *VRChat* vaunts full body avatars that move with your body to simulate real-life emotions. Participants use VR gear or input devices and sometimes a phone. Participants use:

i   VR glasses or goggles,
ii   Data gloves,
iii   Head mounted displays (HMD),
iv   Data suits,
v   Workbenches, and
vi   Joysticks.

Haptic expedients empower users to feel a sense of touch when manipulating objects within a virtual environment. VR gear has become lighter, daintier, and more affordable than that in the past. Head-mounted displays take the form of a pair of goggles or helmet with a screen in front, which displays 3D images. Many contain headphones and/or speakers to receive audio/video output as well. Head mounted displays also contain a tracking device, which means that the images displayed to the wearer change along with users' head motions. When logging in through apps, a user appears to everyone in a chat room, and one can hug or touch others. Although moderators regulate harassment in VR chat-rooms, cases of unwanted kissing and touching have been recorded (Igbokwe, 2016). Thus, haptic communication may also occur with sexual connotations in online-only communication settings.

Unlike face-to-face settings, *Cyber-sexual harassment* (CSH) occurs among individuals who remain *anonymous* by using pseudonyms or false identities when conducting unwanted cyber-sexual behaviors (Ritter, 2013). Anonymity makes it difficult to identify and find online predators. Anonymous individuals are less accountable for their online digital abuse behaviors because they may perceive no negative consequences. *De-individuation* occurs when anonymous individuals perform behaviors they'd normally not perform in everyday life, but because it occurs in online environments, individuals do not take personal responsibility for their uncivilized behaviors (Postmes & Spears, 1998), which explains why online sexual predators may not judge their own actions to be malevolent. Additionally, Blanchard's (2004) Virtual Behavior Setting Theory suggests that online communication is accessible solely through computer communication, and as a result, de-individuation occurs because it lacks the 'physical attributes' used in physical settings.

In VR environments, for example, a female game designer, Renee Gittins, reported the sexual harassment through virtual haptic that she experienced within a VR game Alstpace VR (Roose, 2016). The perpetrator remained *anonymous* using a pseudonym, and since the inappropriate self-touching using an avatar occurred within a social video game, the individual's identity remained hidden. This behavior can be easily dismissed given the *accessibility* of virtual environments since this behavior can only be perceived using the monitor of a television or mobile device screen. After encountering this isolated experience, Gittins felt disturbed, but powerless because she did not know her own civil rights as an online victim, or how to cope with this type of situation (Roose, 2016). Also, when a perpetrator engages in this behavior *one specific time* with this random user, it is unlikely to be punished by the law or by a moderator of the video game. As a victim, Gittins reported feeling negative visceral experiences that felt 'too real' to her personally because she empathized with her avatar while wearing her VR gear in a VR environment (Roose, 2016).

Another victim of video game harassment reports a severe form of tactile online harassment via QuiVR, an online multiplayer (co-op) VR game about using archery in teams to defeat invading monsters. Jordan Belamire blogged about her emotionally traumatic experience with online sexual harassment. She recalls a floating player named BigBro442 with a helmet, bow in hand, and another free-roaming hand, which he used to virtually 'rub' her chest. When this happened, she cried, 'Stop!' while laughing from the embarrassment, which only made things worse.

As soon as she ran away, he chased her around and kept virtually grabbing and pinching the chest of her avatar. When he got closer to her avatar, he "shoved his hand toward [her] virtual crotch and began rubbing" (Belamire, 2016). As this was occurring, her husband and brother-in-law witnessed the incident, but both laughed since the behavior was easily dismissed as a 'joke' as they only saw it through a computer screen and did not feel the emotional distress that she was feeling through the VR system, which felt more real (Belamire, 2016).

Similarly, the perpetrator adopted an *anonymous* name, BigBro442. The *accessibility* of the virtual environment dismissed the seriousness of the online sexual harassment incident. As Belamire (2016) noticed that the avatar was harassing her, she felt shocked and for a moment could not immediately react. After a few seconds she ran away, but the avatar kept chasing her and continued to grope her avatar's genitals. In this instance, once the predator is within a victim's perceived personal distance, victims might not know how to 'escape' or 'stop' the unwanted virtual groping behavior. After similar online sexual harassment incidents were reported by the media, the QuiVR developers responded by adding a 'power gesture' feature to the QuiVR game to prevent and cope with online sexual harassment via their video game (D'Anastasio, 2016). This 'power gesture' enables players to add a 'personal bubble' option to make sexual offenders' avatars disappear from the 'personal bubble' of the victims (D'Anastasio, 2016). Additionally, if victimized players click two triggers, the predators will disappear from the screen of the victims and the predators.

Online gender harassment involves "a range of misogynist behaviors directed at women or men because of their gender" through the use of communication technology (Biber et al., 2002, p. 34). Barak (2005) conceptualized *active graphic gender harassment* as intense tactile and nonverbal behaviors that occur in online environments, such as displaying pornographic pictures or videos and engaging in cybersex or sexting. Active graphic gender harassment can involve haptics when individuals feel psychologically coerced into engaging in self-touching or masturbating rituals in front of a web-camera, while a predator or multiple predators are witnessing the behavior. For instance, an individual user may receive requests to display or witness sexual videos via Chatroulette, which is a website that enables users to meet random individuals via a webcam and microphone. Another example can include touch simulations in mobile dating applications (e.g., Virtual Girlfriend) that enable the intimate virtual touch of an avatar's body parts. If one consents to receiving virtual touch, then this behavior is appropriate. However, if a user coerces another to use touch simulations using technology, then this behavior becomes involuntary, forced, and unwanted. Predators may bribe helpless victims who are in need of money, by providing cash or gifts in exchange for sexual videos or engaging in cyber-sexual activities. Thus, active graphic gender harassment involves sending and receiving inappropriate touch behavior through technological devices. While some platforms have adopted policies and rules of conduct to reduce virtual haptic harassment, these approaches are not always effective.

The Effects of Online Sexual Harassment

Online sexual harassment can have several effects on the victims. Online harassment has led to negative mental outcomes such as anxiety, depression, and social problems (Hawker & Boulton, 2000). Targets of online sexual harassment report feelings of emotional distress, which harmed their overall quality of life (Staude-Müller et al., 2012). Further, adolescent victims of online sexual harassment via Internet or mobile phone reported experiencing psychiatric symptoms, lower self-esteem ratings, and a low sense of coherence (Priebe & Svedin, 2012). Another study by Van Royen et al. (2015) found that adolescents suffer emotional consequences depending on the severity of the online sexual harassment on social networking sites. For instance, severe forms of online harassment such as receiving pornographic images, being asked to send nude images, or witnessing the noncensual use of their normal pictures that were modified to be sexually appealing in a public forum triggered emotional distress (Van Royen et al., 2015).

Several studies highlight the severity of mental health effects caused by these unwanted behaviors. Duggan (2014) reported that 14% of online harassment victims reported being extremely distressed right after the incident, and when comparing the genders, 38% of the harassed women reported being extremely upset in comparison to 17% of the harassed men. A more recent study of female video game players reported ruminating about sexual harassment offenses during and after playing video games with aggressors, even after withdrawing from the video game (Fox & Tang, 2017). Also being victimized, LGBTQ individuals experienced psychiatric symptoms, lower self-esteem, and a lack of coherence (Priebe & Svedin, 2012).

Online sexual harassment can also impact relationships negatively. For instance, a study found that females were more likely to experience feelings of envy, anxiety, and fear due to having their male romantic partner being sexually harassed by another woman through pictures being shown through the post walls within social networking sites (Miller et al., 2014). Some individuals report online sexual harassment from their ex-partners after terminating a romantic relationship through *doxxing*, or the public posting of intimate information without permission (McIntyre, 2016). Victims of doxxing may feel humiliated and threatened by the images or videos posted through social media, text groups, and websites by a former romantic partner (McIntyre, 2016). Cyber stalking, especially unsolicited hate, vulgar, or threatening email can be very distressing, at times. Other methods of cyber stalking include sending the target noxious viruses or even large quantities of junk emails.

Biber and colleagues (2002) examined the gender differences of the effects of online sexual harassment based on discourse medium, finding that both men and women found misogynist comments toward women and comments about one's dress to be more harmful when received online (e.g., Facebook) than in face-to-face settings. However, when examining online-sexualized pictures and online sexual jokes, women felt those were more offensive to them than did the men of the study (Biber et al., 2002). These findings suggest that intense forms of online sexual harassment including haptic harassment or the experience of inappropriate virtual touch may impact women and men quite differently. For instance, women may experience and perceive haptic sexual harassment to be more disturbing than men do. Future studies need to examine the impact of haptics in online sexual harassment.

Future Directions

Future directions can advance gender scholarship in the area of virtual haptic sexual harassment. First, gender-based theories may expand understanding of cyber-harassment given that the Internet has become a hostile environment for gendered digital abuse. For instance, cyber-feminism theories may help to understand intersections of online sexual harassment including gender, race, and sexual orientation (Morrow et al., 2013). Cyber-feminism can extend Dill et al.'s (2008) research findings that long-term exposure to virtual sexual harassment through video game characters transferred over to being more tolerant toward face-to-face sexual harassment and the acceptance 'of rape myths.' Future studies can adopt cyber-feminism by examining the role of power dynamics and heterogeneity in the transferal of attitudes towards digital abuse from online to physical settings. Cyborg feminism, the idea that identity is socially constructed by our interactions with other users' virtual avatars or physical representations in online environments can also help to understand how individuals respond to digitized bodies in cyberspace environments through gendered lenses and how these digital responses impact individuals' attitudes toward physical bodies in real life (Paniagua, 2012).

Sexual objectification is evident in the digital sphere, and feminist scholars can advance this scholarship by scrutinizing the cultures and norms that lead to the trivialization of online sexual harassment through haptics. For instance, Fox et al.'s (2013) study found support of the Proteus effect and objectification theory, indicating that women treat their bodies as objects, and they suffer psychological consequences from their selection and identification of 'sexualized' avatars that display virtual cleavage, revealing clothing, and hyper-attractive bodies. Also, users exhibited blame attitudes toward others who become sexually harassed online. Thus, future scholars can extend this research by examining specific psychological effects of online sexual harassment through haptics that occur via sexualized avatars in social virtual environments based on perceived harassment intensity across sexes and sexual orientations. Future studies can also investigate the harmful sexist language involved in digital dialogues between men and women via chat rooms, social media, or virtual realities to explain the perpetuation of virtual haptic sexual discrimination.

Second, scholars may investigate the legal ramifications of online sexual harassment through haptic communication. Since online sexual harassment is considered a cyber-crime in some US states such as California and New Jersey and also in some European and Asian countries, understanding the implications of cyber-harassment laws can be beneficial. If aggressors perceive a negative cost to engaging in cyber nuisance, such as paying a large fine or spending time in jail, then aggressors might avoid cyber-harassing individuals based on their gender, which might prevent subsequent digital abuse behaviors. With the passage of anti-cyber harassment laws protecting victims against cyber-harassment through haptic communication, managers and officials may take this issue more seriously in personal matters and the workplace (Citron, 2009). Cyber-harassment laws can also empower victims and witnesses to report these virtual touch violations as they emerge in online environments (Citron, 2014).

Third, investigating technological strategies to prevent online sexual harassment can be fruitful. For example, several mobile apps can prevent and reduce online sexual harassment. Apps such as 'Not Your Baby App' can be used through the iPhone to indicate the social environment and the aggressors to warn other potential victims about these digital aggressors with pseudonyms. The *OnWatch* mobile app can be used to send messages through text messaging or social media directly to the police or to obtain emergency services. Another technological strategy to cope with cyber harassment can be social media pages or websites that serve to educate individuals about the behaviors that correspond with digital gender abuse. For instance, the Sexual Harassment Watch page on Facebook monitored by the Gender Friendly Organization provides several educational videos, images, and quotes to educate its followers about digital sexual harassment through haptics. To combat the potential online sexual harassment that has emerged in the Virtual/Multiple Reality (VR/MR) space, Walker (2015) suggests using virtual reality simulated interventions such as 'My Voice, My Choice' (MVMC) training program to prevent and cope with sexual harassment that occurs in online settings.

Conclusion

This chapter has provided an overview of the issue of online sexual haptic harassment, delivered examples illustrating the wide range and prevalence of such abuses, examined some common outcomes of these behaviors, and discussed legal and policy approaches, especially in India and the United States, to combat them. Sexual harassment that takes place using physical touch behavior in amalgamation with virtual touch in both physical and virtual settings in everyday parlance have been delineated in this chapter in detail. In reality, sexual harassment has been ubiquitous in most forms of online and gaming environments from the early days of their existence. Yes, until very recently, it was restricted to verbal and visual communications. But with the advent of haptic virtual technology, gender persecution has become more persistent and intimidating in nature, affecting both women and men. Victims of both face-to-face and online haptic sexual harassment may experience mistreatment within the context of romantic, work, and acquaintance relationships. Again, the current research has also emphasized cyber-stalking as an offence in which the cyber-criminal pesters or stalks a potential target using electronic or digital resources, for example email, social media, messages or instant messaging (IM) and thereby indulging in sexual misconduct. Often, the experiences of digital sexual harassment emphasized in this chapter may have long-term effects on the mental, emotional, and social well-being of a victim.

Online sexual haptic harassment is clearly a vast and expanding area of abuse that warrants further investigation. Distinguishing the conceptualization differences between traditional and online haptic sexual harassment is challenging, and scholars need to continue to refine these constructs. Future scholarship may continue to scrutinize this issue by using feminist theories, investigating current digital anti-abuse laws, and assessing innovative technological solutions against digital gender abuse. The field of such abuses will likely continue to expand with further technological developments, presenting an ever-urgent need for careful study to inform useful problem-solving.

Note

1 Kissinger is a mobile kiss messenger that transmits kissing sensations to the lips of one's partner. Individuals can use force sensors under a silicon lip, which is a technological tool that transmits vibrational kisses in two-way interactions over Internet or a mobile/tablet device.

References

Allendale, D. (2007). *How exactly does 'virtual rape' even occur in second life?* http://www. vtoreality.com/2007/how-exactly-does-virtual-rape-even-occur-in-second-life/909/

Andersen, P. A. (1999). *Nonverbal communication: Forms and functions.* Mayfield.

Barak, A. (2005). Sexual harassment on the internet. *Social Science Computer Review, 23*(1), 77–92. https://doi.org/10.1177/0894439304271540

Barker, K., & Jurasz, O. (2019). *Online misogyny as a hate crime: A challenge for legal regulation.* Routledge.

Behm-Morawitz, E., & Schipper, S. (2015). Sexing the avatar: Gender, sexualization, and cyber-harassment in a virtual world. *Journal of Media Psychology, 28*(4), 161–174. https://doi.org/10.1027/1864-1105.

Belamire, J. (2016). *My first virtual reality groping.* https://medium.com/athena-talks/my-first-virtual-reality-sexual-assault-2330410b62ee.

Biber, J. K., Doverspike, D., Baznik, D., Cober, A., & Ritter, B. A. (2002). Sexual harassment in online communications: Effects of gender and discourse medium. *Cyber psychology Behavior, 5*, 33–42. https://doi.org/10.1080/109493102753685863.

Blanchard, A. (2004). Virtual behavior settings: An application of behavior setting theories to virtual communities. *Journal of Computer-Mediated Communication, 9*(2), 1. https://doi.org/10.1111/j.1083-6101.2004.tb00285.x.

Brewster, M. P. (2001). Legal help – Seeking experiences of former intimate – stalking victims. *Criminal Justice Policy Review, 12*(2), 91–112. https://doi.org/10.1177/0887403401012002001

Bugeja, M. (2010). *Avatar rape.* https://www.insidehighered.com/views/2010/02/25/avatar-rape.

Chawki, M., & Shazly, Y. (2013). Online sexual harassment: Issues and solutions. *JIP-ITEC, 2,* 71–86. https://www.jipitec.eu/issues/jipitec-4-2-2013/3742.

Citron, D. K. (2009). Law's expressive value in combating cyber gender harassment. *Michigan Law Review, 108,* 373–415. http://digitalcommons.law.umaryland.edu/cgi/viewcontent.cgi?article=1687&context=fac_pubs.

Citron, D. K. (2014). *Hate crimes in cyberspace.* Harvard University Press.

Cooper, A. L., Golden, G. H., & Kent-Ferraro, J. (2002). Online sexual behaviors in the workplace: How can human resource departments and employee assistance programs respond effectively. *Sexual Addiction & Compulsivity, 9,* 149–165. https://doi.org/10.1080/10720160290062293

Cuen, L. (2016). *Is Facebook policing how women respond to sexual harassment?* https://mic.com/articles/146116/is-facebook-policing-how-women-respond-to-sexual-harassment#.OjosOhKOd.

D'Anastasio, C. (2016). *VR developers add 'superpower' to their game to fight harassment.* https://kotaku.com/vr-developers-add-personal-bubble-to-their-game-to-fi-1788237241.

Dill, K. E., Brown, B. P., & Colllins, M. A. (2008). Effects of exposure to sex-stereotyped video game characters on tolerance of sexual harassment. *Journal of Experimental Social Psychology, 44*(5), 1402–1408. https://doi.org/10.1016/j.jesp.2008.06.002.

Duggan, M. (2014). *Online harassment.* http://www.pewinternet.org/2014/10/22/online-harassment/

Duggan, M. (2017). *Online assessment 2017.* http://www.pewinternet.org/2017/07/11/online-harassment-2017/

EPA. (2017). *Title IX of the education amendments act of 1972.* https://www.epa.gov/ocr/title-ix-education-amendments-act-1972.

Equal Employment Opportunity Commission. (2016). *Sexual harassment.* https://www.eeoc.gov/laws/types/sexual_harassment.cfm

Equal Employment Opportunity Commission. (2017a). *What you should know about EEOC and the enforcement protections for LGBT workers.* https://www.eeoc.gov/eeoc/newsroom/wysk/enforcement_protections_lgbt_workers.cfm.

Equal Employment Opportunity Commission. (2017b). *Dollar general sued by EEOC for sexual harassment.* https://www.eeoc.gov/eeoc/newsroom/release/2-9-17.cfm

Floyd, K. (2014). Relational and health correlates of affectionate deprivation. *Western Journal of Communication, 78*(4), 383–403. https://doi.org/10.1080/10570314.2014.927071.

Fox, J., Bailenson, J. N., & Tricase, L. (2013). The embodiment of sexualized virtual selves: The Proteus effect and experiences of self-objectification via avatars. *Computers in Human Behavior, 29*(3), 930–938. https://doi.org/10.1016/j.chb.2012.12.027.

Fox, J., & Tang, W. Y. (2017). Women's experiences with general and sexual harassment in online video games: Rumination, organizational responsiveness, withdrawal, and coping strategies. *New Media & Society, 19*(8), 1290–1307. https://doi.org/10.1177/1466144816635778.

Frommholz, I., Khateeb, H. M., Martin Potthast, M., Ghasem, Z., Shukla, M., Short, E. (2016). *On textual analysis and machine learning for cyber stalking detection.* The National Centre for Cyberstalking Research.

Griffiths, M. (2000). Internet addiction – Time to be taken seriously? *Addiction Research, 8,* 413–418. https://doi.org/10.3109/16066350009005587.

Hawker, D., & Boulton, M. (2000). Twenty years' research on peer victimization and psychological maladjustment: A meta-analytical review of cross-sectional studies.

Journal of Child Psychology and Psychiatry, 41(4), 441–455. https://pubmed.ncbi.nlm.
nih.gov/10836674/.

Hornstein, E. (1984). *The Guide to American law: Everyone's legal encyclopedia.* West.

Igbokwe, I. (2016). Sexual harassment now has a new name; It is called virtual reality.
Tech Point. https://techpoint.ng/2016/07/21/sexual-harassment-vr/.

Joshi, D. (2013). *India's criminal law amendment to include cyber stalking, harassment and voyeur-
ism.* Centre for Internet and Society.

Kidd, L. (2007). *Sex in second life.* https://thegreenlanterns.wordpress.com/new-resident-
help/sex-in-second-life/.

Kilgore, E. L. (2018*). EEOC sues United Airlines for sexual harassment based on employee
"Revenge porn."* https://www.louisianalawblog.com/labor-and-employment-law/
eeoc-sues-united-airlines-sexual-harassment-based-employee-revenge-porn/.

Kopecky, K. (2017). Online blackmail of Czech children focused on so-called "sextor-
tion" (analysis of culprit and victim behaviors). *Telematics and Informatics, 34,* 11–19.
https://doi.org/10.1016/j.tele.2016.04.004.

Li, Q. (2006). Cyberbullying in schools: A research of gender differences. *School Psychology International, 27*(2), 157–170. https://doi.org/10.1177/0143034306064547

Mainiero, L. A., & Jones, K. J. (2013). Workplace romance 2.0: Developing a communication ethics model to address potentially sexual harassment from inappropriate social
media contacts between coworkers. *Journal of Business Ethics, 114,* 367–379. https://
doi.org/10.1007/s10551-012-1349-8.

McIntyre, V. (2016). "Do(x) you really want to hurt me?": Adapting IIED as a solution
to doxing by reshaping intent. *Tulane Journal of Technology & Intellectual Property, 19,*
111–134. https://journals.tulane.edu/TIP/article/view/2667.

Miller, M. J., Denes, A., Diaz, B., & Buck, R. (2014). Attachment style predicts jealous
reactions to viewing touch between a romantic partner and close friend: Implications
for Internet Social Communication. *Journal of Nonverbal Behavior, 38,* 451–476. https://
doi.org/10.1007/s10919-014-0196-y.

Mitchell, K. J., Finkelhor, D., & Wolak, J. (2007). Online requests for sexual pictures
from youth: Risk factors and incident characteristics. *Journal of Adolescent Health, 41*(2),
196–203. https://doi.org/10.1016/j.jadohealth.2007.03.013.

Mitchell, K. J., Finkelhor, D., Wolak, J., Ybarra, M. L., & Turner, H. (2011). Youth
internet victimization in a broader victimization context. *Journal of Adolescent Health,
48,* 128–134. https://doi.org/10.1016/j.jadohealth.2010.06.009.

Morrow, O., Hawkins, R., & Kern, L. (2013). Feminist research in online spaces. *A
Journal of Feminist Geography, 22*(4), 526–543. http://dx.doi.org/10.1080/09663
69x.2013.879108.

Ontario Human Rights Commission. (2020). *Identifying sexual harassment.* http://
www.ohrc.on.ca/en/policy-preventing-sexual-and-gender-based-harassment/2-
identifying-sexual-harassment.

Paniagua, M. Z. (2012). Cyberfeminist theories and the benefits of teaching cyberfeminist literature. In A. Lopez-Varela (Eds.), *Social sciences and cultural studies – issues
of language, public opinion, education and welfare* (pp. 243–264a). Intechopen. https://
www.intechopen.com/books/social-sciences-and-cultural-studies-issues-of-
language-public-opinion-education-and-welfare/cyberfeminist-theories-and-the-
benefits-of-teaching-cyberfeminist-literature.

Postmes, T., & Spears, R. (1998). Deindividuation and antinormative behavior: A meta-
analysis. *Psychological Bulletin, 123,* 238–259. https://doi.org/10.1037/0033-2909.
123.3.238.

Powell, A., & Henry, N. (2017). *Sexual violence in a digital age.* Palgrave.

Preventing Sexual Harassment. (1992). *SDC IP.73 1992 Manual*. BNA communications, Inc.

Priebe, G., & Svedin, C. G. (2012). Online or off-line victimization and psychological well-being: A comparison of sexual-minority and heterosexual youth. *European Child & Adolescent Psychiatry, 21*(10), 569–582. https://doi.org/10.1007/s00787-012-0294-5.

Project deShame. (2019). *Tackling online sexual harassment – the start of project deShame II*. https://www.childnet.com/blog/tackling-online-sexual-harassment-the-start-of-project-deshame-ii/.

Punyanunt-Cart, N. M. (2009). Development and validity testing of a measure of touch deprivation. *Human Communication, 12*, 67–76. https://psycnet.apa.org/record/2017-27194-001.

Raskauskas, J., & Stolz, A. D. (2007). Involvement in traditional and electronic bullying among adolescents. *Development Psychology, 43*(3), 564–575. https://doi.org/10.1037/0012-1649.43.3.564.

Ricotta, & Marks, P. C. (2017). *What to know about internet sexual harassment in the workplace*. http://www.queensemploymentattorney.com/blog/2017/12/internet-sexual-harassment-in-the-workplace/.

Ritter, B. A. (2013). Deviant behavior in computer-mediated communication: Development and validation of a measure of cybersexual harassment. *Journal of Computer-Mediated Communication, 19*, 197–214. https://doi.org/10.1111/jcc4.12039.

Roose, K. (2016). *Virtual reality has a huge sexual harassment problem*. https://splinternews.com/virtual-reality-has-a-huge-sexual-harassment-problem-1793856248.

Saadatian, E., Samani, H., Parsani, R., Pandey, A. V., Li, J., Tejada, L. et al. (2014). Mediating intimacy in long-distance relationships using kiss messaging. *International Journal of Human-Computer Studies, 2*, 736–746. https://doi.org/10.1016/j.ijhcs.2014.05.004.

Sexual harassment on the Internet. (2010). *Internet harassment*. https://www.unc.edu/courses/2010spring/law/357c/001/internetharassment/internet-harassment.html.

Society for Human Resource Management (SHRM). (2009). *Federal statutes, regulations and guidance*. https://www.shrm.org/resourcesandtools/legal-and-compliance/employment-law/pages/federal-statutes-regulations-and-guidance.aspx.

Solon, O. (2005). *These sex tech toys will blow your mind*. http://www.wired.co.uk/article/sex-tech.

Spector, N. (2017). *Victims of sexual harassment often experience emotional and physical symptoms for years to come*. https://www.nbcnews.com/better/health/hidden-health-effects-sexual-harassment-ncna810416.

Staude-Müller, F., Hansen, B., & Voss, M. (2012). How stressful is online victimization? Effects of victim's personality and properties of the incident. *European Journal of Developmental Psychology, 9*(2), 260–274. https://doi.org/ 10.1080/17405629.2011.643170.

Stockdale, M. S., Visio, M., & Batra, L. (1999). The sexual harassment of men: Evidence for a broader theory of sexual harassment and sex discrimination. *Psychology, Public Policy, and Law, 5*, 630–664.

Stop Online Abuse. (2018). *Stop online abuse: Case studies*. http://www.stoponlineabuse.org.uk/case-studies.

Tsetserukou, D. (2010). HaptiHug: A novel haptic display for communication of hug over a distance. In D. Tsetserukou (Eds.), *International conference on human haptic sensing and touch enabled computer applications* (pp. 340–347). Springer. https://link.springer.com/conference/eurohaptics.

Tyler, K. (2008). Sign in the name of love: Can "love contracts" decrease an employer's litigation risks and keep office romances in check? *HR Magazine, 53*(2), 41–43. https://www.shrm.org/hr-today/news/hr-magazine/pages/hr-magazine-archive.aspx.

U.S. Equal Employment Opportunity Commission. (2016). *Sexual harassment.* https://www.eeoc.gov/sexual-harassment

Vanacker, B., & Heider, D. (2012). Ethical harm in virtual communities. *Convergence: The International Journal of Research into New Media Technologies, 18*(1). http://journals.sagepub.com/doi/abs/10.1177/1354856511419916.

Van Royen, K., Vandebosch, H., & Poels, K. (2015). Severe sexual harassment on social networking sites: Belgian adolescents' views. *Journal of Children and Media, 9*(4), 472–491. https://doi.org/10.1080/17482798.2015.1089301.

Varma, A. (2020). *Dealing with sexual harassment in the virtual workplace.* https://www.thehindubusinessline.com/opinion/dealing-with-sexual-harassment-in-the-virtual-workplace/article31403719.ece#.

Vossler, A. (2016). Internet infidelity 10 years on: A critical review of the literature. *The Family Journal, 24*(4), 359–366. https://doi.org/10.1177/1066480716663191.

Walker, L. (2015). *Virtual reality training for sexual harassment?* http://www.newsweek.com/virtual-reality-training-sexual-harassment-303612.

Wheeler, C. (2020). Katz, Marshall & Banks, LLP. *Victims of anonymous online harassment suffer serious consequences.* https://www.kmblegal.com/employment-law-blog/victims-anonymous-online-harassment-suffer-serious-consequences.

Whitty, M. T. (2004). Should filtering software be utilized in the workplace? Internet in the workplace. *Surveillance and Society, 2*(1), 39–54. https://doi.org/10.24908/ss.v2i1.3326.

Wolak, J., Finkelhor, D., Mitchell, K. J., & Ybarra, M. L. (2008). Online "predators" and their victims. *American Psychologist, 63*(2), 111–128. https://doi.org/10.1037/2152-0828.1.S.13

Wolak, J., Mitchell, K. J., & Finkelhor, D. (2007). Unwanted and wanted exposure to online pornography in a national sample of youth internet users. *Pediatrics, 119*(2): 247–257. https://doi.org/10.1542/peds.2006-1891

Yee, N., & Bailenson, J. (2007). The Proteus effect. The effect of transformed self-representation on behavior. *Human Communication Research, 33*(3), 271–290. https://doi.org/10.1111/j.1468-2958.2007.00299.x.

PART II
Practices

4

FEMALE CORPOREALITIES OF BLAME & INVASION IN CASES OF SEXUAL & SEXIST CYBERBULLYING IN THE BASQUE REGION

Estibaliz Linares Bahillo, Maria Silvestre Cabrera and Raquel Royo Prieto

Introduction

This chapter examines in detail the experiences of adolescent girls in relation to their corporealities and sexualities as well as the cultural mandates projected onto them from cyberspace. Adolescence must be understood in its socio-cultural context; in the contemporary world, this means understanding it within the digital framework, since the management of relationships and (in)formation is conducted through relation, information, and communication technologies (RICTs) (Marsh, 2010; Megias & Ballesteros, 2014; Ruiz, 2014).

In this way, this chapter brings together some of the results and conclusions from the research project the "Third Digital Gender Gap" (Tercera Brecha Digital de Género), carried out over two years, from 2017 to 2019, by the Social Values Research Team at the University of Deusto in Bilbao, Spain[1]. In particular, the chapter analyzes the testimonies and stories gathered from nine discussion groups carried out with adolescent girls between the ages of 11 and 13 (80 girls in total), and nine groups with mothers (50 women in total). It should be noted that the fact that the discussion groups were composed only of mothers does not reflect the available options or intentions of the research team, which extended invitations, via school parents' associations, to fathers as well as mothers. However, in the end, only mothers attended the groups; for that reason, the discussion groups collected only mothers' testimonies. The aim of the research is to draw attention to and study the experiences and pressures faced by adolescent girls in the digital age.

Female Corporeal and Social Mandates during Adolescence

In order to understand female cultural codes during adolescence, we must compre-hend them within complex and contradictory frameworks. Buckingham & Bragg

DOI: 10.4324/9781003260851-6

(2004) argue that the construction of femininity begins with identification with the community, that is, feeling and recognizing oneself as "we" before "I." Femininities take shape in an atmosphere of patriarchy and capitalism, dependent upon an outside gaze for self-affirmation (Martino & Pallota-Chiarolli, 2005, p. 99).

At this stage, corporeality is at the epicenter of the perception and construction of identity; though, in the case of girls, it becomes a special source of self-affirmation and self-worth. Girls start to realize that within a patriarchal and heteronormative structure, their bodies become an important factor in their success, and, at the same time, a source of self-affirmation (Renold, 2007). This all happens in a hypersexualized and hypereroticized context, assuring in turn that "being sexy" is highly valued in adolescent culture (Buckingham & Bragg, 2004, p. 103; Egan & Hawkes, 2012; Megias & Ballesteros, 2014; Renold, 2007; Renold & Allan, 2016).

In other words, while boys remain in a more flexible system in which to explore and exhibit (or not) their sexuality, the system for girls has tighter limits, where normativity can easily be transgressed; as a result, girls can find themselves stigmatized by other girls as much as by boys (Egan & Hawkes, 2012; Renold, 2007). As Renold (2002; 2007) notes, the "good woman"/"bad woman" dichotomy is therefore complicated in the case of girls. This last point is especially important because, as Martino & Pallota-Chiarolli (2005, p. 99) and Renold (2002; 2007) indicate, girls tend to use it to mark out their own status and to differentiate themselves from "those other girls" who break the gender mandate, and in order to gain male approval. Other words that arise from patriarchal scrutiny and that sustain power imbalances include, for example, "whore," "bitch," or "slut." These sexist and macho words are regularly used not only by boys but also by girls, and their use helps to construct a more restrictive and oppressive structure for girls' sexuality (Renold, 2007).

Another mechanism found in relationships between girls and boys is the force of symbolic violence, which is distributed through audiovisual channels, such as the media or RICTs. These channels feature stereotypical corporealities, and messages sent through them promote the cult of the body (Vázquez et al., 2013), provoking an increase in corporeal vulnerability at this age (Bragg et al., 2011; Capdevila et al., 2008; Rovira, 2001). It should be observed that adolescence is also an important stage for symbolic violence or, as defined in the study by Vázquez et al. (2013), as "beautiful violence." This violence favors unequal spaces and the reproduction of stereotypes, creating not only obsessions and a cult of the body but also serious eating disorders such as anorexia or bulimia, especially in the case of adolescent girls.

Blame, Shame, and Dishonor in the Construction of Female Identities

When we speak of the construction of female identities, we must mention as well other cultural mandates, such as the blame inflicted by patriarchal "dishonor."

Feminist anthropology relates the rise of honor culture to the need to preserve scarce resources (Gilmore, 1982, p. 175; Narotzky, 1995, p. 22–23). Men, and the community itself, need to guarantee the legitimacy of descendants by blood, meaning that they must preserve (control and monitor) women's virtue (their virginity before marriage and their fidelity after it). Attacking a woman's honor becomes a way to attack the community as a whole (Friedl, 1963; Schneider, 1971).

Cyber Space: A Space of Invasion as Well as Corporeal Resistance

According to the Basque Youth Observatory report (Gazteen Euskal Behatokia, 2019), the channels most used and present in the lives of adolescents in the Basque Country are as follows: video games (50%), YouTube (80%), and social networks (99.7%). Furthermore, the most popular activities among people between 15 and 30 include listening to music on smart phones (81.9%); watching movies (52%); watching videos on YouTube, Vimeo, and other platforms (43.1%); and playing video games (14.8%). The report also mentions that the networks most used by adolescents are WhatsApp (96.7%) and Instagram (89.9%).

With regard to how girls live with and confront these spaces, and in relation to their corporeal experiences in the digital world, different studies allude to the fact that images and corporealities are gaining increased importance in the identification of adolescence itself. For example, Thelwall & Vis (2017) claim that girls tend to take more selfies than boys. In the culture of simulation and images, adolescent girls expose their bodies much more than boys (Gobierno Vasco, 2013; Thelwall & Vis, 2017). As mentioned by Flores & Browne (2017), Thelwall & Vis (2017), Tortajada et al. (2013), and Zafra (2005, 2010), we are dealing with a digital symbolic violence that uses images as a method of coercion. Such conditioning has a notorious effect on girls' feelings, at a time when they face important corporeal and socio-cognitive changes which provoke anxiety (Rodriguez & Hernandez, 2018).

Furthermore, as Flores & Browne (2017), Rodriguez & Hernandez (2018), and Tortajada et al. (2013) recount, girls have to confront a generalized, hyper-sexualized, and hypereroticized image of their bodies (thin with tight waists, but pronounced backsides and breasts). On Instagram in particular, a female corporeal image, used as an object of advertising and eroticism, has become widespread. We are dealing with a misogynist culture in which female corporealities are valued and devalued by men as well as by other women (Mujeres en Red, 1999; Zafra, 2010).

In open contradiction with everything said so far, some sources insist that social media has had a positive and subversive effect on adolescents and the management of their identities. The argument here is that these networks have given a voice to people who transgress norms, making diverse bodies and sexual identities more visible, as is the case with transrealities (Rutten, 2018; Waterloo et al., 2018).

But other research stresses that a more profound study from a gender perspective shows a percentage difference between attacks on adolescent girls and boys in social networks. In these studies, we find that girls are more cyber bullied than boys—9% vs. 6%, respectively, according to the European Institute for Gender Equality (EIGE, 2018) and 12% vs. 8% according to UNESCO (2017). And according to the study by Jane (2018), the probability of experiencing harassment is 27% higher for girls than for boys (76).

Nevertheless, the empirical evidence demonstrates that the problem is more structural and qualitative than quantitative, given the gender differences in the targets of harassment and the forms adopted by them. From this perspective, different sources confirm that girls are the objects of different methods of cyber bullying, depending on the case, creating intimidating spaces for their bodies and their sexuality (Delegación del Gobierno para la Violencia de Género, 2014; EIGE, 2018; Lenhart, 2009; Navarro, 2016; Powell & Henry, 2014).

For example, studies by the Basque Government (Gobierno Vasco, 2013), Megias & Ballesteros (2014) and Ryan (2017) testify to the fact that young girls are more scared than boys of being targeted for abuse in relation to the circulation of images, photos, or videos of themselves (typically in sensual, semi-naked, or naked poses), and/or of being more shamed, denigrated for their bodily image, and sexually harassed.

In light of these results and those of our own research, and in the interests of appropriating feminist terminology, we propose the use of the term "sexist cyber bullying," defined as the attitudes, articulations, or behaviors produced in RICTs and supported by gender stereotypes. These include attacks on bodily image, insults, comments or images that reproduce gender stereotypes (such as sexist images uploaded onto a social network platform that denigrate women because of their sex), and sexual cyber bulling, which is marked out as all those attitudes, articulations, and behaviors of a sexual nature that are produced in RICTs and that have the impact of attacking a girl's dignity, especially when this creates an intimidating, degrading, or offensive atmosphere. This includes, for example, sending and distributing a girl's private photos or videos without her consent (Linares, 2019).

In reality, we need testimonies that gather together young women's experiences in order to reconstruct, from the perspective of their gaze and their bodies, the forms of oppression that have been practiced on them, and how this patriarchal memory—which damages and objectifies girls—permeates the construction of their identities. For this reason, this chapter seeks to identity the inter- and extrasubjective pressures in cybernetic spaces that are suffered by adolescent girls.

Methodological Framework

The following objectives have acted as a guide for the most applied part of this study:

O1: To draw attention to the corporeal and sexual experiences of adolescent girls in the online world.

O2: To identify the cultural pressures, such as symbolic cyber violence and sexual and/or sexist cyber bullying, that threaten female corporeality.

O3: To recognize the cultural mandates (such as shame, dishonor, and excessive demands on bodies) which condition young women's corporealities and sexualities.

O4: To identify the discourses and emotional resources available to mothers to confront the patriarchal mandates that condition adolescent girls' corporealities and sexualities.

In order to meet these objectives, we use a qualitative methodology because this allows us to go into depth about the meaning of the things each informant considers important and significant when recounting her experiences (Ruiz Olabuénaga, 2012).

We have employed the interpretative technique of the discussion groups aimed at "the study and recognition of the group as a primary social unit: sometimes as a context or means whose influence determines relationships and individual behavior, and at others as an organizational whole or entity in society" (Gutiérrez, 2008, p. 15). This technique allows us to get inside the imaginaries and cultural codes present in the discourses and experiences of the girls and their mothers.

In precise terms, we formed nine discussion groups with adolescent girls between the ages of 11 and 13 years (a total of 80 girls) and nine groups with their mothers (a total of 50 women), all residents of the Basque Autonomous Community in Spain.

It is important to note that all measures were taken to ensure ethical criteria were met: informed consent of all the women participating; family consent in the case of all minors; and anonymity through the coding of the interviews, which involved eliminating the participants' names and substituting them with alphanumerical codes to identify each one. In the same way, we should make clear that this article does not aim to make generalizations based on the results, but rather to demonstrate an emerging reality in a concrete context.

Corporeal and Sexual Digital Disciplines Among Adolescent Girls in the Basque Country[2]

The analysis of the girls' discussion groups illustrates how the system dominates and conditions their bodies and their imagination of "beauty." These codes and imaginaries are adjusted to proconsumerist interests which, furthermore, stipulate and indicate which "trends" to follow. That is, the channels used most by adolescents provide the economic system with a privileged medium through which to expand its commercial interests.

These messages are spread by a variety of routes: YouTube; advertising; and social networks, as is the case of fashion social network 21 Buttons or, as already mentioned, Instagram. The latter network prioritizes the image as a relational medium. Thus, as the girls who participated in the research recount, Instagram generates heteronormative cultural codes and schema, based on the false premise of showing "the best of yourself." Through the image, the photo shows the public what Zafra (2010) identifies as the keys to personal success: trips, feelings, new relationships, and so on.

These ideals are basically held up by frivolous and false principles, in a constant "posturing" aimed to simulate an eternal state of happiness—"always be happy"—which in turn creates anxiety. This proposed happiness is governed by what is considered desirable and desired, which coincides with attributes of white, upper-class people living in the Western world. Girls admit to adding and following "influencers" or "Instagrammers" whose profiles promote a beauty ideal as well as the consumption of certain products and brands.

In this world made up of what is "desired, imagined, and consumed," adolescence is confronted with a social display window which normalizes corporeality in accordance with gender codes. As indicated by their own words, girls are required to be thin and sexy, but also shy, as well as made up, and so on. Boys, on the other hand, are called upon to show masculinity, strength, toughness, etc. Let's look at a few examples:

CA4 (GIRL): In the case of girls (they're valued), most of all if they're half naked or you can see half a boob ... For boys, it's if they're all hunky (Basque original).

FB4 (GIRL): Girls usually post pictures with cleavage and boys with their shirts off, so they can show off their muscles (Basque original).

The informants' descriptions of the differences between girls' and boys' photos show that these are maintained within the parameters of masculinity and femininity outlined above. These gendered canons are preestablished by masculine dominance.

According to the words and codes used by the adolescents themselves, this homogenization of the image (Zafra, 2010) requires "posturing"; this "posturing" in turn determines the definition and value of female corporealities. Here are some examples:

CA6 (GIRL): Yes, everyone postures, but especially girls. We're always anticipating and thinking about how we'll look (Basque original).

BA2 (GIRL): We girls do more photo sessions, and boys do more group photos (Basque original).

There is a visual structure concerning female embodiment in particular, situating girls as objects rather than subjects in this relational medium. These messages saturate girls' self-perception and self-esteem, influencing their existential positionality on the internet.

In this way, conditioned by a wide range of channels and by the need to belong to a peer group, the girls project these same categories of submission, ultimately feeling like objects on the media catwalk. The girls themselves tell us about how they get together with one another in order to take photos in a place where they can project "the best of themselves." Here are some of their commentaries:

AA10 (GIRL): We do a lot of "photosessions." I mean, you meet up with your friends and you take photos, like with a camera and everything. And you go to places you've chosen carefully …

DA5 (GIRL): I like (Instagram) because in the end you get to see photos of people and then you can copy them. In the end, almost all us girls take photos like that. I don't know why, but in the end we all take them.

A "symbolic body" (Bourdieu, 2002: 86–88) is constructed, and this creates anxiety. Thus, a rigid and constrained gender construction is self-inflicted, and this is projected, felt, and experienced. Girls don't feel their bodies as their own; they experience them as incomplete and perceive them as "lacking." In their words:

AA12 (GIRL): Well, I do it so it comes out well, so I don't look average. I think it's important how people see me. It's true, I think about it a lot.

HA11 (GIRL): We're, like, stricter when it comes to photos, because we take a lot of care about how we turn out, how everything is, because we want to look good.

HA10 (GIRL): One day you do something unusual and you wonder what they'll think, and when they post something bad in the comments it affects you. Even if you say it doesn't, it does.

GA1 (GIRL): Boys don't care how they look in photos. We're the opposite. We take 50 photos, because we worry about how we look and how we'll turn out.

EA1 (GIRL): Girls are the ones who show more, because in the end it's the boys who notice more.

Girls question their bodies, break them into fragments, and attack them through messages that are extremely damaging to their self-image. They suffer, therefore, from a cultural distortion which limits their self-perception. They experience themselves through the public opinion of the internet and look at themselves through the eyes of others and through a multi-filtered camera. In this way, female corporeality becomes a territory of control and submission. Girls' bodies are objects which are instrumentalized to generate inequality and imbalance.

This kind of violence generates totally contradictory sensations because, on the one hand, it coexists in a universe where the objectification and hypersexualization of female corporeality are obvious, and, on the other, there are still social restrictions that send out contradictory messages about how female sexuality should be experienced (look flirtatious and, at the same time, submissive).

The cultural dichotomy established by Lagarde (1990) between the "good" and the "bad" woman is divided, therefore, by a fine line, given that those who surpass this line distinguishing what is desirable from what is out of order will be stigmatized as "bad women"— or, as the girls in our study put it, "whores or sluts." Ultimately, this confers a dangerous and oppressive cultural ambivalence that is concerned with and damages female corporeality. In the words of the girls interviewed:

AA4 (GIRL): But some of them do it to get lots of followers or to flirt with guys… I mean, some of them are a bit slutty.
GA12 (GIRL): No, in terms of your private parts, it's fine when you don't show those parts, but when you can see your butt or your boobs or whatever, it's like "don't show that," I mean you look like a whore.

Nevertheless, a very interesting point to emphasize is the fact that some girls resist and rebel against this stigmatization, making sisterly links with their friends and rejecting the competition for the male gaze that de Beauvoir wrote about (1949). From this critical questioning, girls talk about appropriating their bodies and exercising agency over them. In their words:

HA5 (GIRL): Everyone does what they want with their own body. You show what you want.
GA14 (GIRL): You show whatever you want of your own body. Nobody should tell you to upload a photo. You upload photos the way you want, the way you like them.

On the other hand, the research participants view sexual cyber bullying towards girls as a fairly regular occurrence. In fact, when we mentioned a case of this kind of cyber bullying to them—a girl sends a naked photo of herself to a boy and he makes it go viral—they tell us this is a "typical" action and that they know of similar cases in their close circles. Here are some examples:

BA5 (GIRL): Yea, this girl called Juana posted a photo in her bra and underwear, and over a hundred people saw it and she had to take it down. And all the comments…
HA4 (GIRL): So, this girl goes around like … with a lot of clothes on, right? And she's done stuff with a guy and now she's pregnant. Now she's 14, but at the time she was 13. And in the video, she was doing things, and she got really bullied. I don't know, they said all sorts of stuff to her, like she's a whore. Even the teachers know about it.
IA5 (GIRL): Here there was a case where between the two of them, they had a deal to exchange photos. So what happened was that the girl erased the photo and the guy sent it to his friends (Basque original).

The testimonies show that female corporeality and sexuality are always assigned a central place. Even at a relatively young age, these become sites of patriarchal invasion and appropriation. We find that girls who express their sexuality freely on the internet are condemned, and their bodies are surrounded by serious social stigmatization and domination.

These ways of harassing and oppressing girls tend to follow a similar path. First, a video is taken or circulated; second, without the girl's consent, these photos go viral, and thus begins the process of objectification: the girl ceases to be herself and is turned into an erotic object—similarly to what happens in advertising or pornographic content (de Beauvoir, 1949; Lagarde, 1990; Megias & Ballesteros, 2014). In the third phase, the girls are heavily stigmatized and start to suffer ongoing and constant (cyber) bullying, expressed in words such as "slut, floozy, easy, whore, cunt…," which operate as fixed forms of control and domination. As a result, sexual and sexist cyber bullying are tightly entwined, becoming forms of patriarchal oppression.

In this final phase, a mass audience becomes the judge of the girl's behavior, and hers only. Even in those cases where a sexual video appears with both a boy and a girl, she is the one who will be condemned and stigmatized. He, on the other hand, is seen as a hero, a macho guy; he might even be congratulated for his "great feat." As we see in the following extracts, in the online world, girls undergo violence transferred from the world offline. Girls' sexuality complies with the mandate of the patriarchal system, which constrains women's experiences, even when they are very young:

CA4 (GIRL): Imagine a guy with lots of girls. People say, "What a freakin' boss! With all those girls," or whatever. But if it's the other way around, it's "Ah, what a slut, you'll catch gonorrhea." That kinda thing (Basque original).
AA5 (GIRL): Whore! I swear, seriously! Whatever you do, "slut!" Not silly or anything else. If it's a girl, "whore."

The use of words that oppress and constrain female sexuality is a regular exercise on social media, and girls learn and are aware that any one of them can be condemned with this stigma. In fact, in one of the discussion groups, they recount how, even at the age of 11, they had already been confronted by these words. This is how one of the girls put it:

It (sexist cyber bullying) can happen to any of us. For example, we put a video up on YouTube from the other school, and they insulted us. It was about a Christmas rap song we did at school, and they called us sluts.

(HA9)

Another issue we should take note of is the revictimization girls have to confront. Faced with this kind of situation, from 80 adolescents in our study, only five girls gave support to and empathized with those girls who have suffered cyberbullying. The others placed responsibility on the girls who sent the photos in the first place. The concept of the "bad woman" becomes a thick cloak hiding women's suffering and the oppression carried out on them. The girls' arguments come from an essentially individualistic perspective, and they do not reference the macho or patriarchal structures that perpetuate these attitudes. This prevents us from focusing on the issues from a more holistic point of view. Here are some commentaries taken from the girls' groups:

BA4 (GIRL): It's the girl's (fault), because if you don't know the guy well, what are you going to send them for? She shouldn't send them. She could just show them directly from her phone (Basque original).

GA7 (GIRL): It's like, why are you uploading that? Why are you uploading that? I mean, you have to be an idiot to send a photo like that.

HA2 (GIRL): She was wrong. If she shows her boobs, too bad. Why is she sending them? It's your private parts, yea? You shouldn't even send them to your friends.

AA9 (GIRL): She's to blame for doing that, she was really stupid, we know what happens.

HA11 (GIRL): I think it's bad and you shouldn't send the photos to anyone.

In their words, we can observe that in some of them, the process of objectification means they perceive themselves as sexually passive (de Beauvoir, 1949, p. 467), and they expect other girls to fulfill this mandate as well. This acceptance (to be objects, not subjects) prevents them from empathizing with other girls, and sometimes, it even makes them want to distance themselves from them (Egan & Hawkes, 2012; Martino & Pallota-Chiarolli, 2005; Renold, 2002, 2007).

In the language of the majority, we find a sense of responsibility for safeguarding their own sexuality. As de Beauvoir (1949) and Lagarde (1990) theorized, women are taught from girlhood to hide their sexuality, as well as shame. This creates anxiety and the surrender of their own expectations to patriarchal demands, which in turn crushes the free experience of their sexuality. The following commentaries demonstrate this point:

AA10 (GIRL): If you send a photo to someone it should be a photo anyone can see. A photo your boyfriend or your mother could see.

AA9 (GIRL): Even if you send a photo that only lasts a few seconds, someone can take a screen shot and send it all over the place.

GA12 (GIRL): Even if it's your boyfriend, you shouldn't send them to him because if you send them to him, they end up all over the place.

HA11 (GIRL): But just think if you break up. Who knows what he'll do with that.

GA10 (GIRL): Once you've sent photos to someone, they can end up anywhere.

Nevertheless, it is important to highlight that, although they are fewer in number, there are some girls who do not place the blame on other girls, and who break the gender codes. Even though many of the informants themselves speak from a perspective of privacy and sexual restraint, others take a more critical stance. This allows them to empathize with other girls and question patriarchal demands and, accordingly, the invisible forms of oppression exercised against them. In their words:

AA2 (GIRL): Most of the photos that get spread around are of girls and not of boys. We can be trusted more than the boys.
AA12 (GIRL): When a guy in the class uploaded a photo of a naked girl, I kicked him out of the group.
IA1 (GIRL): I think the woman suffered a lot and people marginalized her quite a bit (Basque original).
FA1 (GIRL): But it was the guy's fault, he should know you shouldn't send that … You have to put yourself in the girl's place. It's not her fault at all.

Maintaining such positions becomes an act of resistance. This is because, as the girls themselves tell us, they are confronted not only by this kind of cyber bullying, but also by all the symbolic violence inflicted on their bodies. As we said in the previous section, female corporeality becomes a patriarchal product, used to oppress and subdue women. In this way, as evidenced from the Basque Government (Gobierno Vasco, 2013) study demonstrated, girls get more disrespectful comments about their appearance—for the mere fact of being girls. As they themselves remark:

CA (GIRL): A girl uploaded a photo of herself in a bikini and she was told to "cover up" and stuff like "don't show off your body, we're not interested…" (Basque original).
CA2 (GIRL): Maybe a girl tends to gets more comments about her body.
EA6 (GIRL): A girl who was a bit fat was often called "fat whore," "whale…" And someone on ThisCrush commented, "Fat slut – go to an orca orphanage, let's see if you kill yourself."

For the girls who maintain a more critical discourse, such behavior is annoying and exhausting; they draw attention to the fact that the violence inflicted on women takes many forms. They call for change and for reclaiming their own sexualities, bodies, and lives. As they themselves put it:

AA2 (GIRL): Me personally, on social media, no. But I have a friend in México, a guy, and a friend of his, a girl, was on a bus with a short dress and the men started to whistle. And instead of standing up to them people just sat there and watched. I mean! Why? A girl dresses that way because she wants to, not because she wants to be whistled at.
BA3 (GIRL): The other day I saw a photo on Instagram and there was a photo of someone in a bikini, with a comment that said "so it's no surprise you girls get raped …" Everyone can do what they want with their body, that's why it's theirs, and they shouldn't care what people say.

GA11 (GIRL): The other day I saw a photo with a girl wearing a dress that was like this, here it was like a bathing suit and that was it. And she started to get tons of comments: "Cover up!" and stuff. And she replied with things like, it's her body and she'll upload what she likes and if they don't like it you should stop following her.

The messages hurled at girls' bodies are extremely aggressive, keeping in mind as well the high levels of objectification they're exposed to online and offline. As was expressed in the different groups, adolescents are exposed to endless sexual stimuli, in which female corporeality is reduced to an erotic and sexual object. However, in this complicated atmosphere, we can also see that some of the girls showed awareness of and resistance to gendered objectification and bullying.

Guilt and Dishonor as (hetero)Patriarchal Mechanisms: The Discourses of Adolescent Girls' Mothers in the Basque Country

Faced with these issues, it is especially interesting to understand and get closer to the emotional and social resources that mothers draw on to challenge and counteract the (hetero)patriarchal mandates that fall onto girls' sexualities and corporeality—or to know whether, in contrast, mothers reproduce the same messages and cultural pressures.

The risk of sexual and/or sexist cyber bullying is something the families worry about. The majority of the mothers have heard of or know a case of cyber bullying, not necessarily sexual or sexist, and they are conscious of the risks. Nonetheless, when we listen to their discourses in depth, we find gender schema and mandates that project the same patriarchal cultural imaginary that restricts female bodies.

The main prejudice and stereotype detected in the family discussion groups from the participating schools was the blame many mothers put on women for distributing a naked or semi-naked photo. For many of the mothers in our discussion groups, sending the message is a serious mistake, and for that reason, wider circulation of it is also the fault of the person who sent it in the first place.

I2 (MOTHER): I think it's about this eagerness to show off, I think it's a question of upbringing. You have to tell girls that it's private and they should know it's private, and you can't just go casually showing it off.

I5 (MOTHER): I think girls need to learn to value themselves a bit, to learn that even if there are a lot of demands on them … it's about respecting themselves.

G3 (MOTHER): It's true, what you say, that girls, I mean, they're more eager to show themselves off, display themselves, and I think they send more of that kind of photo.

E2 (MOTHER): My son also sends them, but of course, then he receives them. And of course, maybe the girl's mother doesn't know her daughter isn't so good. At least I know my son isn't so good, well, good … it's more natural and he shows you.

B4 (MOTHER): I'm going to start from the beginning: what's that girl doing sending that photo?

B3 (MOTHER): The one who started sending it is just as bad as the one who circulates it after. So, in the end, they're equally guilty.

Here, there is no power imbalance between the one who takes the photo and sends it and the one who receives and circulates it. In divvying up the blame, it is as if that prior power imbalance did not exist. But the imbalance is clearly revealed when the photo is stolen (in a changing room, for example); in this case, the blame disappears and the victim and the victimizer are much more obvious.

H2 (MOTHER): But the case you talked about is different, because that girl had her photo taken in the changing room without her knowing it. I think that's much worse, because it's against her will. But in the other case it's something you've done voluntarily, you've passed it on to someone, you didn't want it to go anywhere else, but well, you did it, the girl who did it is bad, maybe she just wanted to show it to her friend.

Given a hypothetical situation in which their sons and daughters are victims or aggressors, the majority of mothers clearly demonstrate empathy for the girls who are victims and total rejection of the boys who are the aggressors.

However, in hypothetical cases of someone sending and circulating a photograph, the compassion for the possible victims of sexist cyber bullying is seen especially when the assumption is that the "harm" is already done, that an "error" has already been committed, and it is time to "face the consequences" and support the girl who finds herself in a complicated and painful predicament.

A7 (MOTHER): What are we going to do? Well nothing... I, if someone takes a photo of my daughter and sends it to her and she's upset she has to put up with it... well, what can I do? Am I going to get angry at her? I mean, it's already done...

The rejection of the aggressor is practically unanimous, and in the majority of cases there is talk of punishing and denouncing him. Here, we show one response that expresses intolerance for such behavior as well as one that assumes responsibilities.

G4 (MOTHER): I think that's the first thing you need to know. He's committing an offense and end of story. I mean, it's an offense, you can't pass on that photo, right? It's an offense.

G2 (MOTHER): You have to tell him he's committing an offense and that's something very, very serious. Someone trusted in you and on top of breaking that trust, they're committing an offense. So, I have no idea what would be... Listen, faced with these two situations, I couldn't tell you which is more serious.

F3 (MOTHER): Look, I can only tell you that they can have Instagram at age 16, everything else is your responsibility because you've let your daughter or son have Instagram on their phone. From there it's your responsibility.

In a minority of cases, though, we found a justification and exoneration of the ones who circulated the photographs.

H2 (MOTHER): I also think, OK, we shouldn't make such a big deal and say, OK, this has happened, you shouldn't do it again, it's serious, but that's it.

H4 (MOTHER): But I'm sure if you're the mother of the kid and maybe you don't see it as so bad, that he wouldn't have sent it (…) But he's your son and he's not so bad, he wouldn't have sent it.

F5 (MOTHER): Most likely he did it as a joke. I know a kid and he's a whiz kid, but I'm sure he did it as a joke. But it wasn't funny for the other person.

On more than one occasion, mothers mentioned that it would be worse to have a son or daughter who was an aggressor than a victim and that it would be much more upsetting and much more complicated to deal with. However, on the opposite perspective, there are other mothers that focused on the victim.

H2 (MOTHER): It's easier to be the boy's mother because it's easier to tackle him – what you did was really bad and you have to be punished. But if you're the mother of the girl, what can you really do? Teach her, don't take that kind of photo. But once the photos have been circulated what can you do? Make a complaint, sure, but…

E4 (MOTHER): I think it hurts you more when your child hurts someone else than when someone hurts your child. In the end, you know you can support your child, you can help. But when it's your child who's causing the harm …

The fact is that the vast majority of mothers who participated in the groups have their own internalized biases. They reproduce patriarchal processes and then share them, as reflected in the discourses of the girls.

Conclusion

On social networks, reality is filled with insecurities, where unequal power spaces and relationships are projected. From childhood, girls receive contradictory messages about their own bodies: On the one hand, they are persuaded to display their bodies and feel like female objects, while, on the other, they are surrounded by a patriarchal atmosphere that inhibits and oppresses them, making them feel ashamed of bodily display or blaming their self-presentation when they are targeted with harmful words and behaviors.

Among the girls, we have found an obvious discomfort with themselves. The meanings they give to their corporealities are limited to negative and incomplete categories. They are exposed to objectified images of female corporeality, which means that they examine and intervene with themselves from an outside, consumerist, and patriarchal lens. Female corporealities become territories of invasion and oppression, and their bodies' memories are imbued with harm and self-contempt.

Likewise, based on this constant contradiction that interpellates and coerces them, we find a fine line between what is considered desirable for a girl and what is punishable for her.

In a digital world, where a significant objectification of female corporeality occurs on all platforms, it is revealing that for girls, the ideal of preserving their sexuality and corporeality persists in order not to find themselves stigmatized by machista norms. In fact, for their own resignification as "good girls," it is the girls themselves who differentiate themselves from other girls who take decisions to reveal more of their bodies.

In order to conform to the patriarchal schema of the "good woman," many girls reject and judge girls who send photos of themselves, and they don't question male actions as strategies for coercion and control mechanisms. In this way, from a young age they not only (re)experience fear on the street but also online, and this fear situates them as passive agents.

This discourse of fear, as we have seen, has been projected not only by society as a whole but by their own families. From this patriarchal mandate of blame and dishonor, mothers continue to legitimate the fact that girls experience their sexualities from a position of fear and anxiety, even while they conceal these feelings. Of course, this mechanism causes girls to experience constant contradictions in their own corporeality.

Female corporeality becomes a territory of control and submission. Girls' bodies are objectified and instrumentalized to create inequality and imbalance. They are more insulted, instrumentalized, denigrated, and coerced because of their bodies and sexuality. In the spaces they live in, they learn not to love them, to detach from them, and to hide them from a very young age if they do not want to become targets of cyber bullying.

Notes

1 The research was financed by the Basque Government through its funding for basic and applied research. Análisis de la tercera brecha digital de género de las personas adolescentes de la CAE. Ref.: PI2016–2029. Proyectos Investigación Básica y/o Aplicada 2016. Gobierno Vasco. 2016–2019.
2 As indicated in the text, some of the discussion groups were conducted in Basque; these were translated from Basque to Spanish before the article as a whole was translated from Spanish to English.

References

Bragg, S., Buckingham, D., Rusell, R., & Willett, R. (2011). Too much, too soon? Children 'sexualization' and consumer culture. *Education*, *11*(3), 279–292. Doi: 10.1080/14681811.2011.590085

Bourdieu, P. (2002). *Masculine domination*. Stanford University Press.

Buckingham, D., & Bragg, S. (2004). *Young people, sex and the media: The facts of life?* Palgrave Macmillan.

Capdevila, A., Figueras, M., Gómez, L., Jiménez, M., Luzón, V., & Ramajo, N. (2008). La construcción de la identidad adolescente: Imagen de los adolescentes en prime time televisivo. In M. García, S. Nuñez, & A. García (Eds.), *Comunicación, identidad y género*. Fragua (pp. 102–114).

De Beauvoir, S. (1949). *El segundo sexo*. Feminismos.

Delegación del Gobierno para la Violencia de Género (2014). *El ciberacoso como forma de ejercer la violencia de género en la juventud: Un riesgo en la sociedad de la información y el conocimiento*. Ministerio de Sanidad, Servicios Sociales e Igualdad.

Egan, E. D., & Hawkes, G. L. (2012). Sexuality, youth and perils of endangered innocence: How history can help us get past the panic. *Gender and Education, 24*(3), 269–284.

European Institute for Gender Equality (EIGE) (2018). *Gender equality and youth: The opportunities and risks of digitalisation*. Lithuania: EIGE.

Flores, P., & Browne, R. (2017). Jóvenes y patriarcado en la sociedad TIC: Una reflexión desde la violencia simbólica de género en redes sociales. *Revista Latinoamericana de Ciencias Sociales, Niñez y Juventud, 15*(1), 147–160.

Friedl, E. (1963). Studies in peasant life. In B. Siegl (Ed.), *Biennial review of anthropology*. Stanford: Stanford University Press (pp. 276–306).

Gazteen Euskal Behatokia. (2019). *Diagnóstico de la situación de la juventud de euskadi*. Observatorio Vasco de la Juventud.

Gilmore, D. (1982). Anthropology of the mediterranean area. *Annual Review of Anthropology, 11*, 175–205.

Gobierno Vasco. (2013). *La desigualdad de género y el sexismo en las redes sociales. Una aproximación cualitativa al uso que hacen las redes sociales las y los jóvenes en la CAPV*. Departamento de Educación de Gobierno Vasco.

Gutiérrez, J. (2008). *Dinámica del grupo de discusión*. Cuadernos metodológicos, CIS (Centro de Investigación Sociológicas).

Jane, E. (2018). Cyberhate, feminist flight and fight responses to gendered. In M. Segrave & L. Vitis (Eds.), *Gender, Technology and Violence*. New York: Routledge (pp. 45-61).

Lagarde, M. (1990). *Los cautiverios de las mujeres. Madrespoas, monjas, putas, presas y locas*. horas y HORAS.

Lenhart, A. (2009). *Teens and sexting*. Pew Internet & American Life Project.

Linares, E. (2019). *El iceberg digital machista. Análisis prevención e intervención de realidades machistas digitales que se producen en la adolescencia de la CAE*. Emakunde (Instituto Vasco de la Mujer).

Marsh, J. (2010). Young children's play in online virtual worlds. *Journal of Early Childhood Research, 8*(1), 23–39. Doi: 10.1177/1476718X09345406.

Martino, W., & Pallota-Chiarolli, M. (2005). *Being normal is the only way to be: Adolescents perspectives on gender and school*. University of New South Wales.

Megias, I., & Ballesteros, J. C. (2014). *Jóvenes y género. Estado de la cuestión*. Centro Reina Sofia.

Mujeres en Red (1999). *Mujeres en RED: ADAS*. Diputación de Córdoba.

Narotzky, S. (1995). *Mujer, mujeres y género*. Consejo Superior de Investigaciones Científicas.

Navarro, R. (2016). Gender issues and cyberbullying in children and adolescents: From gender differences to gender identity measures. In R. Navarro, S. Yubero, & E. Larrañaga (Eds.), *Cyberbullying across the globe. Gender, family, and mental health*. Springer (pp. 35–44).

Powell, A., & Henry, N. (2014). Blurred lines? Responding to 'sexting' and gender-based violence among young people. *Children Australia, 39*, 119–124. Doi: 10.1017/cha.2014.9.

Renold, E. (2002). Presumed: (hetero)Sexual, heterosexist and homophobic harassment among primary school girls and boys. *Childhood, 9*(4), 415–434. Doi: 10.1177/0907568202009004004.

Renold, E. (2007). *Girls, boys and junior sexualities.* Taylor & Francis.

Renold, E., & Allan, A. (2016). Bright and beautiful: High achieving girls, ambivalent femininities, and the feminization of success in the primary school. *Discourse: Studies in the Cultural Politics of Education, 27*(4), 457–473. Doi: 10.1080/01596300600988606.

Rodriguez, N. S., & Hernandez, T. (2018). Dibs on that sexy piece of ass: Hegemonic masculinity on TFM girls Instagram account. *Social Media + Society,* (Jan–Mar), 1–12.

Rovira, M. (2001). Los códigos de género en la adolescencia. In A. Tomé, & X. Rambla (Eds.), *Contra el sexismo. Coeducación y democracia en la escuela.* Síntesis, S.A. (pp. 39–56).

Ruiz, C. (2014). *La construcción social de las relaciones amorosas y sexuales en la adolescencia. Graduando violencias cotidianas.* Diputación Provincial de Jaén.

Ruiz Olabuénaga, J. I. (2012). *Metodología de la investigación cualitativa.* Universidad de Deusto.

Rutten, T. (2018). *Breaking the binary: Exploring gender self-presentation and passing on #Transisbeautiful on instagram.* PhD Thesis, Uppsala University.

Ryan, J. (2017). *Worried about the wrong things: Youth, risk and opportunity in the digital world.* The MIT Press.

Schneider, J. (1971). Of vigilance and virgins. *Ethnology, 9,* 1–24.

Thelwall, M., & Vis, F. (2017). Gender and image sharing on Facebook, Twitter, Instagram, Snapchat and Whatsapp in the UK: Hobbying alone or filtering for friends? *Aslib Journal of Information Management, 69*(6), 702–720.

Tortajada, I., Araüna, N., & Martínez, I. J. (2013). Advertising stereotypes and gender representation in social networking sites. *Comunicar, 21*(41), 177–186.

UNESCO (2017). *School violence and bullying: Global status report. Sustainable development goals.* UNESCO.

Vázquez, N., Estébanez, I., & Herbón, M. (2013). *Violencia Bella. El cuerpo adolescente como territorio de control. Análisis de vulnerabilidad y resistencia a las presiones sobre el autoconcepto y el cuerpo femenino entre las y los adolescentes de seis municipios de Bizkaia.* Medicus Mundi.

Waterloo, S. F., Baumgartner, S. E., Peter, J., & Valkenburg, P. M. (2018). Norms of online expressions of emotion: Comparing, Facebook, Twitter, Instagram, and Whatsapp. *New Media & Society, 20*(5), 1813–1831.

Zafra, R. (2005). *Las cartas rotas. Espacios de igualdad y feminización en internet.* Premio Ensayo "Carmen de Burgos" 2000. Instituto de Estudios Almerienses.

Zafra, R. (2010). *Un cuarto propio conectado. (Ciber)espacio y (auto)gestión del yo.* Fórcola.

5

BUSTING TROLLS

Examining the Hate Campaign Against Actress Leslie Jones

Benjamin Brojakowski and Gabriel A. Cruz

In 2016, the reboot of the 1980s comedy *Ghostbusters* drew intrigue and ire from fans of the original film. The starring cast of Kristen Wiig, Melissa McCarthy, and Kate McKinnon received nearly equal parts praise and scorn from fans and critics, but no one was scrutinized as much as the other lead, Leslie Jones. Jones, a former *Saturday Night Live* cast member, was the only person of color in a starring role. When the first trailer for the film was released in March 2016, many fans who were initially excited about the reboot were disappointed that the only woman of color was playing what was perceived to be a less intelligent character that conformed to many common stereotypes associated with Black roles, specifically the Black best friend (Lang, 2016).

The trailer also inspired the film's detractors to increase their social media presence by supporting boycotts and spreading hateful messages, many of them targeting Jones. The abuse lasted for several months and included tactics such as hacking her personal website, releasing sexually explicit photos, and using racist and sexist messages (Rogers & Bromwich, 2016). These tactics, which Jane (2014) refers to as gendered e-bile, occur more often "in response to feminist activism and perceived feminist gains" (p. 563). Although Jane (2014) focuses on gendered e-bile, we argue that the abuse and insults directed at Jones were more intense because of her status as the only woman of color with a starring role in the film. This belief stems from the common media framing of Black women and girls as hypersexual, aggressive, and uncivilized (Tanksley, 2016). The attacks became so overwhelming that Jones took a hiatus from social media.

On March 4, 2016, the day the trailer was released and the criticism began, Jones responded to the harassment by tweeting, "Why can't a regular person be a ghostbuster. I'm confused. And why can't i be the one who plays them i am a performer. Just go see the movie!" The message indicates that Jones was proud of

DOI: 10.4324/9781003260851-7

her performance and proud to portray a character that showed a "regular person" can be a superhero.

In this chapter, we briefly examine the timeline of Jones' social media abuse from the release of the *Ghostbusters* trailer (March 4) until the time of her hiatus from July 18 to 21, 2016. We specifically focus on the responses to Jones's March 4 tweet and her July 2016 tweets after Milo Yiannopoulos reviewed the film for Breitbart (MILO, 2016). The March 4 tweet came one day after the first Ghost-busters trailer was released, and fans commented on Jones' character in the film. Silman (2016) notes that the July tweet came after she was harassed and trolled by followers of Yiannopoulos after his review of the film was published on the Breitbart website. The abuse Jones received was so extreme that Twitter released two statements regarding offensive behavior on that platform. The latter state-ment noted that several accounts had been warned or suspended. This included the permanent suspension of Yiannopoulos for violation of Twitter's policies. We believe this tweet and review served as critical incidents that sparked fur-ther abuse. We also explore the concept of social media mobbing. This concept explains the phenomenon of people converging on social media to express their dissatisfaction with a person, organization, or event (Blevins, 2016). We identify shaming as a specific tool used by the mob. We define shaming as an instrument of social control that takes place when an individual or mob feels that a social norm has been violated (Ronson, 2015). We also consider Jane's (2014) belief that mobbing can replicate game play. It is possible that mobbers compete against others by trying to create the most offensive content. This is important because, as Phillips (2015) notes, this content calls attention to and challenges dominant cultural norms. Furthermore, the transition into more extreme behaviors, like hacking and doxxing, can become normalized (Sunstein, 2009).

We utilize critical discourse analysis (CDA) in order to examine the data. In this study, we find that the Twitter mob consisted of supporters and detrac-tors. We also found that the commonalities of perceived emotional tone, hyper-bolic language/symbols, and language indicating a relationship with Jones exist between the two groups. We examine subthemes of each group and provide representative examples. We find that detractors used sexist and racist insults, justified their behavior, and referenced the normativity of online harassment. Supporters usually offered unqualified messages of support or included a critique with their message.

Literature Review

A Pew Research Center report (2021) indicates that nearly 72% of Americans use some type of social media, showing its increase across multiple demographics during the last decade. This increase in social media use has led to social prob-lems within social networking sites. In the early years of digital social media, Suler (2004) introduced the online disinhibition effect as a framework for under-standing the psychological reasons people engage in different behaviors online.

Since that time, this digital deviance has allowed online harassment to become an "established norm" for women, more commonly for young and LGBTQ+ women (Hunt, 2016). Felmlee, Inara Rodis, Zhang (2020) also address a high number of tweets from their own study that target women based on both their gender and racial identity and call for more attention to this topic. We examine how these characteristics and stereotypes associated with them are used by digital shamers throughout this research.

Cyberbullying, Mobbing, and Shaming

In this chapter, we aim to explore the ways cyberbullying, mobbing, and sham-ing exist within the contemporary culture of social media. We draw from Suler's (2004) online disinhibition effect, as well as introduce and analyze examples of the messages Jones received in response to the trailer that introduced Jones's role in the film. We examine the ways individuals in social networks and online communities have used hateful language, threats, and hacking to push Jones, and others, off social media. Empowered by anonymity and semi-anonymity, these individuals fit the definition of cyberbullies. Wright (2017) defines cyberbul-lying as "malicious behaviors carried out through a variety of information and communication technologies, such as instant messaging tools, social network-ing sites, gaming consoles, text messages, and cell phones, email, and websites" (p. 189–190).

Cyberbullies are motivated to harass victims for many reasons, but Suler's (2004) online disinhibition effect examines some of the psychological factors that may encourage this type of behavior. The online disinhibition effect proposes that there are six interacting factors that contribute to abusive behavior online. One factor that we specifically highlight is invisibility. In a text-driven envi-ronment like Twitter, abusers remain hidden from their victims. Perhaps more importantly, though, is that the abuser also does not see the physical response of the victim. In this environment, the abuser is unable to witness any physical or nonverbal cues that may inspire sympathy or empathy (Suler, 2004). This invisibility and semi-anonymity allows individuals "to benefit from the fact that their utterances and actions are considered too abhorrent to repeat or discuss in mainstream contexts" (Jane, 2014, p. 559).

When a large group of individuals engage in online abuse, a social media mob forms. These mobs form when groups of people with similar ideologies con-verge on a single issue. Himelboim, McCreery, & Smith (2013) found that highly polarized clusters of social media users emerge because like-minded users fre-quently interact with each other. These mobs can become dangerous when they are exposed to an individual or issue that challenges their beliefs. Poerksen & Detel (2014) note that social media mobs are created when a large group of inter-net users acknowledge a norm violation, are prepared to react to the violation, use the most appropriate communication tool to harm the norm violator, and choose to redress the mob's target. Shaming is a popular tactic used by social media mobs and can serve as an entry point into more extreme and dangerous behaviors. Shaming is defined as critical, threatening, or abusive language used toward an individual or group when a perceived social norm has been violated (Posner, 2015). Shaming also functions as a way of establishing social control when legal action is not necessary or possible. The goal of shaming is to cause a negative reaction as opposed to offering criticism that may lead to dialogue or thoughtful discussion. Shaming is a potent tool that gives a voice to the powerless while allowing individuals to remain semi-anonymous (Ronson, 2015). It can become a harmful practice within groupthink and with the online disinhibition effect. When mobs grow in size and intensity, individuals are more likely to move to extreme opinions or actions (Sunstein, 2009). These actions may include threats, pejorative language, or psychological abuse.

Shamers' actions are troubling for several reasons. First, these digital attacks are often as equally oppressive and damaging as the messages they are challenging. Brojakowski (2016) notes that some of these messages contain threats of death and physical violence and encourage individuals to physically harm or kill themselves. Luxton, June, & Fairall (2012) refer to this as cyberbullicide. Ronson (2015) addresses the issue of copycat and parody accounts. Owners of these accounts impersonate others in hopes of damaging their reputation or proliferating harmful misinformation. This tactic is more subversive than threatening language but may have a similar negative impact on the victim. In a timeline of Jones' harassment, Silman (2016) embedded a tweet by Jones that includes images of photoshopped content that was attributed to her account. This tactic was subtler than creating parody accounts but had the ability to damage her reputation through easy proliferation.

A second characteristic of shamers are the tools and accounts they use to find individuals. Social media accounts such as @YesYoureRacist and websites such as NoHomophobes.com are well-intentioned and strive to raise awareness for social inequalities but do not always lead to productive encounters. These tools exist to expose individuals who do not support politically correct language or may be overtly hateful to a larger audience. These tools can implicitly encourage shaming by drawing attention to accounts they identify as problematic. Furthermore, these accounts and tools encourage victims and activists to address e-bile and hateful rhetoric publicly. Jane (2016) raises ethical concerns about these behaviors. She notes that these behaviors "may well resemble vengeance-motivated lynching or even sadism" (p. 289). As we explain later, many well-meaning individuals tried to tweet support for Jones, but these comments "fed the trolls" and emphasized the issue instead of challenging the abusers.

A third negative characteristic of shaming culture involves offline consequences for victims. Ronson (2015) highlights several examples, such as relationship problems, loss of jobs, and inability to find work. Threats against physical safety after being doxxed are also a concern (Hern, 2014). One example from the comedy industry involved Kathy Griffin. After participating in a controversial photoshoot, backlash from the public caused her to lose endorsements, comedy performances, and TV spots. Griffin later argued that her penalty reflects a double standard in the entertainment industry (Chen, 2018).

Steadfast opponents of social justice activism use similar shaming tactics. For example, #GamerGate supporters felt that their rights were being restricted by social justice activists, specifically feminists, and lashed out with threats of rape, murder, and other forms of violence (Chess & Shaw, 2015). These threats become more real when victims are doxxed and their personal information and home addresses are made public online (Hern, 2014). In August 2016, Jones' website was hacked, sexually explicit photos were leaked, her passport and driver's license were made public, and she was taunted with photos of a dead gorilla that was meant as a racial insult (Silman, 2016).

This understanding of mobbing and shaming practices leads us to ask the following research question:

> **RQ1**: How do members of the mob use shaming to reinforce racist and sexist ideologies in their messages?
> **RQ1a**: What discursive strategies do shamers use?
> **RQ1b**: How do they position themselves relative to Leslie Jones in terms of power?

Method

We utilize CDA to examine the data we have gathered from Twitter. Twitter is an appropriate social network for this study as it is widely used (Twitter, 2022), encourages incivility (Ott, 2017), and users can easily respond or retweet with minimal offline consequences due to its semi-anonymous nature. Our data include public responses to Jones' aforementioned tweets. Tweets that were deleted, made private, or independently directed at Jones without being part of the larger conversation could not be included in this study. CDA is useful for revealing how social structures are produced and influence the way meaning is created (Pulos, 2013) and operates under the assumption that "ideologies are representations of aspects of the world which can be shown to contribute to establishing, maintaining and changing social relations of power, domination and exploitation" (Fairclough, 2003, p. 9). In short, discourse can contribute to the reinforcement of social power relations and various forms of domination (Fairclough, 2003). By applying CDA, we examine the ways in which discourse is used to reinforce the ideologies of racism and sexism in terms of a Black American female identity.

Our project examines online behavior and the use of mobbing tactics to harass Jones, specifically as those insults reify the stigmatization of her identity as a Black woman. Previous research indicated that CDA can be appropriately applied to this form of cyberbullying to understand the reinforcement of oppressive ideologies (Albert & Salam, 2013). Within the context of this research, this means that individuals on Twitter were able to interact with a known and verified celebrity in a way that reinforced misogynist and racist ideologies while enjoying complete or partial anonymity and avoiding repercussions. This power dynamic allowed the users to exert force and domination over Jones. Domination is defined as "the exercise of social power by elites, institutions or groups, that results in social inequality, including political, cultural, class, ethnic, racial and gender inequality" (van Dijk, 1993, pp. 249–250). The lack of inhibition when it comes to discursive practices made possible by the anonymity of the platform allows for easier analysis of ideologies than in other contexts where individuals can be easily identified and are thus more inclined to use coded or subtle language.

Our Application

Our units of data included tweets that were components of two threads initiated by Jones. These tweets were analyzed for meaning and the presence of ideologies according to a set of criteria that we developed. That criteria include (1) tone, (2) content of message, (3) specific insults, and (4) the positioning of the author relative to Jones and others. The criterion of tone refers to the apparent emotional state of the author. Twitter provides text that is frequently accompanied by signs and symbols, such as emoticons, abbreviations, and pictorial signifiers. This allows readers to infer the emotional tone of a typed message (Baym, 2015). The criterion of analyzing the content of the message involves evaluating the apparent meaning of the tweet and the goal of the communication. For instance, a negative tweet may be interpreted as intending to do harm, but it is important to understand whether that message was meant to be a malicious negative comment, a productive negative critique, or a message bringing a concern held by the author to the attention of the recipient. The criteria of evaluating specific insults attempts to discern the presence of ideological forces. Different vulgarities reinforce harmful ideologies, that is, racial slurs reinforce racial superiority/inferiority dynamics, and homophobic epithets help to normalize both the marginalization of LGBTQ+ and the understanding of them as disordered. The final criterion interprets the ways the author appears to be positioned in relation to Jones and others. This is an important consideration for understanding the social dynamics of this virtual space. When individuals tweet at others, they align themselves with the target's supporters or detractors. Through this behavior, they reinforce, oppose, or modify ideologies regarding race and gender. This aspect of the evaluation provides insight into the ways cyberbullies form mobs and play off each other in order to create a hostile environment that facilitates the normalizing of racist and misogynist practices. We found that Twitter users were normally divided into two groups, supporters and detractors; however, there are important commonalities between the two groups.

Our method involved collecting publicly available data and analyzing each tweet according to the established criteria. We analyzed the data, respectively, and compared our findings. These data mean that each tweet analyzed for this study was not deleted or protected at the time of data collection. The results were organized in terms of the themes that emerged during analysis. We detail the ways in which the ideologies of racism and misogyny were made manifest. We also explain the mobbing and cyberbullying practices utilized by Twitter users and the ways they normalized racism and misogyny through the construction of a virtual environment that is consistent with the real world in terms of microlevel oppressive practices that reinforce the macrolevel sociocultural positioning of marginalized groups with multiple stigmatized identities, that is, Black females (Weber, 1998).

Results

After applying our criteria for CDA to the tweets from the two selected Twitter threads generated by Jones in response to the backlash from *Ghostbusters* (2016), we found data that both met our expectations as well as revealed unexpected information. We disclose our findings regarding the various tones utilized by the Twitter users, the positionalities they assumed relative to Jones, and the content of the tweets. The results are divided into three sections: (1) detractors, (2) supporters, and (3) commonalities between the two groups. We first address the most common aspects that characterized the tweets and then describe the ways users expressed support or hostility. We included examples of the tweets we analyzed to provide context. To ensure content fidelity, we did not alter tweet content, but user handles of all individuals were changed to provide confidentiality. We conclude this chapter by examining the ways the discursive formations within these tweets support problematic ideologies and their real-world implications.

Commonalities

While many of the tweets contained various types of content that ranged in complexity, the perceived tones utilized by the Twitter users were fairly simple. Twitter users were generally positive or negative in their perceived tone; and even when users mixed condemnation with support, the overall tone of the message seemed to fall within that binary. For example, @TwitterUser1 wrote, "I'm excited for the opportunity 4 u, but that looks like some Hollywood stereotypical shit 2 make blk ppl look inferior mentally." The tweet indicates some degree of support for Jones, but the overall message is that of negativity. The user asserts that the role appears to be in keeping with racist typecasting and the use of stereotypes within the entertainment industry. When analyzing the tweets for evidence of tonality, we found common signifiers associated with online text, specifically elements such as insults, overt praise, using ALL CAPS, and punctuation. These text-based cues increase the media richness of the tweets by working as proxies for social cues that are typically absent from text-alone communications that obey the normative rules for grammar (Baym, 2015). In addition to these signifiers, we considered the presence of emoticons/emojis, linked news articles, images, memes, and GIFs. These additional signifiers reduced ambiguity as to the users' intent, whether in terms of clarifying the tone of a tweet that was somewhat vague or by adding emphasis to a clearly expressed message.

One of the most important findings from our analysis in regard to the perceived tone expressed by Twitter users was the hyperbolic nature of the tweets. In addition to being hyperbolic, Ott (2017) notes that Twitter communication is "simple, impetuous, and frequently denigrating and dehumanizing" (p. 60). Users utilized profanity, strong language, ALL CAPS to signify yelling, as well as imagery that emphasized their points. Jane (2016) argues that these communicative strategies are designed to evoke the strongest emotional response from victims. Both supporters and detractors used still images and GIFs to express their perspectives. One example of the ways imagery was used to emphasize a message was the hostile tweet from @TwitterUser2. It read "#Ghostbutthurt #FreeMilo" and was accompanied by an image of the original ghostbuster logo of a ghost inside the international prohibition symbol with a smaller version of the ghostbuster logo placed over the mouth of the ghost. Beneath the logo was the word "Ghostbusters" with "busters" crossed out and "butthurt" written underneath. The term "butthurt" is an insult that asserts a person is too emotionally sensitive and is behaving in a way that is disproportionate to the original offense. A contrasting example that illustrates a positive message conveyed by a supporter was the tweet sent by @TwitterUser3. It read "love you girl. keep your head high [emojis: winking-kiss face, person with a raised hand, and a heart]" and an image that represented the word "haters" as an acronym for "Having," "Anger," "Towards," "Everyone," "Reaching," and "Success." Emojis were almost exclusively used by supporters, such as @TwitterUser4 who tweeted, "I'm so sorry ignorant hateful people are terrible. Your movie is a beacon of hope to so many girls right now, We love you." The message included several emojis of a purple heart. This tweet illustrates how the heart emoji is used to reinforce the seemingly obvious message of support and positivity, conveying a sense of enthusiasm along with the message.

In addition to the use of emojis and images, Twitter users often utilized typeface to convey extreme sentiments. For example, @TwitterUser5 manipulated the typeface in the tweet "You know what FUCK HER SHE GOT FUCKING MILO BANNED BECAUSE HE CALLED HER FAT." In this tweet, @TwitterUser5 conveys displeasure with Jones by using profanity and emphasizes the sentiment by typing a portion of the tweet in ALL CAPS to indicate extreme anger. This is consistent with the profanity in conveying a sentiment of hate and rage. Closely linked to the criterion of tone is that of positionality and how users understand their relationship with Jones. Their perspectives on that relationship heavily influence the tone that they take in their exchanges with her.

User Positionality

When supporting or condemning Jones, users often did so with a sense of familiarity. Baym (2015) points out that text-based mediated communication allows for room in terms of interpreting messages and creating a conceptualization of others that may or may not be true to reality. We contend that users who interacted with Jones fabricated an image of her in their minds that lent itself to communicating with a sense of familiarity. The normative method of address that users employed when tweeting at Jones involved referring to her as they would a person with whom they were having a conversation. This most often took the form of referring to Jones as "you" within their messages. Furthermore, the content of the messages often conveyed a sense of familiarity or equality when positive. Twitter users who criticized and condemned Jones may have viewed themselves as superior to her in some capacity, since one does not generally rebuke or scold a superior. This is consistent with the assertion made by Ott (2017) that Twitter fosters incivility. For example, @TwitterUser6 tweeted "Give hate, get hate. You racist bigot" and included a link to the Breitbart article "Double Standards: Leslie Jones' Racist Twitter History," which details the Twitter exploits of Jones and highlights past incendiary remarks. In this example, the user expressed an opinion of Jones that places her beneath them by virtue of the qualities associated with bigotry, particularly ignorance, closed-mindedness, and intellectual inferiority. Individuals may infer that the users value themselves as superior to Jones. The lack of titles used, that is, calling her "Ms. Jones," in addition to tweeting at her use of poor grammar, conveyed a sense of familiarity. Another example by @TwitterUser7 read, "[image of five pink hearts] New levels, new devils. Love you sis be strong & stay focused you're inspiring women everywhere! #BlessUp." @TwitterUser7 expresses a sentiment of support and encouragement as well as familial support and solidarity. This is signified by typing as though they were speaking directly to Jones, indicated by "you" and using the term "sis" to emphasize an emotional connection felt by the author. Some users included her full name, but that was almost always as a part of the hashtag #loveforlesliejones. As users take advantage of the informal nature of Twitter they implicitly and simultaneously express solidarity with Jones as a Black woman or reassert the degradation of her identity.

Content

The data yielded from analyzing the content of the tweets shed light on how digital discursive formations are used to reinforce harmful ideologies that have real-world consequences. We classified users into two categories, "detractors" and "supporters." These categories are divided into subcategories that describe the types of behavior expressed by Twitter users. The function of using subcategories is to distinguish between ideological constructions that may overlap but have distinctions. The category of "detractors" includes subcategories: sexist/racist insults; justification for sexist/racist behavior; and the normativity of online harassment. The value of each subdivision in this category is to distinguish between perspectives that function differently in terms of discursive mechanics but all advance the legitimization of online abuse. "Sexist/racist insults" focus on the specific linguistic manifestations; "justification for the sexist/racist behavior" shifts the focus to the rationalization of such attacks; and "normativity of online harassment" attempts to naturalize this element of the artificial digital environment. The category of "supporters" contains two subcategories of behavior: unqualified supportive messages and support with critique. These subdivisions delineate between types of support, so that we can identify the complexity of online praise that can still be connected to chastisement, which while not as overtly harmful as slurs and insults still presumes a level of emotional accessibility that is similar to derogatory attacks.

Detractors

Sexist/Racist Insults

We first examine the racist and sexist insults aimed at Jones. These often involved allusions to racial stereotypes that were likely to demean an actor who is a person of color. These types of interactions were among the most prominent and appear to be the impetus behind Jones' departure from Twitter. Jones indicates this with a tweet wherein she asks for help in stopping fake accounts that claim to be her. The account she referenced tweeted messages that are homophobic. They also use grammar and language that is uncharacteristic of Jones and is consistent with racist representations of African-American speech patterns. The fake account writes "uncleTom fag @nero needs to get his racist ss out my mentions. Shit liek dis make me think that we need to gas dese goddamn faggots to death"; while the real Jones wrote later on the same day that she asked for help with the fake account, "I leave Twitter tonight with tears and a very sad heart. All this cause I did a movie. You can hate the movie but the shit I got today...wrong." While the genuine quote is not grammatically correct, it is clear that the fake quote is a parody of the actress meant to convey that she is uneducated.

In terms of race, Twitter users referenced what they perceived to be the stereotypical nature of Jones' character. As @TwitterUser8 tweeted, "your playing a loud unfunny obnoxious stereotype. Not a funny relatable everyman that the audience can relate to." Others echoed this assertion by remarking that Jones' character leaned heavily on racist tropes and stereotypes that denigrated the African-American community. Accompanying the criticism of her portrayal of the character was the assertion that the character was predicated on a racist trope regarding African-Americans in film; ostensibly that of the "coon" trope characterized by outlandish antics, mannerisms, and mangled English (Bogle, 2016). Users often took issue with the idea that the only Ghostbuster that was not a scientist and was the only person of color worked as an employee of the Metropolitan Transportation Authority. Many believed that this job is less prestigious than those held by the other three lead characters who are scientists and academics. This was a point of contention with some of the users, such as @TwitterUser9. @TwitterUser9 wrote "@Lesdoggg A regular person can be a Ghostbuster.

The question is, why's the blk woman the non-scientist & there are 3 white women scientist?" It is clear that racial slurs and comments were also a part of the harassment that Jones encountered. This was evidenced by references made by other users such as @TwitterUser10 who tweeted "Harambe memes are funny, are they not? @Lesdoggg." The reference to Harambe alludes to the memes comparing Jones to a gorilla killed at the Cincinnati Zoo in order to save the life of a child during an emergency situation. This type of comparison implies that Black Americans are similar to apes intellectually and physically (Goff, Eberhardt, Williams, & Jackson, 2008).

Misogynist attacks made against Jones often involved connections between the film, feminism, and/or political correctness. Some assaults on Jones used misogynist terms such as "witch" and "stereotypical bitch." Others referred to the film as endorsing political correctness and feminism so much so that it became unfunny. One example comes from a conversation in one of the threads mocking the idea that there needs to be more representation of women heroes/leads in science fiction. @TwitterUser11 tweeted that "Before #Ghostbusters there were no strong female characters in movies. FACT. Now, we have changed this. YESSS! @TwitterUser4 @Lesdoggg." Later in that same conversation, @TwitterUser12 remarked that "Ripley was a weak, sassless character. Time for an Aline reboot? @paulfeig." These remarks mock the need for more positive representation of women in the action and sci-fi genres by dramatically over-emphasizing the significance of a having an all-woman lead cast and by insulting the character Ellen Ripley, the famous heroine of the *Alien* franchise. @TwitterUser12 even incorporated a racial component to their harassment by referencing the need for "sassiness" in a strong female character. Sassiness is an element found in stereotypical representations of Black American women going back to the early iterations of the mammy stereotype (Bogle, 2016). This sentiment was echoed by at least one other participant in the conversation. These comments illustrate the presence of both overt sexism as well as implicit racism combined with sexism. In the earlier comments, users utilize terms such as "witch" and "stereotypical bitch" that are meant to denigrate Jones in a traditionally misogynist manner. The latter comments regarding a reboot of *Alien* mock the need for appropriate representation by implying that a postsexist media industry has already been achieved via characters such as Ellen Ripley, the protagonist of *Alien*. By mocking the need for female representation and incorporating racist elements of historical representation, that is, sass, the users denigrate Jones and frame her as irrelevant.

Justification for Racist/Sexist Behavior

Users were not always content to simply insult Jones. They occasionally provided explanations for why the attacks were warranted. Users justified the harassment in three ways. First, they claimed she was in fact a racist and that fact warranted her mistreatment. Users posted screenshot images of tweets attributed to Jones as evidence of her inclination to make racist remarks. Jones claimed that most of those tweets were the result of her account being hacked or photoshopped. Others referred to tweets that involved apparent criticism of White individuals as the rationale for supporting the treatment of Jones. These tweets typically involved benign if insensitive messages remarking that White females look alike or that the term "Black Republicans" is an oxymoron and conceptually idiotic. To be clear, these comments display prejudice in some capacity, but they do not rise to the level of offensiveness of the tweets from fake accounts such as the tweet that gay people should be exterminated. Yet, for the mob, these tweets were license to condone the attacks on Jones as a digital eye-for-an-eye style of punishment.

Users also justified the digital abuse of Jones through her involvement in the Ghostbuster reboot. They tweeted that the film was terrible and that she should be ashamed. An example of this type of vitriol comes from @TwitterUser13 who commented that "when your unoriginal movie bombs, you've only got yourself to blame. #FireJackDorsey #FreeMilo." Tweets such as this one connect the issue of Milo's ban along with criticism of the film. @TwitterUser13's remark implies that the two are connected and that Jones should be blamed for attracting so much hate.

The third prominent justification for the abuse directed at Jones was the issue of Milo Yiannopoulos being banned from Twitter. The users blamed Jones for Milo's ban and, as with the matter of her being perceived as racist, used this as justification for harassing her. Users seeking to harass Jones utilized the hashtag #FreeMilo to express their support for Yiannopoulos. The hashtag was almost always combined with a message that ridiculed her for her racially charged tweets or for having been involved with the film, such as the tweet "good! No more 'white people' tweets from you #FreeMilo" by @TwitterUser14.

Normativity of Online Harassment

Another type of discursive formation that often occurred was the idea of the Internet as an arena wherein abuse and policing are norms (Hunt, 2016). As Brock (2012) notes in a description of the "Too Much Nick" blog, some internet users create norms for how the technology should be used and work to reclaim the digital space if those norms are challenged. Several users tweeted messages that downplayed the significance of the harassment by asserting that abuse online was normal and/or that online harassment was a matter of little consequence. Two examples of this are @TwitterUser15's tweet, "Welcome to the internet. FYI there's a clear difference between what's said to you online and IRL. If you don't get that, leave" and @TwitterUser16's tweet, "I guess your new to the Internet but everyone here gets treated like trash by children, no red or green carpet here sweetie." These messages highlight the idea that abuse should be expected online and that such abuse is inconsequential as compared to harassment that occurs in real life. This perspective regarding the nature of online communication supports the type of harassment that results in the psychological trauma endured by Jones and others.

Supporters

Unqualified Supportive Messages

Within the content of the supportive messages, we encountered various terms of familiarity, primarily along the lines of "girl" or "queen" coupled with praise and concern for Jones' well-being. This is consistent with the earlier discussion on the inherent informality of the platform as articulated by Ott (2017), and the idea that users position themselves relative to the recipient of the tweet in a manner that is closer than they would position themselves normally in real life. In both of the threads that we analyzed, the supportive tweets appeared to be the most prevalent of the responses. While it would be irresponsible to speculate without more data and altering the scope of the project, it seems that at least in terms of personal significance, the negative tweets were more salient for Jones as indicated by her desire to leave Twitter. The notion that negative comments are more salient to Jones than the positive comments is consistent with the concept of negativity bias. This concept asserts that people generally pay more attention to negative information instead of positive (Park, 2015). Many of the tweets celebrated her ability and prowess as a comedic actress, but some voiced support for the part she played in the removal of Milo from Twitter. One such example is @TwitterUser17 who tweeted "I'm sorry that we are racist misogynistic folks Leslie Jones. Thank you for being real and saying what happened." Several other tweets echoed the sentiment that some of her followers were appreciative of Jones for helping to remove Milo from Twitter. These messages of support often simultaneously acknowledge the marginalized social position that Jones occupies while attempting to rebuff that ideology. By praising Jones and offering comments that reaffirm her value as a female of color while acknowledging sexism and racism, the supporters are attempting to undermine the stigma that attracted the negative attention to Jones in the first place. In essence, these tweets help to make visible the ideological forces that facilitated the hate toward Jones.

Support with Critique

The final category that we encountered while analyzing tweets was that of messages that combine condemnation with support. These tweets are characterized by support for Jones and the apparent level of success she has achieved while also condemning her role within the film. An example of this sentiment is the message tweeted by @TwitterUser18, "I'm happy for you! I know roles do not get handed out everyday, but this is some 1916 'Step and Fetch it.'" This tweet simultaneously expresses support for Jones and her professional accomplishment in managing to get a primary role in a major film while also comparing her character to the 1930s actor of color Lincoln Perry. Perry's infamous stage persona Stepin Fetchit served as a hyperbolic representation of negative stereotypes about Black Americans being lazy, unintelligent, and underachievers (Regester, 1994). While not as common as most of the other types of content encountered during analysis, this form of criticism occurred often enough to be noteworthy and represents a sort of cognitive nuance in the minds of her supporters.

Discussion

In this research, we used CDA to examine Twitter data related to the shaming and abuse of Leslie Jones in 2016. We were first drawn to this topic after criticism of her role surfaced during the debut of the *Ghostbusters* trailer. We then followed the way the mob of abusers grew during the promotion and release of the film. Our goal was to examine the ways these cyberbullies and shamers reinforced common racist and sexist ideologies in their messages. We also examined their discursive strategies and the ways they positioned themselves in relation to Jones, a well-known celebrity.

We found that supportive and abusive Twitter users utilized common computer-mediated communication strategies to imply a specific tone. A common strategy was using ALL CAPS language to emphasize content. We found that this tactic was most often done to express outrage or insults. Another strategy was emoji use. These small images provided visual clues as to the tone of the messages. We found that users were not often "star-struck" by their interactions with a celebrity. They frequently interacted with her in an informal manner and used language that indicated they felt their communication mirrored common face-to-face synchronous interactions. This mode of address is consistent with the underlying assertions of Ott (2017) and Suler (2004) that in digital spaces, people behave in a manner that differs from how they would in real life as they are not subject to the same consequences that would come from face-to-face interactions. The value of this understanding is that we can then give proper weight to the messages from both the supporters and detractors as evidence of actual ideological perspectives that are not as subject to social desirability bias as in-person communication.

We also found that many abusive messages contained language that reinforces several racist and misogynistic beliefs. These messages contained victim blaming and justifications for the abuse. For example, messages containing comparisons to gorillas were an obvious attack on her Black identity (Goff, Eberhardt, Williams, & Jackson, 2008). Additionally, terms such as "witch" were coupled with comments mocking the need for strong female characters in film. We discovered that shamers and cyberbullies justified these dehumanizing behaviors. This dehumanization tactic is sometimes used in response to outgroup wrongdoing (Leidner, Castano, Zaier, & Giner-Sorolla, 2010). Many shamers used this strategy by justifying their abuse by Jones' wrongdoings of ruining a male-led film (original *Ghostbusters*) and having Milo Yiannopolous banned from Twitter. Users also minimized the internet as a medium for abuse. A pattern emerged of users mentioning that abuse was common on the internet and noting that their messages did not matter in this setting. The abusive messages combined with the fake accounts that were created to misrepresent her ultimately led to her temporary departure from Twitter on July 18, 2016. Her message read, "Twitter I understand you got free speech I get it. But there has to be some guidelines when you let spread like that. You can see on the Profiles that some of these people are crazy sick. It's not enough to freeze Acct. They should be reported." This was followed by the aforementioned tweet about leaving Twitter. These tweets indicate that the hateful attacks on Jones crossed her emotional threshold of what she could endure.

It is encouraging that Jones received positive messages as research indicates abuse against women is often underreported (Alhusen, Bloom, Clough, & Glass, 2015). This suggests that individuals other than the target are willing and able to notice and respond to abuse in digital settings. This is supported by research from Shaw (2016). In the Leslie Jones case, women were able to interact in the comments section of Instagram and provide suggestions for how digital abusers should be punished. Suler (2004) also suggests that the same components of the online disinhibition effect that contribute to negative digital behaviors may also contribute to users' willingness to provide support as well.

The data indicate that ideological beliefs pertaining to marginalized positionality rooted in physical appearance and the immediate access provided by Twitter are at the crux of the mobbing and cyber-shaming experienced by Jones. The detractors of Leslie Jones often resort to racial and sexist slurs that are rooted in the problematic notion of women of color being worthy of neither dignity nor respect. These detractors are able to voice those insults via Twitter which significantly reduces real-world barriers that ordinarily insulate celebrities from the public. Ostensibly, the supporters recognized the nature of these attacks and offered messages of support that reaffirm her identity as a woman and/or Black actor. Without more research, it would be irresponsible to ascribe motives to the detractors, such as whether they attacked Jones out of hatred for women, Blackness, or the movie, out of boredom, competing with/against other trolls, as a means of obtaining gratification by exercising some small amount of power, or other motives. Based on the data analyzed along with the understanding that Jones' character was singled out as "the worst of the lot" (2016) in Yiannopolous' Breitbart article "Teenage Boys with Tits: Here's My Problem with *Ghostbusters*," and the apparently disproportionate hate that Jones received compared to her co-stars, it seems that her status as Black woman provided the most exploitable material for hate by the abusers. In essence, we assert that the reason for the mobbing and abuse toward Jones was that out of all of the possible targets for vitriol relevant to the film, she was the most easily assailable due to preexisting ideologies regarding the inferiority of Blackness and womanhood. Her marginalized identity acted as a sort of lightning rod for cyberbullies who identified her as an exploitable target and then compounded each other's messages by interacting with one another or by emphasizing certain themes by articulating them again.

Practical Implications

Unfortunately, online abuse is evolving. This abuse is becoming more dangerous and leading to more significant offline consequences. In our examination of Jones, we found that in addition to utilizing real-world racist and gendered insults in a digital space (and thus blurring the line between the "real" and digital), abusers used dehumanizing tactics, hacking, photo manipulation, and widespread release of personal and nude images (Rogers & Bromwich, 2016). We also recognize other dangerous behaviors such as doxxing, cyberstalking, and SWATing that have occurred in other scenarios. As previously written, Keats Citron (2014) described that engaging with harassers online may provide short-term relief but do not protect victims from more dangerous behaviors. The use of such strategies in conjunction with the constant berating in the form of digital discourse that we have examined indicates the means in which harmful real-world ideologies that are rooted in the oppression of various demographics manifest in digital spaces. In doing so, these manifestations traumatized Jones and compelled her to temporarily leave Twitter. In short, negative ideologies permeated her digital space and left her to deal with the real-world consequences of digital abuse. Although the supportive messages found in this study are valuable, our research shows that more education about services available for victims of digital abuse is necessary. Our research also raises questions about the ways Twitter and other social media sites respond to abuse. Although Yiannopolous was banned, the backlash by less influential individuals was enough to drive Jones away from the platform. This chapter shows that more effective and swifter consequences are needed in these spaces to limit digital and offline abuse. Additionally, we believe that further investigation into the phenomenon of cyber abuse perpetrated against public figures from marginalized backgrounds may yield information useful for developing theoretical concepts related to the function of privilege online and selection of targets by shamers and bullies.

References

Albert, C. S., & Salam, A. F. (2013, August, 15–17). *Critical discourse analysis: Toward theories in social media* [Conference Submission] Proceedings of the Nineteenth Americas Conference on Information Systems, Chicago, IL. https://citeseerx.ist.psu.edu/viewdoc/download?doi=10.1.1.665.6834&rep=rep1&type=pdf 1–8.

Alhusen, J., Bloom, T., Clough, A., & Glass, N. (2015). Development of the myplan safety decision app with friends of college women in abusive dating relationships. *Journal of Technology in Human Services, 33*, 263–282.

Baym, N. K. (2015). *Personal connections in the digital age* (2nd ed.). Cambridge: Polity Press.

Blevins, J. (2016, August 28). *Social media mobbing diminishes the quality of public discourse.* Retrieved from http://thecincyproject.org/2016/08/28/social-media-mobbing-diminishes-the-quality-of-public-discourse/

Bogle, D. (2016). *Toms, coons, mulattoes, mammies, and bucks: An interpretive history of Blacks in American films*. New York: Bloomsbury.

Brock, A. (2012). From the blackhand side: Twitter as a cultural conversation. *Journal of Broadcasting & Electronic Media, 56*(4), 529–549. doi:10.1080/08838151.2012.732147

Brojakowski, B. (2016). #BostonStrong: Exploratory research of twitter impression management. In S. Gibson & A. L. Lando (Eds.), *Impact of communication and the media on ethnic conflict* (pp. 162–178). Hershey: IGI Global.

Chen, J. (2018, January 31). *Kathy Griffin calls fallout after Trump photo scandal a 'double standard'*. Retrieved from https://www.rollingstone.com/culture/news/kathy-griffin-on-trump-photo-scandal-fallout-a-double-standard-w516187

Chess, S., & Shaw, A. (2015). A conspiracy of fishes, or, how we learned to stop worrying about #Gamergate and embrace hegemonic masculinity. *Journal of Broadcasting & Electronic Media, 59*(1), 208–220.

Fairclough, N. (2003). *Analysing discourse: Textual analysis for social research*. London: Routledge.

Felmlee, D., Inara Rodis, P., & Zhang, A. (2020). Sexist slurs: Reinforcing feminine stereotypes online. *Sex Roles, 83*(1–2), 16–28. doi:10.1007/s11199-019-01095-z

Goff, P. A., Eberhardt, J. L., Williams, M. J., & Jackson, M. C. (2008). Not yet human: Implicit knowledge, historical dehumanization, and contemporary consequences. *Journal of Personality and Social Psychology, 94*(2), 292–306.

Hern, A. (2014, October 23). *Felicia day's public details put online after she described Gamergate fears*. Retrieved March 23, 2016, from http://www.theguardian.com/technology/2014/oct/23/felicia-days-public-details-online-gamergate

Himelboim, I., McCreery, S., & Smith, M. (2013). Birds of a feather tweet together: Integrating network and content analyses to examine cross-ideology exposure on Twitter. *Journal of Computer-Mediated Communication, 18*, 154–174. doi: 10.1111/jcc.4.12001

Hunt, E. (2016, March 07). *Online harassment of women at risk of becoming 'established norm', study finds*. Retrieved from https://www.theguardian.com/lifeandstyle/2016/mar/08/online-harassment-of-women-at-risk-of-becoming-established-norm-study?CMP=share_btn_tw

Jane, E. A. (2014). Online misogyny and feminist digilantism. *Continuum: Journal of Media & Cultural Studies. 30*(3), 284–297. doi:10.1080/10304312.2016.1166560

Jane, E. A. (2016). 'Back to the kitchen, cunt': Speaking the unspeakable about online misogyny. *Continuum: Journal of Media & Cultural Studies. 28*(4), 558–570. doi:10.1080/10304312.2014.924479

Keats Citron, D. (2014). *Hate crimes in cyberspace*. Cambridge, MA: Harvard University Press.

Lang, N. (2016, March 4). *The new "Ghostbusters" and race: Why it matters that Leslie Jones isn't playing one of the scientists*. Retrieved from http://www.salon.com/2016/03/04/the_new_ghostbusters_and_race_why_it_matters_that_leslie_jones_isnt_playing_one_of_the_scientists/

Leidner, B., Castano, E., Zaiser, E., & Giner-Sorolla, R. (2010). Ingroup glorification, moral disengagement, and justice in the context of collective violence. *Personality and Social Psychology Bulletin, 36*(8), 1115–1129.

Luxton, D. D., June, J. D., & Fairall, J. M. (2012). Social media and suicide: A public health perspective. *American Journal of Public Health, 102*(2), S195–200.

MILO. (2016, July 18). Teenage boys with tits: Here's my problem with ghostbusters. *Breitbart*. Retrieved March 31, 2022, from https://www.breitbart.com/tech/2016/07/18/milo-reviews-ghostbusters/

Ott, B. (2017). The age of Twitter: Donald J. Trump and the politics of debasement. *Critical Studies in Media Communication, 34*(1), 59–68. 10.1080/15295036.2016.1266686

Park, C. S. (2015). Applying "negativity bias" to Twitter: Negative news on Twitter, emotions, and political learning. *Journal of Information Technology & Politics, 12*(4), 342–359. 10.1080/19331681.2015.110025

Pew Research Center. (2021, April 7). *Social media fact sheet.* Retrieved August 1, 2022, from http://www.pewinternet.org/fact-sheet/social-media/

Phillips, W. (2015). *This is why we can't have nice things: Mapping the relationship between online trolling and mainstream culture.* Cambridge, Massachusetts: MIT Press.

Poerksen, B., & Detel, H. (2014). *The unleashed scandal: The end of control in the digital age.* (A.R. Koeck & W.K. Koeck, Trans.). La Vergne, TN: Ingram Book Company.

Posner, E. (2015, April 9). *Are the benefits of our new shaming culture worth the costs?* Retrieved February 02, 2016, from http://www.slate.com/articles/news_and_politics/view_from_chicago/2015/04/internet_shaming_the_legal_history_of_shame_and_its_costs_and_benefits.html

Pulos, A. (2013). Confronting heteronormativity in online games. *Games and Culture, 8*(2), 77–97. doi:10.1177/1555412013478688.

Regester, C. (1994). Stepin Fetchit: The man, the image, and the African American Press. *Film History, 6*(4), 502–521.

Rogers, K., & Bromwich, J. E. (2016, August 24). *Hackers publish nude pictures on Leslie Jones's website.* Retrieved from http://www.nytimes.com/2016/08/25/movies/leslie-jones-website-hacked.html?_r=0

Ronson, J. (2015). *So you've been publicly shamed.* London: Pan Macmillan.

Shaw, F. (2016). "Bitch I said hi": The Bye Felipe campaign and discursive activism in mobile dating apps. *Social Media & Society, 2*(4), 1–10.

Silman, A. (2016, August 24). *A timeline of Leslie Jones's horrific online abuse.* Retrieved, November 9, 2017, from https://www.thecut.com/2016/08/a-timeline-of-leslie-joness-horrific-online-abuse.html

Suler, J. (2004). The online disinhibition effect. *CyberPsychology and Behavior, 7*(3), 321–326. doi: 10.1089/1094931041291295.

Sunstein, C. (2009). *Going to extremes how like minds unite and divide.* Oxford: Oxford University Press.

Tanksley, T. C. (2016). Education, representation, and resistance: Black girls in popular Instagram memes. In S. U. Noble & B. M. Tynes (Eds.), *The intersectional internet: Race, sex, class, and culture online* (pp. 243–259). New York: Peter Lang Publishing.

Twitter. (2022). *Company about.* Retrieved March 31, 2022, from https://about.twitter.com/company

van Dijk, T. A. (1993). Principles of critical discourse analysis. *Discourse & Society, 4*(2), 249–283. doi:10.1177/0957926593004002006

Weber, L. (1998). A conceptual framework for understanding race, class, gender, and sexuality. *Psychology of Women Quarterly, 22*(1), 13–32.

Wright, M. F. (2017). Parental mediation, cyberbullying, and cybertrolling: The role of gender. *Computers in Human Behavior, 71,* 189–195.

6

DRIVERS AGAINST THE MACHINE

Reproductive Labor and Reproductive Justice in a Phantom Public

Kasturi Ray and Julietta Hua

Introduction

By the time New York City taxi drivers headed into a 15-day hunger strike in October 2021, they had already been organizing for 3 years for medallion debt forgiveness. Buying one's own medallion, or license to operate a passenger-ride vehicle, had once been imagined as a pathway toward individual financial freedom and economic security: in the absence of other alternatives for the mostly immigrant male drivers, medallions could be seen as an expensive but worthwhile investment in retirement, in that drivers could imagine renting out their medallions when they themselves could no longer drive. As John Henry Assabill, a taxi driver, put it,

> If you are a young man … and you have a medallion … you have a lot of energy to work more hours. By the time you get weak, your medallion is paid for. And then you can retire on it.

But then he added, "We didn't know it was going to be like this" (Badger, 2014). Drivers like Assabill who had once invested in their individualized "right to drive" by financing a medallion saw the value of their medallions plummet from a peak of over $900,000 to under $200,000 in a matter of a couple years, mostly due to the influx of unregulated "gig" rides provided by Uber, Lyft, and other ride-hail app companies entering the New York City market (Laughlin, 2018).[1]

The financing of expensive medallions has not enabled drivers to make a livable wage, much less retire. While app-hail companies that gig driving (like Uber and Lyft) marketed their difference from the traditional taxi as a matter of safety and innovation of an outdated (taxi) industry, they not only employed

DOI: 10.4324/9781003260851-8

former taxi drivers but relied on the same structures of debt and labor as traditional taxis. In fact, gigged driving companies' marketing sells its difference from taxis as giving drivers freedom around their "right to drive." In the taxi industry, the medallion, which represents a drivers' ownership of the "right to drive," is exactly what the hunger strikers point out as keeping drivers in precarity. Medallions are marketed to drivers as a way to have greater freedom over their right to drive, yet they have yoked drivers who try to purchase a medallion with inescapable debt.

Thus, finding themselves debilitated by both the regulatory structures of the traditional taxi industry (medallions) and the entry of ride-hail gig companies that exacerbated already existing exploitations in the industry (driving down earnings), several drivers committed suicide in the opening months of 2018. These drivers left behind communications that living under conditions of indebtedness and declining wages were unbearable (Furfaro & Jaeger, 2018).[2] These ongoing struggles led up to the 2021 hunger strike wherein driver-organizers took it upon themselves to starkly dramatize the draining of their bodies and hopes, making demands for city accountability and redress. Drivers' demands explain that,

> Owner-drivers, overwhelmingly immigrants of color, personally guarantee medallion loans. This means that in the event of a foreclosure, the lender will pursue the owner-driver for any balance that remains after the sale of the medallion. After years of poverty income, and loss of retirement, owner-drivers are further at risk of losing their savings, assets, and livelihood... A solution to this crisis is possible. The addition of a government guarantee, or backstop, to a city program of $20k cash down payments to use toward debt restructuring would facilitate real debt forgiveness. A mostly immigrant workforce that has served this city 24x7 would have their life back. As the cause and benefactor of the crisis - the city collected over $850 million from medallion sales from 2004 to 2017- the City has a moral obligation to right this injustice.
>
> *(New York Taxi Worker Alliance [TWA], 2021)*

Led by their collective union, the New York Taxi Workers Alliance (TWA), driver-organizers had been arguing that ballooning predatory interest rates on medallion purchases, debt-collecting practices based on shock tactics, and the precipitous decline in value of the medallions themselves were unduly onerous to drivers even while they enriched banks and lending companies, taxi leasing and ride-hail app companies, and the city ("over $850 million" collected by and for the City in medallion sales fees and taxes). This, the driver union argues, makes it a moral obligation of the city to address and a means for the mostly immigrant workforce to "have their life back."

That taxi and other long-duration (eight or more hours a day), professional drivers sacrifice their lives, not simply livelihoods, is our focus in this chapter. Our broader research, which has followed the organizing work of taxi drivers in the era of the gig economy, has drawn from legal documents, the archives of the TWA (they are a national taxi driver union that goes by New York Taxi Worker Alliance in New York City), urban planning and congestion studies, as well as interviews and surveys of taxi and gig (or ride-hail app) drivers. From this broader research, we argue that long duration, professional passenger driving is best understood through the framework of reproductive labor. Like household work, child care, and service work in general, driving requires emotional labor; professional passenger driving is service work, and as such, much of the driver's labor attends to the needs of the passenger. The hunger strikers also point to this aspect of their profession; it is work that serves the city "24x7," and the industry, we argue, is predicated on the sacrifice of worker life (the driver suicides perhaps provide the starkest evidence of the life cost of the work).

We think about the issues that professional passenger drivers (whether traditional taxi or gigged) have been facing through the lens of reproductive labor precisely because the masculinized bodies of drivers have occluded the reproductive nature of driving labor. Going beyond the "feminization of labor" allows us to consider reproductive labor through its broadest scope: as a type of biopolitics. We argue that as reproductive labor, professional passenger driving across industry sectors (taxis and ride-hail app transportation companies like Uber or Lyft) enables accumulation by structuring some lives antagonistically, where driver lives are valuable *only* insofar as they flourish the lives of others (passengers/consumers):

> We define reproductive labor as exertions enabling the flourishing of another's life, the tending of the body, home, and well-being of another (and thus the nation) that is often de-monetized and generally undervalued because such work is constructed as natural and expected.
>
> *(Hua & Ray, 2021, p. 5)*

Yet, companies like Uber and Lyft build their brand on their difference from, rather than similarity to, the taxi industry; this is the other focus of our chapter.

The second part of this chapter argues that the marketing of Uber, Lyft, and other gigged driving companies only further obscure the gendered violence endemic to the industry. Specifically, companies that gig driving argue they are technology companies innovating transit through the app and algorithm. Marketing hides how the gigging of driving further casualizes it by rendering the ride simply "people connecting with each other." This casualization is also marketed as providing a safer alternative to taxis and other forms of transport despite taxi's high level of state surveillance and regulation. For example, Uber has long sold itself as the "safer choice" specifically for women passengers (*Jane Doe v. Uber Technologies*, 2020, p. 23); Uber does so by using gender to mystify the harm and violence of the passenger ride-for-hire industry that impacts drivers most intensely. In other words, the violence endemic to the passenger ride-for-hire industry, which impacts drivers most acutely, operates through the deployment of gender to sever subjects (i.e., men drivers against women passenger). The result is an individuating of harm, which ignores the societal violence enacted through, for example, changing expectations and access to public transportation.

We bring a feminist lens to the ongoing work of driver-organizers like the hunger strikers and the members of the TWA who continue to insist that we see the life sacrifice of professional passenger drivers as a matter of public concern, whether we ride taxis or not. To the work of TWA organizers, who have recognized that all professional passenger drivers whether they are in the traditional taxi industry or the gigged driving sector experience similar labor conditions (debilitating debt, falling wages, increased surveillance, incursions into the ability to live), we add that centering a feminist and reproductive justice lens can expand the ways we think about gendered labor and its violence. Thus, our chapter ends with a consideration of reproductive justice, especially in light of recent state incursions to *Roe v. Wade*. What driver-organizers and the TWA continue to teach us is that centering collective well-being and life-chances for all drivers, whether taxi or gig, is a successful strategy for material change, as their recent wins for debt-restructuring and forgiveness, *and* minimum wages for all drivers, including gig drivers, attest. Following their cue, we add that centering reproductive justice enables us to trace how the passenger ride-for-hire industry, whether taxi or gig, enacts gendered violence, both in hiding the reproductive nature of driving behind masculinized drivers and in severing the safety of drivers from the interests of passengers. We begin by examining how gender violence is narrowly conceived in a series of Jane Doe legal cases filed against Uber in order to argue for the broadening of considerations of both gender violence and reproductive labor.

The "Safer Choice:" Narrowing What Counts as Gender Violence

By 2020, a series of high-media-profile cases recounted multiple Jane Does' petitions for jury trials against their Uber drivers who were accused of sexually assaulting women passengers.[3] While these cases point to the uneven gendered vulnerabilities of women to sexual violence, they also enable Uber to use gender to mystify the harm and violence endemic to the passenger ride-for-hire industry, harms that tend to impact drivers most intensely, as the New York hunger strikers argue. One *Jane Doe* case explains:

> Uber markets itself extensively to young women as the best option for a safe ride home after a night of drinking, making a safe ride for young women always within reach, and drunk driving a thing of the past. But what Uber does not share with passengers is that making the choice to hail a ride after drinking also puts them in peril from Uber drivers themselves.... Uber owed a duty to implement a thorough and effective background checking process, carefully hire qualified drivers and supervise drivers for the protection of its passengers.
>
> *(Jane Doe v. Uber Technologies, 2020, pp. 13, 25)*

In order to bring Uber to account for the actions of their drivers, who raped their passengers, the *Jane Doe* case must argue false advertising of Uber as "the best option for a safe ride home" as well as Uber's failure to properly vet drivers. As the case points out, Uber's "profits over safety" approach makes Uber responsible: "Female passengers continue to pay the price for Uber's ruthless pursuit of income. Tragically, the model of 'profits over safety' is also responsible for the tragedy at the center of this litigation" (*Jane Doe v. Uber Technologies*, 2020, p. 2). While we agree that both Uber and the drivers assaulting passengers should be held accountable for enacting and facilitating violence, we also recognize that Uber, Lyft, *and* traditional taxi companies harm drivers as well. Even while the *Jane Doe* cases and subsequent media coverage focus on the passenger at risk of harm from drivers, we argue that this limits how we can account for violence. Working from an antagonistic relation required by the legal system where a plaintiff (harmed) must be named against a defendant (harming), affirms Uber's "safer choice" paradigm where "safety" is too narrowly conceived as individual rather than more broadly allowing us to think about community safety and systemic harms (or rethink public safety altogether).[4]

The *Jane Doe* cases expose an often-hidden reality of sexual violence and assault, which in the context of patriarchy unevenly distributes harm in gendered ways (women, nonbinary, and LGBTQ communities are disproportionately impacted). Yet rather than provide an occasion to consider harm more broadly, the legal system required that the *Jane Doe* cases make narrow arguments around individual harm (victim versus perpetrator), where corporate accountability could only be framed as peripheral to the central focus (rape) – negligence in not policing and surveilling the named drivers enough, negligence in false advertising. Here, the expectation is for Uber to better police their drivers, an expectation that presumes criminality and therefore scapegoats individual drivers. And, in fact, Uber and Lyft have been quick to admit that they need better surveillance practices because this position allows the companies to refuse any accountability for gender-based violence beyond negligence. Instead, we might take direction from Susan Fowler, the former Uber employee whose 2017 blog entry chronicled the many systemic ways Uber's corporate practices facilitate and entrench patriarchal power hierarchies. In contrast to the ways individual drivers were scapegoated by Uber in the *Jane Doe* case, Fowler chronicles how the company protected their non-driver/office employees who sexually harassed those they were supervising, pointing out the systemic ways patriarchy shapes the corporate practices at Uber. In contrast, Uber's attitude toward their driver-employees is one of disposability. The drivers accused of rape shift the focus away from the corporate structures that abuse employees like Fowler as well as passengers like Jane Doe *and* extract from and abuse drivers. How can we recognize the *entwined systems* that unevenly distribute harm to both passengers like Jane Doe and to drivers without pitting the realities of one against the other?

We hope that by considering long-duration, professional driving from the frame of reproductive labor, and with attention to the broader goals of reproductive justice, the case of Jane Doe allows us to reconsider: whose safety? Uber and Lyft use safety to distinguish themselves as different from traditional taxis, yet as the *Jane Doe v. Uber Technologies* (2020) case points out, drivers are in all aspects of their employment, acting under

> Uber's control and serve to carry out the performance on behalf of Uber. In connection with this, all money is exchanged between passengers and Uber. ... Uber, not its drivers, is the sole decision-maker when it comes to pricing, rates, fares, or payments provided.

and we include driver work and life conditions. Despite advertising otherwise (as a safer choice to taxis), Uber not only acts as a taxi but uses long-standing rhetoric of "dangerous taxi drivers" for its own profit. As we have discussed elsewhere, taxi drivers have long been caricatured as potentially dangerous (the 1976 film *Taxi Driver* plays on this construction), racialized figures.[5] Uber and Lyft's marketing of the Uber and Lyft driver as a sympathetic figure is thus not only gendered but racialized; the marketing toward women passengers, specifically, resonates in part because of the long-standing characterization of the racialized threat of the driver, who, in New York and most major U.S. cities, continues to be mostly immigrant and non-white.[6] This use of safety to pit passenger against driver is a strategy long used in the passenger ride-for-hire industry in order to obscure corporate accountability for workplace safety *and* to enable industry profit.

The historical reality, structured into the industry, is that drivers are more likely to experience on-the-job injury, stress, harm, and debility. Drivers, not passengers, are more likely to be robbed (Smith, 2005) and murdered while on the job (Sygnatur & Toscano, 2000)[7]; they are also more likely to be the targets of discrimination (Blasi & Leavitt, 2006; Mathew, 2005). In many conservative accounts, the driver's other is most often depicted as the passenger, rather than corporate capital, a logic reproduced in the *Jane Doe* cases in part because the legal system leaves little room to argue otherwise. One effect of the *Jane Doe* case, for example, is to inadvertently weigh the status of drivers as Uber controlled employees against the claims of harm and exploitation experienced by the Jane Does. Without dismissing the real accountability of Jane Does' rapists, how can we also acknowledge the harms of the industry on drivers? One method that TWA organizers and drivers have taken is to continue to insist on exposing the false dichotomies that run through both the app-hailed and taxi industries (e.g., Uber driver vs. cabbie; passenger vs. driver).

The *Jane Doe* cases provide an opportunity to reexamine the narrow framing of gender violence as individual acts and gender as framed mainly in terms of oppositional subjects (men drivers, women passengers). In contrast, gender might instead be taken as an analytic of power, a way to organize power and situate subjects in antagonism so as to ensure patriarchy. Gender violence might broadly include both masculinized and feminized subjects. The narrow framing of gender violence, one used by Uber to market its opposition and difference from traditional taxis, distracts us from the systemic ways Uber, Lyft and other gigged driving corporations act in common with the traditional taxi industry to appropriate the reproductive labor of drivers, which we explore in what follows.

Driving as Reproductive Labor: Broadening What Counts as Gender Violence

Passenger driving has historically been an aspect of household labor, particularly for the economically well-to-do whose households included chauffeurs or drivers. In the context of the 20th-century United States, the rising image of the middle-class household also included a passenger vehicle to complete the picture. Passenger driving has historically been identified as a household task, alongside cooking and cleaning, for which many state disability support programs reimburse clients (Wynn & Boustead, 2015). In addition to being part of the picture of the middle-class household, the automobile functions as both an intimate, privatized space at the same time its function is to traverse publics. Like the workspaces of "domestic work," driving is work that takes place in the intimate space of the automobile and part of the expectation is not simply a ride, but that this ride is comfortable and takes care of the passenger. Thus, the labor entails what Arlie Hochschild explains in an analogous case as "performing emotions for customers … [where] the 'product' of a flight attendant's labor is a positive, satisfied emotional state of feeling in the consumer, the customer" (Vora, 2017, p. 211). Although gig rides are briefer, the driver is tasked not only with driving but also with the comfort of the customer.

While this attention to service is a hallmark of gig driving, it has also been central to the regulation of taxis. For example, former mayor of New York City, Michael Bloomberg, took on projects focused on ensuring that the "taxi system should offer taxi services that are safe, *comfortable*, and easy to use for all passengers and drivers" (italics ours; Design Trust for Public Space, 2007).[8] Safety, comfort, and ease here appear together, and as remains the case, customer service is one category that the New York City Taxi and Limo Commission (TLC; the regulatory body overseeing taxis and limos in New York City) regulates, polices and fines. Riders can complain to the Taxi and Limo Commission if they are unhappy with a driver's service or if the cab itself is wanting, and passenger complaints can precipitate tickets and fines for drivers. Similarly, in gigged driving, passenger ratings of drivers are a key mechanism of the app algorithm and determine whether drivers receive future requests for rides. These concerns around the personal comportment of drivers and the aesthetics of the cab continue to demonstrate the centrality of care to the professional task of passenger driving. They also make the work in part about how drivers' bodies impose (or not) on others; being an immigrant driver, for example, can potentially impact the comfort of a passenger, making the labor of driving more precarious for some.

We follow the important work of many feminist scholars who have approached our "investment in labor as intentional and embodied activity that has social and material consequences" (Vora, 2017, p. 205). Specifically focusing on the gendering of productive labor, this rich literature takes the activities that reproduce life "as productive in itself, as producing immediate life and not just supporting the male worker who earns the means to support immediate life," according to Kalindi Vora (2017, p. 206). In more traditional approaches to labor, "productive" labor has historically been understood as the work of men who earn wages that support families. This form of labor structured a hierarchy of labor-value to the dismissal of the labor of reproducing the lives of wage-earning men (i.e. reproductive labor). In other words, the labor of supporting life, which most frequently includes household and domestic work, child-rearing and tending to another person's body and emotions is "productive in itself" and intentionally under-valued or dismissed out of formal systems of labor compensation precisely because of logics that collapse the work with the bodies that perform it. The established logic argues, for example, that because wombs birth *as a matter of nature*, child birthing is not work that need accrue external, monetized value (and when it does, as with surrogacy, it brings to the fore this premise, often resulting in moral consternation); feminist scholars use reproductive labor to critique the gendered and often racialized presumptions of such established logics.

While passenger driving is a historically masculinized profession earning a wage outside the home, the conditions of driving-labor are, we argue, more aligned with frameworks of reproductive labor. Like other forms of domestic work, professional passenger driving blurs distinctions of public and private and works from the premise of reproductive value. Like domestic work, where the worker is both ensconced in the "private" space of the home even while subject to hyper-surveillance, the driver is highly exposed even while in an intimate space seen as an extension of the household (the car). Yet the cab or app-hailed car is never quite just a workplace, given the influx of cameras, GPS, automated messages, and the constant vulnerability (of taxis, in particular) of being pulled over by police. App-hailed transportation companies have embraced this model of pseudo-privacy, swapping the third eye of the police for the omniscient eye of the app. Thus, rather than thinking of the tools of reproductive labor as brooms and dustpans, we continue a feminist investigation into capital processes by considering instead equipment such as top-of-the-line dash cams, discreet personal cans of pepper spray, cheerful t-shirts that read "tips appreciated," and heavy-duty emesis bags with which drivers are encouraged to outfit themselves (Campbell, 2020). These worker tools evoke the scope – self-defense, careful supplemental labor, and attendance work – entailed in professional passenger driving.

What is interesting in professional passenger driving, across industry sectors, and especially common in the cross-section of long-duration (8 hours/day or more) drivers, is that these tools are heavily regulated by the state in the case of traditional taxis and are extracted as occupational costs from the driver in gigged driving. As Assabill explains about his taxi cab:

> "Everywhere on this car has been regulated… Look at it!" … The car's
> medallion number — 813 — is painted in black plain gothic figures (must

be *black plain gothic figures*) on the driver's-side hood, on both passenger doors and, for good measure, on the rear. Inside, there is a camera mounted over the rear-view mirror, a dispatch radio bolted to the console, a credit-card reader snapped to the passenger headrest. From the back of Assabill's seat hangs a sign — lamination required — spelling out the city's fare structure: $3.25 for the base rate, $2 for the airport departure/arrival tax, $50 vomit cleanup fee. Everywhere, there are mandatory stickers. "That one costs a dollar," Assabill says of a window decal reminding passengers to LOOK! before opening the door into the possible path of cyclists and pedestrians. "The fine for not having it is $100".

(Badger, 2014)

The outfitting of cabs may be familiar to the outfitting of Uber and Lyft cars, wherein the costs of passenger comfort are put upon the driver. Taxi drivers like Assabill risk being ticketed and fined if the cab does not comply with regulations. Additionally, owner-drivers (medallion holding drivers) are individually responsible for outfitting their cars with required equipment, often equipment that makes the cab hypervisible and easier to surveille. And while the taxi equipment consists of regulation-required signage, credit card readers, cameras, and so on, gig drivers bear the individual costs of amenities like phone chargers as well as the individual costs tied to insurance and job loss. These similarities that bridge traditional taxis and the gigged driving sector highlight how the conditions of labor are shared, not different, as Uber, Lyft, and other gig companies insist. Further, many long-duration gig drivers are also, or were prior, taxi drivers.

As two taxi drivers, "Hass" (who also drives for Uber) and "Amr" (who refuses to drive for Uber), explain the conditions of labor shared between traditional taxis and the gigged driving industry:

HASS: We met two years ago when we were both driving yellow cabs. Then I switched over to Uber.

AMR: People who ride with Uber think they are big shots. In a yellow cab, if they don't like you, what are they going to do? I still get paid and get to keep driving. … And let me say this in a straight and honest way: Some people are racist. Okay?

HASS: When I first started with UberX, I was getting a lot of negative ratings. … So then I cut my name in half, to Americanize it, and after two months my rating had jumped up. Now I also make sure I have several phone chargers, auxiliary cords if people want to play their music, and magazines in the back of my car. On special occasions, like Easter, I'll go to CVS and buy chocolate bunnies to hand out. It is in my interest to do this.

AMR: One of the bad things of a yellow cab is you don't have a social life. … That's why I work four months and then go home to Egypt for four months. I'd be dead of a heart attack if I did this year round (Matthew, 2014).

In the early days of Uber's entry into the New York City passenger ride-for-hire landscape (2014), Hass and Amr exchange concerns that now seem prescient. They note that as drivers, whether Uber or taxi, they expect discrimination as a condition of their work. Hass' account of Americanizing his name, and of that helping to raise his passenger ratings on the Uber app illustrates Amr's blunt observation that "some people are racist." Their conversation also points to the reproductive aspect of the labor, where not only does driving require care and attention to passenger comfort (all the "extras" Hass must provide for passengers for his own interest), but it is labor that does not allow for "a social life" (why Amr must take four months off of work). Like the TWA hunger strikers, who put their lives on the line in protest of debilitating structures (debt, employment, policing, etc.), Amr expresses what many surveys of professional drivers have corroborated: long-duration driving is work that you can expect will kill you ("I'd be dead of a heart attack if I did this year round"). In fact, a range of workplace debilities have been chronicled as a matter-of-fact toll of the profession, including kidney disease (often resulting from inability to access restrooms), cancer, liver disease, vision issues, heart attacks, and muscular debilities (Blasi & Leavitt, 2006; Perez & Dang, 2008).

All of this forms the premise of the passenger ride-for-hire industry, and despite Uber and Lyft's insistence otherwise, gigged driving simply further entrenches and obscures these conditions, notably through the cyberoptimism of app and algorithm. By focusing solely on the so-called innovation of the app and algorithm, gig companies like Uber sever the real from the virtual; what is at stake here is thus beyond the labor conditions of drivers and safety of passengers and instead about the reshaping of social expectations and habits. The gigging of driving, in other words, markets app-hail rides like Lyft and Uber as safer and more innovative ways to get around than taxis and public transit, but in fact, this marketing hides both the fact that the dangers of the industry fall disproportionately to drivers, sometimes on passengers, but never on the transportation companies themselves. Cyberoptimism also hides how the gigging of the industry enacts societal violence in changing expectations and access to notions of "the public." For example, in changing expectations for rides away from mass transit to private, individualized rides, the app and algorithm pose potential for harm to society. Without broadening how we think about and analyze gender violence and reproductive labor, we risk overlooking the societal harm brought about specifically through the gigging of driver labor.

Marketing Innovation: Casualization and Other Algorithmic Erasures

If professional, long-duration passenger driving can be understood as reproductive labor, the gigging of the industry has further hidden this reality by focusing on the so-called innovation of the app and algorithm. The app and algorithm are also how the gig driving industry hides its similarity to the traditional taxi.

Algorithms, Cathy O'Neil (2016) explains, are simply historical data used to predict future behavior and as such designed to reproduce what has already existed. Thus, under the guise of mathematical neutrality, algorithms manage digital data to mostly enable long-standing biases and structural inequalities to continue to operate as if common sense, but this perpetuation of inequality is hidden beneath a sense of cyberoptimism. The algorithms that facilitate gigged driving do exactly this – they sediment already existing inequalities and exploitations.

Thus, the fact that long-duration professional passenger driving extracts from the lives of drivers is thus further hidden from view when the industry is gigged; the labor of driving is further de-skilled and casualized when ride-hail app companies market themselves as simply monetizing what is otherwise leisure time. Lyft's "ride in the front seat" and Uber's "drive when you want" exemplify the gig approach. Dara Khosrowshahi (2020), Uber CEO, writes for example that Uber drivers value and desire "total freedom to choose when and how they drive, so they can fit work around their life, not the other way around." Foregrounding the power of the app also pushes driver labor into the background or even out of view entirely; in fact, the driver only appears as someone who works out of choice, whose real, waged life is elsewhere. Uber and Lyft argue that this marks their difference from traditional taxis.

Yet in our research, we discovered that most of the people driving full-time for Uber and Lyft were often, and especially initially, taxi drivers; Hass and Amr are not exceptional. For example, in early legal cases challenging Uber and Lyft's refusal to recognize drivers as employees, testimonies of drivers describe:

> Prior to driving for Uber, Mr. Zadran was a long-time veteran of the taxi industry [and taxi union organizer]. … In March 2014 Mr. Zadran began driving for Uber. He worked roughly 100 hours a week, frequently sleeping in his vehicle.
>
> *(Douglas O'Connor et al v. Uber Technologies, 2015)*

In another example, Mahmood Noori reports that while he drives for UberXL he "hardly ever takes bathroom breaks or stops to eat" (*Douglas O'Connor et al v. Uber Technologies*, 2015). What such testimonies confirm are the industry conditions that the TWA hunger strikers make explicit; Uber and Lyft accumulate capital because they impose work conditions that necessitate that drivers like Noori "hardly ever take bathroom breaks, or stop to eat." Uber's marketing to "drive when you want" so as to "fit work around life" is not the experience of drivers like Zadran and Noori, who find themselves "frequently sleeping in his vehicle" due to driving 100 hours a week.

The flooding of streets with potential rides, once regulated through the medallion, not only means that drivers drive longer and harder but also that the value of their labor in aggregate and across the traditional taxi and gig driving sectors is also pushed down. The industry "disruption" was thus mostly experienced by drivers who could no longer earn as much income per shift as they had previously, given that there were fewer rides and more competition at lower rates, as a New York City Council-initiated task force report details (2020). Because drivers are paid by the ride, not by the hour (true for both traditional taxis and ride-hail apps), they must drive longer shifts to find enough fares to make ends meet. And because taxis regulate how long drivers can stay on the road, many taxi drivers migrated or took on second shifts as gig drivers. While the traditional taxi industry regulates and regularizes fares, including the per-cent split between the medallion holder, the driver, and the city, gigged driving set no such floors for drivers; there is no legal guarantee of a set income for any gigged driver, with the only exception in New York City, where the TWA won minimum wages for all gig drivers operating in the city in 2022 (New York Taxi Worker Alliance, 2022). The taxi union in fact makes clear that their members are also drivers for Uber, Lyft, and Via; the union has continued to organize against the ride-hail app company's marketing that they simply allow people to "drive when they want," by representing gig drivers in legal challenges around wage theft and other labor exploitations.[9]

Marketing gigged driving and its app as simply a friendly platform that con-nects part-time drivers with passengers masks both the long-durational driving in which professional drivers must engage, as well as the role of companies like Uber and Lyft as a propagator of uneven social relations. The app enables the disappearance of driving as labor and also de-skills the work, ignoring the ways passenger ride-for-hire is a profession and industry, long recognized as such by municipalities, which treat passenger ride-for-hire as part of the public trans-portation landscape (hence regulating the industry) (Mathew, 2005). Money, for example, never changes hands in the Uber and Lyft ride since fares are collected via the app. Distancing the consumer from the exchange of money for services also hides how Uber controls all aspects of the exchange; drivers have no way to negotiate fares and often cannot verify that their promised cut of the fare is received.[10] The app, in other words, propagates uneven social relations; drivers have no way to negotiate any aspect of the fare structure. Pricing is also mysti-fied; unlike in a traditionally regulated taxi, the same ride (distance and time) can with the app-hail cost different passengers different fare rates and the result for the driver is a destabilization of earnings. "Dynamic pricing," the model of algorithmic pricing introduced through the gigging of driving, operates on the premise that individual user data determine the price of a ride. Studies of dynamic pricing, which is illegal in the regulated passenger ride-for-hire sector and considered a discriminatory practice, point to aspects like the customer's phone battery life (Calo & Rosenblat, 2017) and zip code as factors that deter-mine pricing (and thus earnings) rather than the traditional time and distance of a ride (Pandey & Caliskan, 2020). It is also likely that something like dynamic pricing determines a driver's take-home earnings; gig drivers earn different rates for different rides, even when the distance and time-of-ride are the same.

Arguing the innovation of the app and algorithm, Uber, Lyft, and other ride-hail app companies thus further deepen the extractive terms of labor for drivers, exacerbating long-standing industry practices. These practices are purposefully obscured through legal claims of algorithmic propriety, where the so-called innovation of the app further hides the reproductive violence of the industry under the claim that the "virtual" aspects of the technology are not only corporate secrets, but what distinguishes gig companies from traditional taxis (this is despite the fact that many traditional taxi companies also use apps to hail rides). The virtual "black box" of the ride-hail algorithm, as scholars like Frank Pasquale point out, is premised on unidirectional extraction: "Corporate actors have unprecedented knowledge of the minutiae of our daily lives, while we know little to nothing about how they use this knowledge to influence important decisions that we – and they – make" (2015, p. 9). The manipulation of knowledge, as Safiya Noble (2012) points out, is dangerous in the ways behaviors are subtly manipulated and social norms reshaped.

With Uber, for example, the harm to any one individual, whose personal privacy is laid bare for the company is not the only or most significant harm. Rather, as Ryan Calo and Alex Rosenblat's research into Uber's algorithmic manipulation points out, the danger lies in how algorithmic manipulation transforms social relations. For example, Uber's app uses visual strategies to show "real-time" availability of rides for both passengers and drivers. Yet as Calo and Rosenblat point out,

> Many users of the Uber app have in fact complained about the app's map of the city full of potential rides, which disappear as soon as one commits to hailing a ride; it happens so frequently that the phenomenon has earned the name 'phantom car'.
>
> *(2017)*

Calo and Rosenblat point out that the icons of cars appearing on the app work not to represent rides available but to change passenger and driver behavior; passengers are more likely to commit to an Uber ride if they see many potential rides near them and drivers are more likely to flood a neighborhood that looks like it has fewer available rides. The work of the app and algorithm is thus to give Uber a way to control supply and demand – to manipulate the market for rides.

Here, the work of the visual representation of potential rides is not to mirror reality but to shape it, specifically by encouraging customers to commit to hailing a ride through the app rather than taking mass transit or a taxi. This impact of gigged driving has been proven in New York City (as well as the San Francisco Bay Area). Congestion and traffic studies reveal how algorithmic incursions into passenger ride-for-hires change expectations around transit and mobility; ride-hail companies are not so much providing rides when other options do not exist but changing inclinations toward individualized, private rides in privately owned vehicles (Schaller, 2018). Studies of traffic patterns connect the rise of gigged passenger rides to both decreases in public transit use *and* increases in personal auto use and ownership (Schaller, 2018, pp. 2, 5). Increasing cars on the road, as one former taxi driver pointed out to us, also correlates to declining air quality.[11] These are the broader stakes: harms to the public hidden by the cyberoptimism offered by the app and algorithm, even as the app-based ride-for-hire sector markets itself as "the safer choice." When safety works narrowly and in gendered ways to only refer to passengers, the harm more likely to be experienced by masculinized drivers is disappeared. To take gender on analytic, rather than solely identitarian terms thus means demystifying the gendered violence endemic to, and impacting most acutely, professional passenger drivers.

Conclusion

This chapter argues that driving is a form of labor in which the reproductive capacities of the driver are seen not so much as a tradeable commodity but, as many of its recipients would have it, as an undisputed resource for capital. This extraction is an intimate one – thus, we are calling driving an intimate labor – both because this operation occurs in spaces where the private and public collide, creating uneasy encounters familiar to service workers, and because the personhood and bodily demands put upon the driver support the flourishing of another's life at the expense of his own, whose own social reproduction remains unfulfilled. The gigging of long duration driving uses the app and algorithm to hide this reproductive violence, which has always been part of the industry of passenger ride-for-hires, at the same time exacerbating it. If anything is new and innovative about gigged driving, it is perhaps how the algorithm deploys the virtual to transform the real in ways that divest from notions of the collective good or the public. Like the advocates of reproductive justice and the TWA driver-organizers, we insist on the need for an otherwise.

Recent incursions on abortion access, ensured through *Roe v. Wade* (1973), like Texas' Senate Bill 8 (SB8), have provided Uber and Lyft another marketing opportunity, selling the companies as supporters of women's reproductive rights. But like earlier marketing attempts to leverage women, these recent tactics hide the reproductive violence on which the industry of passenger ride-for-hires is based and focus instead on selling individualized understandings of rights and freedoms. For example, when Texas Governor Greg Abbot signed into law SB8 in spring of 2021 Lyft and Uber quickly and uncharacteristically released a united message that the companies would pay any legal fees incurred by a driver who might unknowingly provide a ride for someone seeking an abortion. Following Lyft's September 3, 2021 statement that,

> Drivers are never responsible for monitoring where their riders go or why. Imagine being a driver and not knowing if you are breaking the law by giving someone a ride. Similarly, riders never have to justify, or even share, where they are going and why. Imagine being a pregnant woman trying to get to a healthcare appointment and not knowing if your driver will cancel on you for fear of breaking a law. Both are completely unacceptable.

Uber's CEO c Khosrowshahi (2021) announced that the company would follow Lyft's lead and establish a legal defense fund for drivers sued under the new Texas law (Bond, 2021). These responses address a specific and controversial aspect of SB8 that enables private citizens to bring civil suits against persons aiding and abetting abortion, including people who might knowingly or not drive someone to receive an abortion (Texas SB8, 2021).

We look at Lyft and Uber's move to ostensibly "protect" drivers with skepticism and interpret the announcement to "support" drivers as disingenuous marketing that uses reproductive politics to hide how the companies participate in an industry – professional passenger driving – that extracts the reproductive lives and labors of drivers. While Lyft and Uber's SB8 response suggests that drivers are made precarious by the new anti-abortion law, we argue that the industry of professional passenger driving, whether for taxis or for gig companies, needs drivers to always be in precarity; the cost of being a professional passenger driver is the sacrifice of life. As the hunger strikers make clear, driving is a 24/7 profession because of the way the industry is structured – to keep drivers in debt, to drive down wages, to off-load on-the-job risks like injury onto the drivers themselves. Because ride-hail app companies continue to deny that drivers are employees, the companies are able to individualize risk; on-the-job injury or even job loss are simply matters of individual concern, while for many other workers, such matters are public concerns and thereby protected through state unemployment and workers' compensation insurance. The interest in individualization pervades Uber and Lyft's response to Texas' SB8. Uber and Lyft offer corporately controlled funds to drivers to help offset individual costs tied to potential legal challenges. Against these too-narrow foci on individual rights and choice, reproductive justice frameworks emphasize intersecting systems that deny access.

"Reproductive justice" offers an alternative language and framework from that of individualized, privatized choice and responsibility. As early community leader, SisterSong (https://www.sistersong/net/reproductive-justice/), points out, reproductive justice works from centering the disparate racial histories of reproductive politics in the United States, specifically paying attention to the ways reproductive control worked in complex and entwined ways to regulate access to reproduction, parenting and thus family and community formation. For SisterSong, "Reproductive Justice is about access not choice … Reproductive politics in the U.S. is based on gendered, sexualized, and racialized acts of dominance that occur on a daily basis" (https://www.sistersong/net/reproductive-justice/). Loretta Ross names these conditions as "white supremacy, neoliberal capitalism, and population control," holding them central to any reproductive justice intervention (Columbia University, 2021).

As community organizers like Ross have pointed out, we need to broaden the public domestic discourse around reproductive politics, which has, since the passage of *Roe*, tended to be myopically focused around the rhetoric of individual choice and abortion (Luna, 2020). As Angela Davis pointed out in 1981, even when Black and Latina women seek abortion, "the stories they tell are not so much about their desire to be free of their pregnancy, but rather about the miserable social conditions which dissuade them from bringing new lives into the world" (p. 204). Understanding that reproductive justice, which includes access to abortion, is more about addressing "miserable social conditions" than it is about individual freedom or choice, Davis echoes a perspective that provides important insight in to driver struggles over life and labor – for drivers, the issue has never only or necessarily been one of individual "rights." Rather than the "right to drive" (right to own a medallion), the hunger strikers, for instance, point to the public obligation to proactively work on behalf of drivers' who help enrich the city ($850 million; but also in providing daily essential services).

The wisdom of reproductive justice approaches teaches us to look for the interdependent operations of power (whether nationalist, racist, sexist, ableist) that provide a broader social and political context to understanding reproductive control and gender violence. Thus, we consider reproductive labor as a means to situate and understand driving so that we can resist the impulse to treat gigged driving as separate from more traditional forms of passenger ride-for-hires like taxis. Instead of focusing on individual wage-earning workers, reproductive labor also broadens our perspective to consider the multiple ways "productive labor" is supported and enabled, for instance through the emotional labor of another. In that sense, Texas' SB8 targets these support systems, as it criminalizes the communities of support that surround a person seeking abortion. Yet Uber and Lyft's response to SB8 remains within the realm of individual rights; their corporately controlled legal fund in the best light only offers individual drivers support in very limited circumstances. What would it look like to instead support the whole lives of drivers, including their reproductive lives? Against the reproductive politics at play in Uber and Lyft's SB8 marketing, we foreground reproductive justice as a means to rethink how the labor conditions of drivers, as matters of gender violence, concern all of us who are committed to more feminist futures.

Notes

1 Plummeting medallion values holds true in most of the major cities with existing taxi industries "disrupted" by Uber and Lyft. Philadelphia, for example, saw medallion values at approximately $545,000 in 2014 Philadelphia (when app-hails arrived) drop to $80,000 in the mere span of two years.
2 Five New York City drivers in the first five months of 2018 committed suicide, and specifically noted unlivable work and life-conditions. They are: Danilo Corporan Castillo, 57-years-old; Alfredo Perez; Douglas Schifter, 61-years-old; Nicanor Ochisor, 65-years-old; Yu Mein Chow, 56-years-old. The most well-circulated media stories of the suicides involved limo driver Schifter, who left a suicide note on his facebook page. (https://www.facebook.com/permalink.php?story_fbid=188 8367364808997&id=100009072541151). Ochisor reportedly told a fellow driver and friend Dan Nitescu that he planned to commit suicide, having lately struggled to find fares and having watched the value of his medallion plummet. His medallion,

which he and his wife shared, was his retirement plan. Ochisor planned to lease his medallion so that he could retire, however, with the increased availability of rides (facilitated by ride-hail app companies), the value of that medallion was cut in half, making retirement impossible.

3 *Jane Doe 1, et al versus Uber Technologies, Inc.*, 15-cv-04670-SI (ND CA, May 16, 2016). The cases have merged with several others and have led to a 2017 class action filing against Uber. A different set of cases was filed in 2020, which are the focus of this chapter.

4 In 2014, Uber charged passengers a $1-per-ride "Safe Rides Fee," ostensibly to offset the company's safety initiatives. But "the safety plan consisted of little more than a short video course for drivers … Uber was facing increasing costs, so the company came up with the idea … to help boost its margins" (Hawkins, 2019).

5 In our book, *Spent Behind the Wheel* (2021), we trace in detail the criminalization of drivers in Chapter 3.

6 While not many demographic studies of taxi drivers exist, some key municipal and union surveys confirm that in San Francisco and the Bay Area, Los Angeles and New York, drivers continue to be predominantly immigrant men of color. This is in part tied to historical migration and legal reasons, which we explore in more depth in *Spent Behind the Wheel* (2021). For some of this background, please also see Biju Mathew's *Taxi!*

7 The Bureau of Labor Statistics (Sygnatur & Toscano, 2000) reports that on the job homicide rates for professional passenger ride-for-hire drivers is 17.9 fatalities per 100,000, in contrast to police officers, which is 4.4 incidents.

8 Bloomberg championed a project to modernize New York City taxis, called "Taxi of Tomorrow." The focus of this project was to improve the look of the cab and update the fleet. Part of the materials outlining the project include a report commissioned jointly by the New York Taxi and Limo Commission and the Design Trust for Public Space.

9 See for instance the New York Southern District Court case *(Levon Aleksanian et al.)*, which argues Uber committed fraud in the way they calculated driver wages.

10 This is the basis of many of the early class action suits filed against Uber and Lyft that argued they employ drivers, including *Douglas O'Connor, et al v. Uber Technologies, Inc.* This is also the basis of several on-going wage theft suits, notably one in New York filed by the New York TWA on behalf of Uber, Lyft and other gig drivers. That case is *Levon Aleksanian, et al, v. Uber Technologies, Inc.* (2019).

11 Evelyn Engel, as part of Laborfest (Redstone Stone Building, San Francisco, July 11, 2018; attended by Hua), discussed two different traffic congestion studies, which show increased private vehicle use since the entry of Uber and Lyft into the Bay Area. Engel correlates the results of these congestion studies with American Lung Association data indicating worsening air quality in the same period (excluding wild fire impacts). The studies Engel discussed is Clewlow and Mishra (2017).

References

Badger, E. (2014, June 20). Taxi medallions have been the best investment in America for years. Now Uber may be changing that. *Washington Post*. Retrieved from https://www.washingtonpost.com/news/wonk/wp/2014/06/20/taxi-medallions-have-been-the-best-investment-in-america-for-years-now-uber-may-be-changing-that/

Blasi, G. and Leavitt, J. (2006). *Driving poor: Taxi drivers and the regulation of the taxi industry in Los Angeles*. Los Angeles: UCLA Institute for Research on Labor and Employment, 31: taxi-library.org/driving-poor.pdf

Bond, S. (2021, September 3). Lyft and Uber will pay drivers' legal fees if they're sued under Texas abortion law. *NPR News*. Retrieved from https://www.

npr.org/2021/09/03/1034140480/lyft-and-uber-will-pay-drivers-legal-fees-if-they're-sued-under-texas-abortion-la

Calo, R. and Rosenblat, A. (2017). The taking economy: Uber, information, and power. *Columbia Law Review, 117*(6). http://dx.doi.org/10.2139/ssrn.2929643

Campbell, H. (2020, September 1). *59 best car accessories according to Uber drivers (must have).* Message posted to https://therideshareguy.com/11-products-that-every-rideshare-driver-should-be-carrying/

Clewlow, R. and Mishra, G. S. (October 2017). *Disruptive transportation: The adoption, utilization, and impacts of ride-hailing in the United States.* Institute of Transportation Studies, University of California, Davis. Retrieved from reginaclewlow.com/pubs/2017_UCD-ITS-RR-17-07.pdf

Columbia University (2021, April 9). *Reproductive justice: In conversation with Loretta Ross.* Retrieved from https://youtu.be/puasq1tEKVg

Davis, A. (1981). *Gender, race, class.* New York: Vintage.

Design Trust for Public Space (2007, December). *Taxi road forward.* Retrieved December, 19, 2018 from www.nyc.gov/html/tlc/downloads/pdf/taxi_book.pdf

Douglas O'Connor, Thomas Colopy, Matthew Manahan and Elie Gurfinkel v. Uber Technologies, Inc. *Declaration of Veena Dubal.* Northern district of California. 13–3826-EMC (2015, September 1).

Fowler, S. (2017, February 19). *Reflecting on one very, very strange year at Uber.* Message posted to https://www.susanjfowler.com/blog/2017/2/19/reflecting-on-one-very-strange-year-at-uber

Furfaro, D. and Jaeger, M. (2018, March 21). Cabbie blamed Uber, Lyft for financial woes before hanging himself. *New York Post.* Retrieved from https://nypost.com/2018/03/21/cabbie-blamed-uber-lyft-for-financial-woes-before-hanging-himself/

Hawkins, A. (2019, August 23). Uber's $1-per-ride 'safe rides fee' had nothing to do with safety. *The Verge.* Retrieved from https://www.theverge.com/2019/8/23/20829798/uber-safe-ride-fee-margin-mike-isaac-super-pumped

Hua, J. and Ray, K. (2021). *Spent behind the wheel: Drivers' labor in an Uber economy.* Minneapolis: Minnesota Press.

Jane Doe v. Uber Technologies, Inc. and John Kenney, Jr. and Charles Veney, US District Court for the District of Maryland (Baltimore), 1:20-cv-00370. (February 11, 2020).

Jane Roe, et al. v. Henry Wade, District Attorney of Dallas County, 410 U.S. 113. (January 22, 1973).

Khosrowshahi, D. (2020, August 10). I am the CEO of Uber. Gig workers deserve better. The *New York Times*, Opinion. Retrieved from https://www/nytimes.com/2020/08/10/opinion/uber-ceo-dara-khosrowshahi-gig-workers-deserve-better.html

Khosrowshahi, D. (2021, September 3). Message posted to https://twitter.com/dkhos/status/1433894081487273987

Laughlin, J. (2018, March 28). Philadelphia taxis lose another legal challenge to Uber. *The Philadelphia Inquirer.* Retrieved from philly.com/philly/business/transportation/uber-anti-trust-laws-philadelphia-taxi-third-circuit-appeal-court-finds-20180328.html

Luna, Z. (2020). *Reproductive rights as human rights: Women of color and the fight for reproductive justice.* New York: NYU Press.

Lyft. (2021, September 3). Message posted to https://www.lyft.com/blog/posts/defending-drivers-and-womens-access-to-healthcare

Mathew, B. (2005). *Taxi!: Cabs and capitalism in New York City.* Ithaca: Cornell University Press.

Matthew, G. (2014, July 31). Is Uber worth its obnoxious customers? Two veteran cabbies (and friends) debate. *The New York Magazine*. Retrieved from https://nymag.com/nymag/features/uber-2014-7/

New York City Council (January 2020). *The report of the taxi medallion task force.* Retrieved from https://council.nyc.gov/data/wp-content/uploads/sites/73/2020/01/Taxi-Medallion-Task-Force-Report-Final.pdf

New York Taxi Workers Alliance (2021, August 31). *Debt restructuring plan.* Retrieved from https://static1.squarespace.com/static/551c0fb1e4b04e2cba203b00/t/6138d305c3 ed1325fd2714ea/1631113990203/NYTWA+Debt+Forgivenes+Campaign+NYC+Guarantee+2021.8.31.pdf

New York Taxi Workers Alliance (2022, January 18). *NYTWA secured a 5.3% pay-raise for all NYC Uber-Lyft-Via drivers*! Retrieved from https://www.nytwa.org/home/2022/2/11/weve-secured-a-53-pay-raise-for-all-nyc-uber-lyft-via-drivers-drivers-on-average-will-earn-3800-more-this-year

Noble, S. (2012). *Algorithms of oppression.* New York: NYU Press.

O'Neil, C. (2016). *Weapons of math destruction.* New York: Crown/Random House.

Pandey, A. and Caliskan, A. (2020, June 8). *Interactive effect-size bias in ridehailing: Measuring social bias in dynamic pricing of 100 million rides.* Cornell University and Institute for Data, Democracy and Politics at George Washington University. Retrieved from Arxiv.org/abs/2006.04599

Pasquale, F. (2015). *The black box society: The secret algorithms that control money and information.* Cambridge, MA: Harvard University Press.

Perez, B. and Dang, C. (2008). *Los Angeles taxi drivers and restroom access–dignity on the job.* Retrieved from utwsd.org/wp-content/uploads/2012/06/Los-Angeles-Taxi-Drivers-Restroom-Access-Dignity-on-the-Job.pdf

Phillips, M., Phillips, J. (Producer) and Scorsese, M. (Screenwriter/Director) (1976). *Taxi Driver* [Motion Picture]. United States: Columbia Pictures.

Schaller, B. (May 2018). *Making congestion pricing work for traffic and transit in New York City.* Brooklyn NY: Schaller Consulting. Retrieved from http://www.schallerconsult.com/rideservices/makingpricingwork.pdf?source=your_stories_page

Smith, M. J. (2005 March). *Robbery of taxi drivers, problem-orientated guides for police no. 34, Office of Community Oriented Policing Services.* Retrieved from https://live-cpop.ws.asu.edu/sites/default/files/problems/pdfs/RobberyTaxiDrivers.pdf

Sygnatur, E. and Toscano, G. (2000). Work related homicides: The facts. *Compensation and Working Conditions*, p. 3–8. Retrieved from https://www.bls.gov/opub/mlr/cwc/work-related-homicides-the-facts.pdf

Texas Senate Bill 8 & House Bill 1515. (2021 May 19). Retrieved from https://capitol.texas.gov/tlodocs/87R/billtext/html/SB00008I.htm.

Vora, K. (2017). *Labor. MATTER*: Macmillan handbooks: Gender. London: Routledge.

Wynn, B. and Boustead, A. (2015). Home health care for California's injured workers: Options of implementing a fee schedule. *Rand.* Retrieved from Rand.org/pubs/research_reports/RR603.html

7

"SUDDENLY WE WERE THE STORY"

Women Journalists, the #MeToo Movement, & Online Misogyny in India

Paromita Pain

Introduction

Rana Ayyub, an outspoken columnist with *The Washington Post* in India, has been an informed and vocal critic of the current Indian prime minster Narendra Modi. Her deeply investigative features on the government's anti-Muslim policies and sectarian politics have been instrumental in warning the world about the nonsecular politics in the country and have garnered her unprecedented online hate. This has been so relentless that UN human rights experts have gone on record to state that she has been subjected to "judicial harassment," and they have repeatedly urged Indian authorities to investigate "promptly" the "relentless misogynistic and sectarian" attacks on social media against her (Al Jazeera, 2022). Earlier in the year, she had received online threats of physical assault and death, and one person had even been arrested in connection with this.

Gender-based online harassment includes stalking, cyberbullying, hate speech, abusive language, sexual innuendo filled obscenities, targeted smear campaigns, and doxing (Hinson et al., 2018), and Ayyub is no stranger to the different forms of networked persecution. Besides death threats, proprietors of various right-wing journalistic ventures spread misinformation about her and the stories she covers. Two journalists from the online media platform The Scoop Beats were arrested after Ayyub registered a police complaint, seeking justice for "targeted harassment" and "fake news" (International Federation of Journalists, 2022). Today, Ayyub is among the most well-known faces of women journalists from India who experience relentless harassment online for the work they do and for daring to professionally identify as journalists from a minority (Muslim) community (Perrigo, 2021).

Engaging with audiences online sees more women journalists, especially those associated with television reporting face ferocious torment that is rarely focused

DOI: 10.4324/9781003260851-9

on their work but rather targeted at their person, religion, sexuality, and gender (Chen et al., 2020; Pain, 2017). In a comprehensive report on digital journalism and its risks, authors Posetti, Aboulez, Bontcheva, Harrison, and Waisbord (2020) emphasized that online violence was gradually becoming "a new frontline in journalism safety – a particularly dangerous trend for women journalists." A UNESCO supported survey of nearly 1,000 women journalists conducted by the International Women's Media Foundation and the International News Safety Institute showed that 23% of women respondents had experienced some sort of "intimidation, threats or abuse" online in connection to their work. Globally, as various documentation shows, the numbers of these attacks are only increasing (Waisbord, 2020a; Waisbord, 2020b). For India, this has important implications, especially around gender and journalism.

India, a country with a very dynamic media scene that is "driven by a growing middle class..." (BBC India country profile) and a rich relationship with civil society, each gaining from and strengthening the other, suffers from the issue of misogynistic newsrooms (Chen et al., 2020; Pain, 2017). Women journalists must deal with a plethora of "everyday sexism and workplace sex discrimination" (Chadha et al., 2017, p. 20) that often prevents them from fully developing their professional identities. Women also leave journalism due to harassment and the lack of organizational support. India's growing media scene with its rising digital-only newsrooms is still young and has had little impact in addressing this misogyny. Misogynistic newsrooms are no secret, but today as journalists are encouraged to publicize stories, interact with audiences and develop social media identities, another layer of harassment has been added to the experiences of journalists, especially women journalists (Chen et al., 2020; Pain, 2017). Having an online presence can mean gendered harassment that newsrooms have little wherewithal to address. The recent explosion of #MeTooIndia that dragged out into the open horrific narratives of how women reporters, interns, and other positions are treated in the newsrooms finally saw journalists and other media personnel sharing stories of how sexual abuse and harassment perpetuated in the newsroom has further complicated an already complex scenario. While journalists used social media very effectively to out abusers and report harassment, there was little to protect them from the misogynistic vitriol they were forced to encounter online (Chen & Pain, 2017).

As the *New York Times* reported, "After a year of fits and starts, India's #MeToo movement has leapt forward over the past week, getting concrete action in two of the country's most powerful industries: entertainment and the news media" (Goel et al., 2018). Like the US, in India, the movement saw participants from the film, entertainment, and mainstream media sharing stories, advocating on behalf of survivors, and ensuring that different voices found space. Studies on the #Metoo hashtag have focused on how Twitter emerged as a space where participants and activists could name and initiate decisive action against abusers, some of whom were influential men in public positions, and how such digital spaces provided a much-needed impetus to the movement and in the process brought to the forefront and encouraged public deliberation around issues of gendered sexual violence in the workspace. The #MeTooIndia Twitter handle had the word India added to it to differentiate it from the US hashtag. As the movement gained momentum, journalists, and activists organized and presented tweets from all over the country showcasing a variety of experiences and voices. Women from different walks of life created networks to connect and amplify voices. For journalists, it was more than a matter of being a participant. Suddenly, they as a profession were thrust into the limelight. As one reporter with 10 years of experience in a national newspaper said, "Suddenly we were the story" (Personal Interview, 2020).

Journalism may now be recognized as one of the most dangerous professions globally (Jamil, 2020) and with the rise of digital platforms, journalists are subject to a multitude of online harassment, increased surveillance, and other digital threats (*India*, 2019; Jamil & Muschert, 2020; Sohal, 2020). Press freedom is guaranteed by India's Constitution, but as the recently released 2020 World Press Freedom Index has shown, India is now ranked at 142, down two places from 2019. Journalists are murdered with impunity and as the US-based Committee to Protect Journalists has noted, in 2021, four Indian journalists were killed for their work while seven others were imprisoned on various charges. With the #MeTooIndia movement, narratives that focused mostly on women survivors exposed the horrific and gendered nature of crime in some of the country's largest and most influential news dailies. It compelled a reckoning with gender that Indian media had until then been unwillingly to face. Inspired by the work of Waisbord (2020) that has examined how journalists, globally, in the digital realm are trolled and the disadvantages associated with digital publicizing of news and narratives, this study gauges how, in a rapidly digitizing world, journalists deal with publics that have now moved online, and the impact of online harassment and misogyny on their work and professional identities. In the process, it also examines what journalists think about interactivity, the public they are often forced to engage with, and the impact of incivility. This investigation explores the experiences of the journalists who covered the movement and examines the changes that a movement this influential may have brought about in newsrooms through the lens of professional reflexivity and collective professional autonomy.

This study is among the earliest that investigate the impact of the #MeToo movement on newsrooms, journalists, and aspects of digitization on the news media scene in India. As an area of research, investigating how journalists work with uncivil audiences on social media and comment sections may be drawing scholarly attention, but this topic needs more investigation since research has shown that nearly 20% of comments (Coe et al., 2014) are uncivil in nature and both journalists and audiences are concerned about their impact (Diakopoulos & Naaman, 2011; Meltzer, 2015). Documenting the amount, impact, and nature of online harassment is necessary across the globe (Waisbord, 2020a). Focus on the impact of #Metoo, both as a social media movement and as activism that lays bare the abuse that women face in media, provides an opportunity to explore the experiences of journalists in India in a post-#MeTooIndia social and online media space and its implications for the future of journalism in the developing world.

Gender in the Newsroom

A 2017 study (Pain, 2017, p. 1319) quotes a woman political reporter saying that women journalists in India "were not taken seriously" and that "[m]en think that beat reporting is their preserve especially the political beat. It's a complete boy's club sort of situation out there." Over the years, little seems to have changed in this aspect. As Kanagasabai (2016) has shown, the impact of liberalization and globalization on the construction of the gendered self within the space of Indian English-language television newsrooms has made little difference. The newsroom in India continues to be a highly masculine space in which women often enact masculine traits for legitimacy and approval. Kangasabai also emphasized how many younger female journalists want to dissociate from the "feminist" tag, saying they do not need a theoretical label to assert their strength and identity. Media coverage of gender violence does not often show critical engagement with or analysis of issues as social incidents; survivors are often shamed, and most coverage is sensational and patriarchal in nature (Drèze & Sen, 2013). When it comes to sexual assault, media are extremely biased and nonintersectional in nature. Even with the advent of globalization and private television channels, coverage of such crimes is extremely focused on middle class women, such that marginalized women rarely find space and issues of resources, caste, and gender are rarely balanced (Rao, 2014). This leaning toward the urban middle class is reflected on social media and thus perpetuates a bias in the way journalists use social media to report abuse. For example, as Belair-Gagnon et al. (2014) have shown in their interviews with journalists in India, many journalists use Twitter for gathering background information because the most important events are usually city based and involve people with access to technology like Twitter. Rising numbers of digital users ensure that most media outlets have an online presence.

Digitization in India

In 2022, a report by Dentsu International, one of the largest marketing and advertising agency networks in the world, stated that digital media in India was expected to grow at 29.5% compound annual growth rate to reach a market size of Rs 35,809 crore by 2023 (Business India, 2022). India is also considered the second-fastest digital adopter among 17 major digital economies (Kohli, 2021) with Internet penetration pegged at 627 million in 2019. Facebook leads the user base with about 93 million users, with Twitter following closely behind with 33 million users (Statista, 2019). Digital advances have also led to internet-only media startups, which are leading innovation by developing distinct content and social media approaches and mobile first news. Traditional mainstream media and international technology companies are their main competition (Nielsen & Sen, 2016).

Journalism and Digitization

With the emergence of the digital media and with more mainstream media creating a presence online, the professional identity of journalists and the profile of what constitutes the "job" of a journalist have undergone a change. As Santana and Russial (2013) have shown, the rise of digitization has meant that today being a journalist also may include telling stories in videos, pictures, and audio, whereas earlier journalists gathered facts and told stories while audio and photos were the domain of other specialists. Today, all these spheres have connected to create the multimedia journalist who gathers facts, takes photos, and creates videos as well and maintains an active social media presence. This shift has also seen the advent of multimedia gatekeeping which is extremely emphasized in sports journalism (English, 2017), and while journalists can have a vibrant presence online, the information they share and disseminate must be within the bounds set by employer guidelines (Sullivan, 2015). A Hoot survey . . . found that 57% of journalists used both Twitter and Facebook, while an additional 28% used only Facebook and an additional 11% used only Twitter. Only 4% reported using neither Facebook nor Twitter. When it comes to covering rape, Belair-Gagnon, Mishra, and Agur (2014) have shown that both foreign correspondents based in India and Indian journalists in the mainstream media have used Twitter as their dominant social media platform during the Delhi gang rape coverage, more than Facebook, LinkedIn, and others.

Trolling and Online Spaces

Globally, online harassment of women journalists is on the rise (Chen et al., 2020; Waisbord, 2020b). As various studies have shown, female journalists in India have had a long history of facing and dealing with professional harassment (Pain, 2017; Pain, 2021. Digital spaces and the benefits they offer are well understood in India. Thus, journalists are not just encouraged to have social media profiles but also interactions with audiences, promoting stories and exploring sources are job requirements, normalized as part of journalists' routines (Chen & Pain, 2017). While "the mushrooming growth of social media services hugely expanded the scope of content generation and sharing" (Pradhan & Kumari, 2018), the harassment of journalists online has also become routine. Journalists have identified this as extremely harmful to their work, creating unfortunate dilemmas for female journalists. Social media presence is a job requirement, and this also exposes them to harassment that is detrimental to the way they function as professionals (Chen et al., 2020). India has a high rate of internet penetration, with about 93 million using Facebook and 33 million using Twitter (Statista, 2019). The most active users are feminist activists, journalists, students, and young men and women from middle income families (Belair-Gagnon et al., 2014), but most issues arise from the way gender is viewed in the country. In their seminal work on cybercrime in the country, Halder & Jaishankar (2011) have shown that the presence of women online is deemed a threat to masculinity that demands unrealistic notions of chaste behavior. Thus, women online are often trolled with deeply sexual slurs and threats that seek to publicly shame them (Gudipaty, 2017). Men and male journalists too are trolled online, but this is different from the kind of trolling women face. Men are generally shamed for being "stupid" or "bad at their work," but the abuse is rarely sexual.

As Waisbord (2020a) has emphasized, online harassment in the USA has been driven by the rise of right-wing politics and a hatred toward minorities, women, and the mainstream press. In India, we see similar patterns. Muslim journalists who are outspoken against sectarian politics are doxed with alarming frequency. *The Columbia Journalism Review* (2022) recently reported on an app known as "Bulli Bai" that doxed reporters like Ayyub, displaying more than a hundred women "for sale as maids." More than 100 photos of Muslim women including prominent actresses, journalists, and politicians were posted for auction on the application (Jaswal, 2022). The news website Scoop Beats created a video around a manipulated tweet where Ayyub is shown saying that she hates India. Once law personnel got involved, the video was taken down but not before threats against Ayyub intensified. Further exacerbating the problem of online harassment of women journalists, the political regime in power today is aware of the power of social media and utilizes it effectively, working with public relations practitioners and social media experts to increase reach and influence. They also use their digital tools to malign and endanger online spaces for journalists with impunity. In a recent investigation by digital only publication *The Wire*, an app called "'Tek Fog," developed by the ruling party, targeted journalists by creating targeted hashtags, and different WhatsApp groups via this app. Female journalists were clearly targeted and responses to their tweets contained profanity. As Posetti, Aboulez, Bontcheva, Harrison, and Waisbord (2020) note in their global study, online trolls range from mobs with misogynistic intent to state-sponsored campaigns aimed at silencing women and scaring into submission any kind of critical journalism through a multitude of well-designed digital attacks (Ayyub, 2022; Rodrigues, 2019). The Editors Guild of India condemned

> The continued online harassment of women journalists, which includes targeted and organized online trolling as well as threats of sexual abuse…. targeted at journalists, who have been outspokenly critical of the current government and the ruling party, to silence them.

However, news organizations do little to help women journalists deal with online trolling. Many women journalists do not report their online trolling because organizations are often reluctant to help (Gudipaty, 2017).

Ghosh (2020) has shown that when it comes to dealing with online vitriol, women's complaints are often disregarded by the law, and arrests for online hate speech are usually the exceptions. Considering the different factors that play into online harassment, this study uses the concepts of professional reflexivity and collective professional autonomy to investigate and understand the complexities and conflicts professional women journalists must navigate as they deal with ensuring a presence on social media, and the negative fallout this presence entails. Professional reflexivity refers to the ability of journalists to reflect on journalists' capacity for self-awareness (González de Bustamante, & Relly, 2016) and "recognize the different influences and changes in their environment, and alter the course of their actions, and renegotiate their professional self-images as a result" (Ahva, 2013, p. 791; see also Pain & Korin, 2021). The theoretical framework of professional reflexivity is a chance for journalists to contemplate and consider the different influences and impacts on their occupation, specifically in this case the use, identities and the impact of the #MeTooIndia movement on their social and online presence. The study also examines the different strategies that the women use to counter online harassment and thus uses the lens of professional autonomy to understand the level of freedom journalists have, or feel they have, to deal with trolls and other online nastiness. In a global context, Reese (2001, p. 174) has emphasized that "professionalism is a problematic concept, consisting of many values held in tension, which different national groups balance in their own way," for the concept of professionalism has "different levels of meaning," in the hierarchy of influences model (Shoemaker & Reese, 2013) where autonomy as "a fluid concept that is continually adjusted to manage the daily task of reporting the news" (Sjovaag, 2013, p. 1) can add different nuances. In this light, this study asks four research questions:

> **RQ1**: What are the defining themes and discourses raised by the comments that journalists face on social media and online commenting spaces?
> **RQ2**: What are the promises and pitfalls of having an online presence as shown through the experiences of female journalists?
> **RQ3**: To what extent do journalists exhibit the characteristics of professional reflexivity and autonomy when dealing with online abuse?
> **RQ 4**: What strategies do they use to deal with online incivility?

Methods

This study qualitatively analyzes data from 20 in-depth interviews. A qualitative method was deemed the most suitable approach since our purpose was to explore "social reality in subjects' perceptions of their environment" (Bryman, 1988, p. 70). Female journalists who have covered #MeTooIndia were identified from the stories they have covered in different media in India and sent interview requests. Requests were also posted on social media like Twitter and Facebook.

Purposive snowball sampling (Welch, 1975) was also done for referrals to colleagues in order to ensure that a wide range of media organizations were reached. A total of 20 journalists were interviewed at this time with experiences ranging from five to ten years of work with different media as full-time journalists in different mainstream media organizations.

Findings

This study examines four main research questions that investigate the defining themes and discourses raised by the comments that journalists face on social media and online commenting spaces, the promises and pitfalls of having an online presence, strategies used to deal with audiences online, and the extent to which journalists exhibit the characteristics of professional reflexivity when dealing with online abuse. The findings reveal that journalists are trolled mercilessly online. The defining themes of the online trolling focus on their work as women and as journalists and especially on the work they did for the #MeTooIndia movement. Their work on survivors of sexual assault is belittled and there is a distinct right-wing flavor to the content of the vitriol directed at them. Clearly, there are huge drawbacks associated with their online presences, but the journalists have certain approaches that they feel can protect them from online harassment. The sample of journalists interviewed said that their "moves" (Personal Interview, 2021) on social media were reflective of the ways they viewed their professions. They felt that they had professional autonomy, but this certainly could be increased with institutional support. These findings are explicated in detail.

RQ1: Defining Themes and Discourses

#MeTooIndia is a weapon of abuse: Journalist who had covered the #MeTooIndia movement and had specifically mentioned the story on their social media were abused for their work. Their work was used to dehumanize and insult them, and they were called misogynistic names. The word "FemiNAZI" was common, and they were called "sluts" who had "enjoyed the attention." Tweets like "Women already got more privileges and entitlements compared to men and enjoying their over empowerment. #FeminismIsCancer #Feminazis #MeTooIndia" were plentiful. Their coverage of the #MeTooIndia was used as a weapon against them. For example, one journalist, who had recently covered the rape of a minor, was abused as being a "MeToo bitch" who propagated sexual abuse under the guise of news coverage. Her tweet (in support of the # MeTooIndia), "#MeToo #MeTooIndia is the best example in the recent time of women standing up for women together and believing each other against harassment and exploitation at workplace," immediately bought forth a barrage of abusive tweets on Twitter, and later this was linked to different abusive conversations related to the work

done by journalists especially if their stories involved the coverage of sexual abuse. For example:

> Journalist A woke up this morning and thought about how she could attack innocent men. hence her story about the so-called rape of …. But then. What can we expect from her…she after all thinks that the '#MeToo #MeTooIndia is the best example in the recent time of women standing …' Remember? REMEMBER?

A "bad" career choice: Many of the journalists interviewed online had also covered the #MEtooIndia movement where they had done extensive interviews with the survivors of assault and helped amplify their voices. Their work was condemned online. One story titled "India's newsrooms are a den of misogyny" drew extreme ire. The journalist interviewed said she took the story down after a week when the trolling got extremely sexual, and she got tired of blocking out the different direct messages targeting her on all her social media including Twitter and Instagram. Many of the comments focused on how journalism was a bad career choice for women, especially since "women can only see one sides things." Some of the journalists also covered stories on how unsafe public spaces were for women, especially when the #MetooIndia was at its peak and these stories drew a great deal of vitriol. Two journalists candidly confessed that they had reduced the number of stories that had done on women's safety since then. As one participant with five years of print media experience said:

> I really wanted to make women's issues a beat here in my organization. I also wanted to train new journalists joining in and encourage them to be a part of this collective. But clearly the trolling…the viciousness where people often call and start abusing on the phone…it isn't worth it.

Anti-India and anti-national: Some of the abuse directed at specific journalists was distinctly about them covering women's issues, which was viewed as being anti-national and anti-Indian. The right-wing government in India which is pushing a right-wing agenda in the country consisting of emphasizing the superiority of particular religions saw minority journalists being targeted. Just the way Rana Ayyub was targeted, the journalists interviewed for this study also emphasized that issues that were related to women's safety often drew abuse related to their religion and minority status. One journalist with about seven years of television experience said:

> My name clearly spells out my religion. After a story I had done on women and the local trains, my Twitter profile photo was snatched, and false profile was created where I was said to be a slut…my phone number was published, and I had to change my number …the harassment was extreme

and nerve wracking. I was accused of being a traitor and asked to go to Pakistan.

Being asked to go to Pakistan is a common refrain for the journalists targeted, especially if they were from minority communities.

Weak organizational response: As the journalists interviewed said, it was not as if their organizations denied the abuse. Nor did they refuse to listen or demean the complaints. But institutions had very weak responses to the complaints. For example, one journalist with over ten years of experience said that her organization would ask her to get off social media for a few days or block trolls, but they had no social media policy to deal with trolls nor were personnel equipped to find and effectively block them.

RQ2: Promises and Pitfalls of Having an Online Presence

The journalists were very aware that using social media and having a social media presence was helpful in their work. Besides the trolling, a majority of those interviewed said that social media often helped them reach out to audiences they otherwise would not have considered. As one journalist with over 8 years of television experience said:

> I was once doing a story on the police helpline when the Twitter responses to this helpline caught my eye. I realized that while the helpline was very responsive to one part of the state, they were not great with calls to another part. I saw repeated appeals for help from some women and interviewed them for a story that helped improve the reach and effectiveness of the service. This would not have happened without Twitter.

But as the trolling and other ineffective tweets about their work poured in, the journalists in the sample for this study deeply reflected on whether social media was necessary in their work, especially considering its advantage and disadvantages. A common theme in these reflections was the intense emotional labor that they had to undertake as they were forced to deal with trolls and other abuse themselves. The journalists were, however, able to develop strategies to combat the abuse. They created tangible support systems and helped each other. Journalist retweeted the stories that they had done and supported each other during particularly vicious attacks. For example, one reporter with five years of experience posted that her household help was being targeted by a gang on her way to work. Immediately trolls said that she was probably "asking for it since that's what women do to cry rape," and this could have escalated, but other journalists immediately posted helpline numbers to call and requested the police to help by tweeting at legal organizations. But this labor was all their own work and they generously gave their time and effort to protect each other, as they "belonged to the same tribe" (Personal interview, 2022).

RQ3: Professional Reflexivity and Professional Autonomy

The journalists were deeply disappointed in the weak organizational response that they often received. As many of them said, this made dealing with the abuse "worse" (Personal interview, 2022). As one reporter with ten years of multimedia experience mentioned:

> My organization is sympathetic. But they have no solutions. I also think they do not give this issue much thought. Blocking out abusers or not responding is not a solution. Once one troll told me that they knew where my five-year-old went to school. When I complained the organization was sympathetic but took no concrete steps towards rectifying the issue.
>
> *(Personal interview, 2022)*

Reactions of this kind made the women reporters feel "unheard" (Personal interview, 2022). "We are encouraged to interact with the public online," said one journalist. "But what do you say to people who threaten to rape you?" As they reflected on how this impacted their work, they were clear that staying off social media was no solution because "that cut us off from vital public" (Personal interview, 2021). They were aware that with India's internet penetration, people were voicing opinions and speaking up on issues online. They wanted to ensure that trolling did not cut them off from this. Some were even willing to listen to trolls as they felt that "even those who disagreed with us is a part of the audience who we must seek out" (Personal interview, 2022). But they did not want to engage with those comments that were overtly sexual as that made them "deeply uncomfortable" (Personal interview, 2022). Three confessed to having to deal with anxiety and as one of them with six years of television experience said:

> I would keep randomly checking my Instagram feed to see if there were any more…I became twitchy…you know what I mean…I couldn't keep still. Therapy and medication finally calmed me down and I realized that I must learn to let go.

Their relationship with their audiences, the sources, and the people who read their work were clearly of utmost importance. They also realized the value of social media for putting them in touch with voices they would not, perhaps, have otherwise had access to. They were clear that, trolls or no trolls, they did not want to lose touch or in any way disserve their reading public. Their reflections helped to also talk about the strategies they used on trolls and how some of these approaches were successful.

Even in a post-#MeTooIndia world, newsrooms seemed very blind to addressing the harassment these women journalists faced, but something had clearly changed. As the women interviewed for this study emphasized, while it was clear that little was being done, at least "organizations were willing to have a dialogue" (Personal interview, 2021). This made them hopeful that soon they would be willing to put in more technical advancements and expertise that would help them fight these attacks.

RQ4: Strategies and Solutions

The journalists were clear that organizational responses must become stronger. Since organizational responses were lacking, they worked to help each other deal with online torment. As one journalist with 8 years of multimedia experience said:

> When I see a colleague getting trolled whether she belongs to my organization or not I always jump in to help. Once I asked a troll to back off... literally using the words in capital letters. We didn't hear back so I guess it worked!

As one reporter with five years of television experience said, she would block out the trolls when they got personal and used threats of physical assault. But as a majority said, ignoring them did not help. As one journalist with 5 years of experience said: "Ignoring them made them feel that we were scared. They redoubled back with renewed vigor." Three of the journalists interviewed said that they had stopped posting stories on the serious issues they worked on. As one journalist with 8 years of experience said:

> When I had started out earlier there was little demand and requirement on us to post on social media. When I would post my earlier stories, I had a few followers who would either like or ignore the piece. Later this grew to a deluge and so now I often don't post the stories I do because it takes simply too long to sift thorough and find useful comments. Most aren't about the story any way.
>
> *(Personal interview, 2021)*

A few others, especially those with higher years of expertise, said they had stopped posting stories that they had enjoyed the most doing. As one reporter with 6 years of multimedia experience said: "I enjoy doing stories around the heath care concerns of rural women. I also get trolled viciously on them. So, these days I post only the puff pieces online. My emotional investment in them is the least" (Personal interview, 2022).

Some journalists tried to engage in dialogue with trolls. They tried to explain their point of view but, as one reporter with 5 years of multimedia experience said, that "set them off worse" (Personal interview, 2022). Stories that focused on women, politics and sports were the ones that drew the most vitriol. The women wanted better social media managers and social media policies in place that would make clear for all users, including journalists and commentators, which kind of comments would and would not be tolerated. They were clear that better moderation would be beneficial for all, including those who shared and commented on their stories because "we genuinely want to spark conversations with our work" (Personal interview, 2021). They wanted more moderation of what they shared. As one journalist with 6 years of multimedia experience: said:

> I am extremely open to more training about social media use and ways we get the most benefit out of it. It's extremely important to learn the mechanics behind it all and I wish we had more access to training to do this.
>
> *(Personal interview, 2021)*

The journalists clearly believed that they had autonomy, and with more training and more awareness of how to work better with social media they could get the most benefit from that autonomy, as well as provide their audiences with the best benefits as well. There was deep willingness to engage in learning and interacting in healthy ways with audiences and in the process dealing with abuse and trolls. They also emphasized that their professional autonomy was certainly stronger since the #MeTooIndia movement, but they could not display this empathically online because they had few resources to deal with the negative fallout that might follow.

Discussion

Inspired by the work of Waisbord (2020a; Waisbord, 2020b) that looks at how online misogyny and trolling work as "mob censorship," this study explored the online experiences of women journalists in India and examined how online misogyny is impacting their work and professional identities. In the process, it extends the scope of scholarly attention to the international context in the developing world and is among the earliest investigations into the significance of the #MeTooIndia movement on newsrooms and journalists with a digital presence in India.

The journalists interviewed for this study were clearly encouraged to interact with audiences and have active profiles online. But they more than their male colleagues faced online abuse that was clearly aimed at their gender and often religious minority status and rarely focused what the content of their stories (Chen et al., 2020; Pain, 2017). Since these were also reporters who had covered the #MeTooIndia movement in the country, their work was used as a weapon against their professions which was deemed to be a "bad career" selection. They were called feminazis for voicing their rights and some of the attacks were clearly designed to question their right to be in the country. When their stories were critical of the government's policies, especially related to women, the abuse was particularly vitriolic. Some of the uncivil comments aimed at them also called in to question their loyalty toward the country. They were deemed "anti-national" and "anti-Indian" for their efforts and especially if they were from minority religions. Organizational responses in many cases were weak. While the journalists were heard sympathetically, little was done to really help address or resolve the issues. This weak institutional response made some of the journalists feel that this was deliberate and another way of negating the issue as something that affected women alone and therefore was not worth considering at the institutional level.

Posetti, Aboulez, Bontcheva, Harrison, & Waisbord (2020) emphasized that online violence was gradually becoming "a new frontline in journalism safety – a particularly dangerous trend for women journalists" (p. 1). But in India, media organizations have yet to respond to this as strongly as they should, even though the process of dealing with online trolls has certainly taken a negative toll. The #MeTooIndia movement may have forced a consideration of gender that for India media had been a long time coming. As the interviews exhibited, the journalists demonstrated various characteristics of professional reflexivity and autonomy when dealing with online abuse, from examining different strategies to deal with the vitriol, to requesting stronger social media moderation and policies. Journalists worked to create their own support networks and to support each other. They reduced interactions with the public. If they saw one from their "tribe" of fellow journalists being trolled, they banded together to fight the abuse. The journalists emphasized that they wanted to keep communication channels open, but this easy communication path that often led to important sources could also leave them open to harassment that they would rather avoid.

Some journalists stopped posting stories that really mattered to them. A majority said that social media gave them access to publics that they usually would not have had access to, but they were willing to compromise this to avoid trolling. A startling fact was that the journalists did not only want institutional help, but they also wanted to be active agents in their social media use. They wanted to be trained and wanted to be enabled to stop online trolling. For organizations, the message is clear. If they want journalists in tune with their publics, the publics they need, they must have robust social media protocols in place.

This study analyses the social media experiences of women journalists from mainstream media in India. It does not consider women reporters from primarily digital journalism outlets and alternative media. These are acknowledged weakness as is the small sample size that prevents the generalization of results. While the #MeTooIndia movement has at least made institutions more sensitive to the misogyny that women face online, newsrooms must consider more concrete ways of following up on preventing online trolling and abuse. As the impact of #MeTooIndia is felt in more organizations, future research must follow up on its repercussions to document and add to our understanding of gendered harassment and professional journalism.

Funding

This research was supported by a travel grant from the Reynolds School of Journalism, University of Nevada, Reno.

References

Ahva, L. (2013). Public journalism and professional reflexivity. *Journalism*, *14*(6), 790–806.

Al Jazeera. (2022, February 21). India journalist Ayyub Faces 'judicial harassment': Un experts. *Media News | Al Jazeera*. Retrieved April 11, 2022, from https://www.aljazeera. com/news/2022/2/21/india-journalist-ayyub-faces-judicial-harassment-un-experts

Ayyub, R. (2022, January 18). Opinion | an investigation sheds light into Modi's machinery of online hate and manipulation. *The Washington Post*. Retrieved April 11, 2022, from https://www.washingtonpost.com/opinions/2022/01/18/ the-wire-sheds-light-on-india-tek-fog-hate-online/

BBC (2019, February 18). India country profile. *BBC News*. Retrieved April 14, 2022, from https://www.bbc.com/news/world-south-asia-12557384

Belair-Gagnon, V., Mishra, S., & Agur, C. (2014). Reconstructing the Indian public sphere: Newswork and social media in the Delhi gang rape case. *Journalism*, *15*(8), 1059–1075.

Bryman, A. (Ed.) (1988). *Doing research in organizations*. London: Routledge.

Business India (2022). Digital Media is expected to grow at 29.5% CAGR to reach a market size of Rs 35,809 crore by 2023: Dentsu Report. *Business Insider*. Retrieved April 11, 2022, from https://www.businessinsider.in/advertising/ad-agencies/article/digital-media-is-expected-to-grow-at-29-5-cagr-to-reach-a-market-size-of-rs-35809-crore-by-2023-dentsu-report/articleshow/89278244.cms

Chadha, K., Steiner, L., & Guha, P. (2017). Indian women journalists' responses to sexism and sexual harassment. *International Communication Research Journal*, *52*(1), 1–29.

Chen, G. M., & Pain, P. (2017). Normalizing online comments. *Journalism Practice*, *11*(7), 876–892.

Chen, G. M., Pain, P., Chen, V. Y., Mekelburg, M., Springer, N., & Troger, F. (2020). 'You really have to have a thick skin': A cross-cultural perspective on how online harassment influences female journalists. *Journalism*, *21*(7), 877–895.

Coe, K., Kenski, K., & Rains, S. A. (2014). Online and uncivil? patterns and determinants of incivility in newspaper website comments. *Journal of Communication 64*, 658– 679.

Columbia Journalism Review (2022, January 31). *Women journalists in India feel more at risk after 'auction' apps worsen online abuse*. Committee to Protect Journalists. Retrieved April 11, 2022, from https://cpj.org/2022/01/women-journalists-india-auction-apps-online-abuse/

Diakopoulos, N., & Naaman, M. (2011, March). Towards quality discourse in online news comments. In *Proceedings of the ACM 2011 conference on computer supported cooperative work* (pp. 133–142).

Drèze, J., & Sen. (2013). *An uncertain glory: India and its contradictions*. Princeton, NJ: Princeton University Press.

English, P. (2017). Social media boundaries in sports journalism: Individual and organisational gatekeeping in India and Australia. *Asian Journal of Communication*, *27*(5), 480–496.

Ghosh, S. (2020). Decoding gendered online trolling in India. In Mirchandani, M. (Ed.), *Tackling insurgent ideologies in a pandemic world*. *Observer Research Foundation and Global Policy Journal*, 59–64. New Delhi: Observer Research Foundation. Retrieved from https://www.orfonline.org/wp-content/uploads/2020/08/Tackling-Insurgent-Ideologies-in-a-Pandemic-World-for-ORF.pdf#page=59.

Goel, V., Venkataraman, A., & Schultz, K. (2018). After a long wait, India's #MeToo movement suddenly takes off. *The New York Times*. Retrieved from https://www.

nytimes.com/2018/10/09/ world/asia/india-sexual-harassment-me-too-bollywood. html (accessed 15 January 2020).

González de Bustamante, C., & Relly, J. E. (2016). Professionalism under threat of violence: Journalism, reflexivity, and the potential for collective professional autonomy in northern Mexico. *Journalism Studies, 17*(6), 684–702.

Gudipaty, N. (2017). Gendered public spaces. Online trolling of women journalists in India. *Comunicazione politica, 18*(2), 299–310.

Halder, D., & Jaishankar, K. (2016). *Cyber crimes against women in India*. SAGE Publications India..

International Federation of Journalists (2022, March 10). *India: Two arrested for spreading misinformation about journalist Rana Ayyub/IFJ*. International Federation of Journalists. Retrieved April 11, 2022, from https://www.ifj.org/media-centre/news/detail/ category/press-releases/article/india-two-arrested-for-spreading-misinformation-about-journalist-rana-ayyub.html

Jamil, S. (2020). Suffering in silence: The resilience of Pakistan's female journalists to combat sexual harassment, threats and discrimination. *Journalism Practice, 14*(2), 150–170.

Jamil, S., & Muschert, G. W. (2020). Risks to journalists' safety and the vulnerability of media freedom in the U.S. *Agenda for Social Justice 2020*, 135–142. https://doi.org/10.46692/9781447354611.016

Jaswal, S. (2022, January 3). Bulli Bai: India's Muslim women again listed on app for 'auction'. *Islamophobia News | Al Jazeera*. Retrieved April 11, 2022, from https://www.aljazeera.com/news/2022/1/2/bulli-bai-muslim-women-auction-online-india

Kanagasabai, N. (2016). In the silences of a newsroom: Age, generation, and sexism in the Indian television newsroom. *Feminist Media Studies, 16*(4), 663–677.

Kohli, H. (2021, July 4). How Digital India can become a success story. *Fortune India: Business News, Strategy, Finance and Corporate Insight*. Retrieved April 11, 2022, from https://www.fortuneindia.com/opinion/how-digital-india-can-become-a-success-story/105599

Meltzer, K. (2015). Journalistic concern about uncivil political talk in digital news media: Responsibility, credibility, and academic influence. *The International Journal of Press/ Politics, 20*(1), 85–107.

Nielsen, R., & Sen, A. (2016). Digital journalism start-ups in India. *Report of the Reuters Institute for the Study of Journalism*. University of Oxford. Retrieved from https:// ora.ox.ac.uk/objects/uuid:f028366e-4a28-4bb1-bcfb-5ecc8f7eb45a/download_ file?file_format=pdf&safe_filename=Digital%2BJournalism%2BStart-ups%2Bin%2 BIndia.pdf&type_of_work=Report

Pain, P. (2017). "When I ask a question, they look at me strangely:" An exploratory study of women political reporters in India. *Journalism Practice, 11*(10), 1319–1337.

Pain P. (2021). *"IT TOOK ME QUITE A LONG TIME TO DEVELOP A VOICE": Examining feminist digital activism in the Indian #Metoo movement*. New Media and Society.

Pain, P., & Korin, E. (2021). 'Everything is dimming out, little by little:' Examining self-censorship among Venezuelan journalists. *Communication Research and Practice, 7*(1), 71–88.

Perrigo, B. (2021, October 22). Rana Ayyub's fight for truth and journalism in Modi's India. *Time*. Retrieved April 12, 2022, from https://time.com/6108251/rana-ayyub-india-journalism-modi/

Posetti, J., Aboulez, N., Bontcheva, K., Harrison, J., & Waisbord, S. (2020). *Online violence against women journalists*. New York: UNESCO.

Pradhan, P., & Kumari, N. (2018). A study on journalistic use of social media. *Amity Journal of Media and Communication Studies (AJMCS), 8*(1), 49-59.

Rao, S. (2014). Covering rape in shame culture: Studying journalism ethics in India's new television news media. *Journal of Mass Media Ethics, 29*(3), 153–167.

Reese, S. D. (2001). Understanding the global journalist: A hierarchy-of-influences approach. *Journalism Studies, 2*(2), 173–187.

Rodrigues, U. M. (2019). Can Indian journalism survive the onslaught of social media? *Global Media and Communication, 15*(2), 151–157.

Santana, A. D., & Russial, J. (2013). Photojournalists' role expands at most daily US newspapers. *Newspaper Research Journal, 34*(1), 74–88.

Shoemaker, P. J., & Reese, S. D. (2013). *Mediating the message in the 21st century: A media sociology perspective.* New York: Routledge.

Sjovaag, H. (2013). The meaning and function of journalistic ideology. *Past, Future and Change: Contemporary Analysis of Evolving Media Scapes, 135*, 136–146.

Sohal, P. (2020). Shooting the messenger, slowly, but surely: A review of imminent threats to freedom of media and journalistic integrity in India. In Jamil, S. (Ed.), *The handbook of research on combating threats to media freedom and journalists' safety.* IGI Global, pp. 23–37.

Statista. (2019). Retrieved from https://tinyurl.com/yd3nzl4e (accessed 12 January 2022).

Sullivan, R. (2015, April 27). *SBS reporter Scott McIntyre fired over Anzac tweets.* news.com.au. Retrieved from http://www.news.com.au/national/sbs-reporter-scott-mcintyre-fired-overanzac-tweets/story-fncynjr2-1227321537612

Tek fog: An app with BJP footprints for Cyber troops to automate hate, manipulate trends. *The Wire* (n.d.). Retrieved April 11, 2022, from https://thewire.in/tekfog/en/1.html

Waisbord, S. (2020a). Mob censorship: Online harassment of US journalists in times of digital hate and populism. *Digital Journalism, 8*(8), 1030–1046.

Waisbord, S. (2020b). Trolling journalists and the risks of digital publicity. *Journalism Practice 16*(5), 1–17.

Welch, S. (1975). Sampling by referral in a dispersed population. *The Public Opinion Quarterly, 39*(2), 237–245.

PART III
Activism

8

#RHODESWAR

Contesting Institutional Silencing in the Struggle Against Rape in Post-Apartheid South Africa

Gavaza Maluleke

Introducing #RhodesWar

The hashtag #RhodesWar began trending on 11 December 2017 after the public became aware that three female student activists had been expelled from Rhodes University (RU), with two of the students banned for life while the third was expelled for five years (Matshili, 2017). Many of the media reports at the time linked the students' expulsion to their participation as leaders in the anti-rape (naked) protests that took place at RU in 2016 (Maduna, 2017). These protests were a culmination of events that began when university management started taking down posters that were part of the "Chapter 2.12" protests. Gorata Chengeta (2017), a former student who had been a part of the activism during that time, details how Chapter 2.12 came to be:

> Weeks before the reference list appeared, the Unashamed movement at Stellenbosch University had invited students from other universities to help to create a campaign against gender-based violence. The Chapter 2.12 campaign – named after the section of the Constitution that guarantees one's right to safety – would express that the rape culture on our campuses was unconstitutional. The initial plan set out by the founders of Unashamed was to start with a poster campaign and then to make a documentary. Later on, there would be marches at which students would present a list of demands to their respective university administrations.

The activities were organized by members of the Gender Action Project – an activism-based group started by RU feminists in 2007 in response to the silencing of rape survivors in South Africa – with the support of Naledi Mashishi, the Student Representative Council Activism and Transformation officer, bearing

DOI: 10.4324/9781003260851-11

signs that read, "You are more likely to be excluded for plagiarism than you are for rape." These posters were taken down twice by university management, and on 14 April, protestors responded by putting up a sign on the library wall that read: "WE WILL NOT BE SILENCED." A few days later, a reference list of 11 names ending with "et al" (to signify "and others"), made up of former and present students who were alleged perpetrators of sexual violence/assault, was posted on the *RU Queer Confessions, Questions and Crushes* Facebook page (Seddon, 2016). As a result, the hashtag #RUReferenceList began trending on social media.

Following the circulation of the list, a group of student protesters took collective action and went to the different male residences looking for the men on the list (Seddon, 2016). Several newspapers reported that according to witnesses, about 100–2000 student protesters allegedly forced three men who were on the list out of their rooms and held them (Pather & Smit, 2017; Solomon, 2017). Two of the men escaped, but one was held by the group until the next day (Pather & Smit, 2017). It was further reported that in assembling the men on the list, the students called for university management to immediately suspend the men and begin investigating the cases (Seddon, 2016). Instead, the university applied for an interdict against those "engaging in unlawful activities" and those "associating themselves" with such activities, naming three students in particular: Sian Ferguson, Yolanda Dyantyi, and Simamkele Heleni (Staff Reporter, 2016). A narrower interdict was granted following several appeals by the Socio-Economic Institution of South Africa, who were representing the three students and a collection of concerned RU staff members, and was used in the disciplinary hearing where the two women were found guilty of kidnapping, assault, defamation, and insubordination and subsequently banned from RU for life. Using the hashtag #RhodesWar, online users took to Twitter to express their outrage and disappointment at the university's decision (Maduna, 2017). In response, RU released a statement on their Twitter account dismissing these claims, arguing that the matter had been heard in the high court, the Supreme Court of Appeal, and the Constitutional Court and that its decision to expel the students was based on the courts' findings that the student activists had carried out "unlawful acts" that "made serious inroads into the rights and liberties of others" (Rhodes University, 2017).

Locating Rape and Silencing in South Africa's Colonial History

The situation at RU is a microcosm of post-1994 South Africa where rape and femicide debates dominate the public discourse. The reality is that South Africa has consistently recorded some of the highest numbers of reported rapes per capita in the world (Britton, 2006) with violence toward womxn[1] at an all-time high. Until recently, much of the sexual and gender-based violence (SGBV) activism has been spearheaded by nongovernmental organizations. Although much of the discourse has been saturated by media reports that sensationalize the sexual aspect of rape, the era of HIV/AIDS and the women's empowerment discourse shifted the research to focus on the link between the legacy of apartheid violence and its economic ramification to the current rape crisis, in an effort to provide explanations for why men commit violence (Moffet, 2006, p. 131). These efforts highlighted the prevalence of rape, particularly of Black women that had become commonplace during apartheid, whereby "instead of being perceived as an abuse of human rights around which anti-apartheid protesters could mobilise [...] rape was seen as being just part of life" (Armstrong, 1994, p. 35). Within the Black community, Pumla Gqola makes an important link in her analysis of the early Black Consciousness Movement of South Africa and the way they defined the role of the category of "Blackwomen" in *Staffrider* Magazine by suggesting that some of these ideas might have contributed to the prevailing discourse that gendered violence is a commonly accepted practice. She explains that

> Representations of Blackwomen were trapped in two stereotypes: the long-suffering, stoic mother who supports her son and/or husband in activism against apartheid; and the hyper-sexualized female character in short stories who is inscribed with gendered violence for her refusal (or failure) to conform to the previous mould of regulated sexuality.
>
> *(Gqola, 2001, p. 48)*

However, as illuminating as these efforts have been in demonstrating the types of silences that pervaded violence during apartheid, they are incomplete as they overlook the colonial structures that form the basis of the apartheid structures they interrogate.

During the colonial period, the normalization of raping Black women was validated by law with the politics of respectability used to determine which rape victims were believed and thus playing an important role in the colonial courts. With Black women already viewed as "always already sexually available to the raping gaze of the White [man] and as fundamentally promiscuous" (Maldonado-Torres, 2007, p. 255), it was easy to institutionalize the invalidation of their rapes. Pamela Scully, in her study on Gender, Labor and Sexuality in rural Western Cape 1823–1853, tells the story of a woman who was raped by her gardener whose race was not identified, but court papers suggested that he was a man of color (1995, p. 335). The case was reported and at trial, the man was given the death penalty. However, a few months later, the judge commuted his sentence from death to a term of imprisonment with hard labor. According to Scully, this decision was made after,

> a deputation of 'eight or ten most respectable Inhabitants [read white] of George' had called on the judge and told him that 'the woman and her husband are Bastard colored persons, and that instead of her being a respectable woman, her character for chastity was very indifferent and that it was

strongly suspected that she had on several occasions previously voluntarily had a connection with the Prisoner'.

(1995, p. 336)

Predictably, studies from that period show that no White man had ever been executed for rape and the Black men that were executed, the majority were hanged for raping White women (Armstrong, 1994, p. 35). Consequently, most of the rape cases of Black women at that time involved Black defendants. Moreover, as recorders of history, White men were able to decide what can and cannot be recorded and as such, there are not that many cases involving White men raping Black women. This point is echoed by Thornberry (2016, p. 865) when she suggests that such cases were either not recorded by White magistrates or Black women did not deem it worthwhile to report such cases. However, to only focus on the racialized, sexual violation of Black women is to only consider rape as a violent act, and nothing more. Thornberry explains it best when she argues, "to explain rape in terms of violence alone, without consideration of its specifically sexual nature, is to misunderstand the nature of sexual violence and its relationship to broader claims to control female sexuality" (2019, p. 304).

This aspect is clearly demonstrated in the case of the "Black Peril" of the 1800s in KwaZulu/Natal where there was a moral panic in the White community over what they called the Black menace (Etherington, 1988, p. 36). It was feared that White women were in danger of being raped by Black men. The police and the courts were placed on high alert to ensure that any Black man accused of raping a White woman was promptly arrested and, in many cases, found guilty. Although it did not result in a marked increase in the prosecution of rape cases in the colonial courts, the Black rape scare went on for 4 years starting in 1860 (Etherington, 1988, p. 41). Etherington (1988), a historian, argues that the rape scare in Natal was akin to the Zulu invasion scares that circulated within the community from time to time but never actually materialized. He goes on to explain that it soon became clear that this scare was more related to White men's fears over property and social control within the ruling class (Etherington, 1988). For Etherington, the criminal rape law that was passed at that time was a way to protect property, so we can easily conclude that "rape amounted to an invasion of the property of fathers and husbands who controlled access to the bodies of the women in their care" (Etherington, 1988, p. 41).

The Promise of Hashtag Activism

Recent scholarship in feminist media studies has underscored the different ways in which digital platforms have become creative spaces for the public to gain insight into, and be involved in sexual violence discourse (Mendes et al., 2018, p. 237). Using digital media to call attention to the struggles of young women to retain control over their bodies is a relatively recent phenomenon. Black feminists see these digital platforms as having the potential to create safe spaces where their voices and subjugated viewpoints might be heard by those in privileged positions (Rapp et al., 2010, p. 255). Dixon (2014, p. 34) cautions against the idea of safe spaces, especially on Twitter and Facebook, because of the possibility of online harassment, hate speech, and disagreements. In recent years, South Africa has witnessed a rise in feminist hashtags against gendered violence beginning with #PatriarchyMustFall in 2015 and #AmINext in 2019, signaling an increasing belief in the transformative potential of digital platforms for womxn's participation in the public discourse. However, even as scholars celebrate these digital platforms and their potential to engender creative modes of protest, new systems of violence and old, institutionalized forms of silencing targeting activists are exemplified in the interplay between on/offline activism and public spaces. What new and old institutionalized forms of silencing are highlighted? And how are these young, female activists navigating and circumventing these silencing acts?

Drawing on the notion that speech or the act of speaking out is regarded as an important element within feminist circles, especially in anti-rape politics because it is viewed as an act of defiance but more importantly, it can give "voice to the voiceless" (Motsemme, 2004, p. 917), this chapter explores the voices of resistances articulated against these institutionalized forms of silencing under the hashtag #RhodesWar, mapping what is being said, how it is being said, and what techniques, if any, are being used to compel others to listen. These narratives are what makes up hashtag activism, a form of protest that is discursive and occurs on social media under a hashtagged word, phrase, or sentence (Yang, 2016, p. 13). The language used, the stories shared, and the emotions circulated all contribute to the act of speaking out in response to the silencing tactics employed by those in power. It is important to note, however, that even as we focus on those womxn activists who speak out, we acknowledge Motsemme's (2004, p. 926) assertion that to be mute does not necessarily mean to be absent and voiceless, but silence here should be viewed as presence and a form of speaking.

This chapter analyzes data collected on Twitter under the hashtag #RhodesWar. The hashtag began trending on 11 December 2017 and remained a trending topic until 15 December 2017 when Yolanda Dyantyi, one of the student activists, held a press briefing. The tweets analyzed were taken between 11 and 15 December, and the focus was responses to the University's decision by expressing an opinion or thought on the matter and/or recounting a personal story. Undoubtedly, this focus left out the many other voices that responded to or engaged with the hashtag itself; however, this chapter aims to center those who were using the hashtag as a form of activism to fight and challenge the expulsion of the antirape student leaders. This approach can be viewed as a form of purposive sampling in that it identifies and selects those who were deemed to be at the center of creating the hashtag and thereafter maintaining its momentum for it to gain traction. This group of activists were engaged in what Yang (2016, p. 14) calls narrative agency, which she defines as the ability to collectively generate stories on social media using a hashtag such that their efforts are recognized by the public. The dominant narrative published in the newspapers on the hashtag was the public outrage emanating from Twitter, such that RU felt compelled to release a statement. The focus was neither on the number of tweets nor the gender of those tweeting but on what was said and how it was said. Fifty-one tweets were collected, from ordinary people to journalists representing newspapers and nongovernmental organizations focused on SGBV. The majority of the tweets were stories, thoughts, and opinions, and five out of the 51 tweets were retweets. The arguments here are based on a narrative analysis of the collection of Twitter commentary that together formed the #RhodesWar hashtag. Yang (2016) has highlighted that narrative agency is a central component of hashtag activism, and thus, it is also important to pay attention to what narrative agency is visible in this collection of stories. Moreover, the chapter focuses on elements of narrative analysis such as how the stories are told, what function the stories serve, what substance is in the stories, and how the stories are performed (Allen, 2017).

Silencing Tactics and Institutions of Higher Learning

The hashtag #RhodesWar began trending when the news broke that RU had expelled two unnamed students who had participated in the anti-rape naked protests. According to the university, the student activists were both found guilty of kidnapping and insubordination, while one of them was also found guilty of assault and defamation (Pather & Smit, 2017). The immediate reaction from many online users who took to social media was dismay because earlier that year, in May 2017, the University had undertaken the decision that should a student at RU be found guilty of rape, they would be faced with a ten-year expulsion from the university (Pather & Smit, 2017). For many, the decision to expel the two students for life unfairly exceeded the 10-year expulsion intended to punish rapists and as one tweeter lamented, "#RhodesWar. The balance of power are so clear and visible…surely rape should also warrant a lifetime expulsion" (December 12, 2017). This theme was echoed by several people on Twitter, with some arguing that with this decision, RU was punishing those who had protested against rape while normalizing rape culture by protecting rapists. When a newspaper like the Mail & Guardian was given access to the internal papers of the university with regard to the expulsion, it became clear that the discourse on Twitter was spot on. Pather and Smit's article highlighted this:

> the university drew up a draft order that proposed that the two be permanently expelled and that their academic transcripts be endorsed. These endorsements would read: Conduct unsatisfactory – student permanently excluded for kidnapping and insubordination (for McFall); and Conduct unsatisfactory – student permanently excluded for kidnapping, assault, insubordination, defamation (For Dyantyi) […] 'it is unlikely that either of the students will return to the university after this academic year. In the absence of an endorsement, they will be unable to rely on their untainted transcripts at different institutions or for any other purpose. Such a result

would render this entire disciplinary process a wasted exercise. In these circumstances, we submit that it is imperative for the transcripts of the students to be endorsed to read 'conduct unsatisfactory' in the manner expressed in the draft order the university argued.

(2017)

It is important to quote parts of this internal document at length to show the intention behind the sanctions; as some online users had stated, the university was sending a clear message to the protesters: rioting against rape will get you expelled. As more details of the situation emerged, some tweets expressed sadness and disappointment while others expressed anger declaring that universities had become battlefields, and RU was declaring war against those who would dare to speak out. Some noted that an activist protesting rape is expelled while a rapist will get to graduate.

RU responded to the social media outrage by releasing a press statement attached to a tweet where they stated, "Rhodes Exclusions a Result of Criminality, No Student Excluded for Protesting" (December 13, 2017). The press statement expressed concern at the "misrepresentations of facts and cynical attempts at manipulating public opinion" (Rhodes University, 2017). In responding, the university statement offers insight into the changing dynamics that social media brings for those without power or access to resources. Before the advent of social media, the university would have been able to control the public narrative of this story through their access to the media. Journalists would have had to search for activists to get their views. However, with many of them on social media, journalists can locate the most influential, knowledgeable or active participants in a particular hashtag, interview them, or even quote their tweets or Facebook posts.

As shown here in this interview with student activist, Noxolo Mfocwa, who was part of the anti-rape (naked) protests, she had shared her story of exclusion on Twitter when the hashtag began trending, by stating, "After accepting defeat, I asked Mabizela to release my results, just to give me my degree. Frames 1&2 are his responses and 3&4 are sworn affidavits from my lecturers. He lied!! They collected all my scripts and destroyed them" (December 11, 2017). Frames 1&2 consisted of a letter from Dr. Sizwe Mabizela, RU's vice-chancellor, who had rejected her request for clemency and to release her academic results. According to the documents, the student was excluded based on a report submitted by the Disciplinary Review Committee to the Proctor. Her story, unlike the story of the two expelled students that was circulating in the media, would not have made the news as many students are excluded for academic reasons all the time. However, by tweeting this story concerning #RhodesWar, she alerted the public to the possibility that some of the exclusions faced by students might not always be because of the reasons stated in the exclusionary letters but could also be motivated by sinister reasons. As noted here by this Twitter post, "Chatting to a colleague this morning about #RhodesWar as she studied there." She easily said that, "even in my time, we were so scared of speaking up because people were getting excluded all the time" (December 12, 2017). How many students did not speak up about their rape in fear that speaking up could be used against them? Similarly, which students faced academic exclusion like Mfocwa did after speaking about their rape? These are all important questions that begin to circulate when stories are added to the discourse of rape at university.

While speaking to the radio station, Power98.7, Mfocwa maintained that the charges against the students were fabricated. In support of Mfocwa's assertion, Deborah Seddon, a senior lecturer at RU and a member of Gender Action Forum (GenAct), explains that university management argued that the interdict was a necessary intervention in the face of violence that would erupt, should the students take matters into their own hands. But as she further elaborates,

> None of the men on the list rounded up on the night of Sunday 17 April was physically harmed in any way, some escaped quite easily from the angry crowd, ran away, or simply walked off. They were not beaten up, nor injured.
>
> *(2016)*

By sharing the activists' side of the story, Mfocwa was able to show social media's effectiveness in bringing diverse voices and not just those directly affected by the issue at hand. She stated:

> The university has been very good at spinning the story and criminalizing black women who stood up and spoke out against a university that has been oppressing and silencing for the longest of times. All these charges have been trumped up to make it look like we are a violent group of women who decided to just spontaneously attack a group of people. No one was assaulted, and there was no kidnapping.
>
> *(Maduna, 2017)*

Interestingly, Mfocwa chooses to speak specifically to the criminalizing of Black women even though some of the students targeted by the university are White. For instance, Dominique McFall, a White student activist, is one of the two students expelled for life. The foregrounding of Black women could be construed as an exclusion of White women from this narrative. Going by the media coverage, this claim seems valid as the majority of the coverage has been focused on Yolanda Dyantyi, the Black student who was also expelled. McFall's one major appearance was on Cape Talk Radio on 27 August 2018 – 6 months after her expulsion from RU – to discuss her ongoing case with RU when she, along with other student leaders from the university, were invited to attend a Parliamentary public hearing on gender-based violence (Qukula, 2018). However, it could also be argued that the limited media coverage could also be attributed to McFall's lack of social media presence, especially on Twitter where much of the discussion was taking place. It was Mfocwa's Twitter posts that brought her media attention and thus, to view McFall's lack of coverage and Mfocwa's foregrounding of Black women as the exclusion of White women is to overlook the amount of digital labor that Black women are performing in these spaces. As pointed out by Lisa Nakamura (2015), when marginalized groups and racial minorities post, retweet, and comment on social media spaces in an effort to "call out, educate and protest" against racism and misogyny, they should be viewed as performing a type of unwanted labor that is "hidden, often-stigmatised and dangerous" (p. 106). In South Africa, Black women perform this type of labor, not just to gain media visibility but to be able to control their narratives. It is widely acknowledged that South African media tends to hypervisibilize Black women, and Black people in general, while denying said subjects their humanity (Boonzaier, 2017, p. 478; Chiumbu, 2016, p. 427). These acts of erasure are what Mfocwa and other young activists like herself are fighting against by performing digital labor. Dlakavu, expounds on this in her writing alongside Ndelu and Matandela (2017, p. 106), by arguing that for young feminist activists such as herself, to "riot and write and record and film and tweet" is an "imaginative, transformative political project" that guards against Black womxn's erasure to ensure that "our history and humanity is legitimized." It is important to highlight that for these authors, "writing" is not just about text but can be visual or oral (Dlakavu et al., 2017, p. 106).

It is against this backdrop that we can better understand Mfocwa's interview and her need to not just focus on sharing her personal story of academic exclusion from RU (already shared on Twitter) but aimed at pushing back against the narrative being set up by the university to portray these Black womxn activists as criminal and violent. And rightly so because as argued by Chiumbu (2016, p. 427), in labeling the actions of the activists as criminal and violent, the university can direct the public's attention away from the fundamental issues that incited the protests in the first place, to now focus solely on activists' actions. By focusing on the spectacle of violence, the university relies on old but familiar colonial tropes in which Africans can only be rendered visible in the public discourse through their corporeality (Boonzaier, 2017, p. 478) in order to silence these young feminist activists.

Universities are often regarded as sites of instrumental transformation in many societies. In South Africa, the restructuring of the post-1994 higher education sector was guided by the notion that higher education has an important role to play in the political, economic, and cultural reconstruction and development of the country (Reddy, 2006, p. 128). Ever since the call to decolonize the university, initiated by the #RhodesMustFall and then subsequently, the #FeesMustFall movement, the reforms undertaken post-1994 in the higher education sector did not disrupt the foundation and infrastructure of the colonial empire that still underpin South African universities. This is now an accepted reality in the public discourse and as these two tweets show:

> We know all 2 well that unis criminalize us 4 leading protests. Or senikhohliwe [*my translation: have you forgotten*] that during FMF more than 200 students were arrested for "criminal acts"? Even worse, Rhodes

charged them under "Common Purpose', an apartheid law! 'Crimes' of
THOUSANDS on 5 womxn. BS! #RhodesWar.

(December 13, 2017)

Rhodes has a culture of protecting what shouldn't be protected, from mur-
derers, Cecil's colonial legacy and now rapists #RhodesWar.

(December 12, 2017)

For these young activists, RU's link to its colonial roots is made worse by its
name. The reluctance by the institution to rename themselves has many on social
media and in other public platforms calling RU by other names such as the University Currently Known as Rhodes or the University Still Known as Rhodes.
It is commonplace to see these acronyms on social media having gained traction
during the Fallist[2] movements. Despite the university's negative reputation, the
higher education sector has been applauded for its contribution in creating the
new Black middle class (Reddy, 2006, p.130). In South Africa, as in other parts
of the world with similar histories of settler colonies, the position of the middle
class (i.e. respectability) has always been the domain of Whiteness. This is not
to suggest that all White people could attain this position but for many Black
families, it is assumed that sending their children to university is an opportunity
to enter the middle class. These ideas stem from colonial times and if we look at
the Eastern Cape, for example, the divisions between Black people comprised of
abantu abasesikolweni (school people) and abantu ababomvu (red people) were
influenced by British middle-class ideas (Thornberry, 2016, p. 866). Thornberry
(2016, p. 866) argues that this distinction was meant to highlight the difference between those Africans who went to school, viewed as the frontrunners of
respectability, and abantu ababomvu as those who rejected schools and preferred
to continue with the pre-colonial African traditions. Education and by extension
the university as a site of respectability is a colonial discourse that is still in circulation today. This notion is reinforced by what Dlakavu et al. highlights when
paraphrasing Susan Andrade's 2002 essay entitled "Gender in the Public Sphere
in Africa, Writing Women and Rioting Women" by stating that:

> The women who have rioted, who have been on the streets, have been
> women of working class backgrounds, women who have had little to no
> access to education; and writing women were women who had gone to
> university or finished high school or who had formal jobs. These two bod-
> ies or groups of women operated or expressed political ideas differently –
> writing and rioting.
>
> *(Dlakavu et al., 2017, p. 106)*

Highlighting this distinction between rioting and writing Black women is
important as it points to the erasure of those who "riot" such as the Black women

who rioted during apartheid and were consequently left out of mainstream discourse. While those who were able to "write" are given recognition as was done with abantu abasesikolweni in Colonial Eastern Cape. In a way, we could argue that today's Black womxn who are given entry into universities are afforded an opportunity to attain this respectability through the expectation that they will get rid of their "rioting" ways in favor of writing so as to gain recognition and become "middle class." However, Dlakavu et al. (2017, p. 106) cautions against the allure of respectability by emphasizing the need for young, Black, womxn activists to "write and riot" simultaneously.

This is because the tactics used against White, middle-class British women who participated in the politics of respectability during the colonial period are visible in today's policing behavior whereby womxn who report rape (write/speak up) are often asked, "what were you wearing" and "were you drinking"? The suggestion here is that respectable womxn should aim to protect their chastity at all costs and not put themselves in situations where men would be tempted to rape them. As explained by Helman (2018, p.17), claims to respectability make it possible for certain womxn to claim rape, be believed and be afforded protection. This assertion might explain this tweet by a poster who claims to have just realized how difficult it is to be a woman in South Africa "especially if you are black and not privileged" (December 12, 2017). The poster does not elucidate their point any further, however it could be argued that the point being made highlights the complexity of Black women's entry into the university and by extension middle-classness and respectability. In the same way that not all White women could claim respectability, the same can be said about Black womxn at university. The purging of womxn by RU should be viewed in light of the role the universities play as gatekeepers who have the power to determine those who can enter into the space of middle-classness and respectability. There is an expected behavior and those who fail to follow this protocol are punished or expelled. In the statement they released in response to the social media outrage, RU outlined the expected behavior that student activists should follow when engaging in protests against SGBV by stating that,

> There is a clear distinction between vigorously pursuing our common objective of eliminating sexual and gender-based violence on the one hand and using such a noble cause as a cover to commit acts of criminality, which serve to undermine a noble struggle.
>
> *(Rhodes University, 2017)*

By viewing the actions of the protesters that day as criminal, RU may be seen as setting parameters on what is acceptable and befitting their students, and thus, those students who transgress these parameters are deemed unfit to participate in the respectability politics of the middle class.

Speaking Up as a Form of Writing

When the news broke that two female students had been expelled, the students' names were withheld. However, four days after the campaign began, Yolanda Dyantyi held a press briefing in which she introduced herself to the public as one of the unnamed student leaders. With this approach, she simultaneously made herself known to mainstream media, social media and the public at large by becoming the spokesperson for the #RhodesWar campaign. This strategy made her popular with mainstream media and social media platforms such as Twitter where her story has continued to circulate despite the hashtag #RhodesWar losing momentum soon after it went viral. Her social media presence has increased to the point that when Yolanda Zulu, another student feminist activist who was also in litigation with RU over her exclusion, won her case, many on Twitter celebrated thinking the win pertained to Dyantyi's case. Others even tweeted Dyantyi asking, "Who is Yolanda Zulu Yoli?" (June 15, 2021) because they had never heard of Yolanda Zulu. Unlike Dyantyi, Zulu's case was an exclusion, similar to Mfocwa's situation, and would probably not garner the same attention and outrage. In many ways, the court cases that RU is involved in with the student activist leaders from the #RUReferenceList protest, and more specifically Dyantyi's ongoing court case, under the hashtag #StandwithYolanda, have revived the hashtag #RhodesWar campaign several times. For instance, in December 2019, when Socio-Economic Institution of South Africa appeared on Dyantyi's behalf at the Grahamstown High Court for the application to review her permanent exclusion from RU, #RhodesWar circulated on Twitter. And when the Grahamstown high court dismissed her case in March 2020 ordering her to pay the University's costs, an application for leave to appeal was filed in April 2020 and the matter argued on the 7th and 11th September 2020, which led to the creation of the #StandwithYolanda hashtag. The hashtag was trending in September 2020 accompanied by similarly connected hashtags such #RhodesWar, #Chapter212 and/or #RuReferenceList.

The importance of Dyantyi's story in keeping the hashtag relevant is indicative of the ephemeral nature of social media, and the limits of speaking up or what Dlakavu et al. calls "writing," when not combined with offline activism (rioting) that is recognizable to the public (Maluleke & Moyer, 2020, p. 895). Dyantyi's ongoing legal fight with RU not only keeps the #RhodesWar hashtag relevant but also visible to the wider public. Such visibility was demonstrated in the 2019 Sudan revolution when the iconic photo of Alaa Salah went viral. As stated by The Africa Report (2021), "Salah became a symbol of a revolution that was desperate for a figurehead." More importantly, her viral photo made visible the presence of the many women who were participating in the revolution. Today's movements rely on the internet and hashtag activism to enact change and are frequently portrayed as creating new forms of political engagement that challenge the need for hierarchical structures (Honwana, 2019, p. 16). However, figureheads as in the case of Salah and Dyantyi who are physically present demonstrate that narrative tools used in older movements (i.e. the use of Nelson Mandela as a symbol of anti-apartheid struggle), are still used by both the activists and mainstream media to connect a particular struggle with an individual.

In the press briefing titled, "#RhodesWar: Stop the Purge of Female Students/Activists by Rhodes University," Dyantyi discussed the charges against her and the other five activists who were targeted by RU. Therefore, even though Dyantyi became the face of the campaign, she stressed the need to highlight the stories of the others who were in a similar situation. As shown in this tweet shared by Daily Vox Journalist Mihlali Ntsabo, "Expelled Rhodes University student Yolanda Dyantyi: the purpose of this public briefing is to highlight the other women besides myself who have been excluded for participating in the #RUReferenceList #RhodesWars" (December 15, 2017). By calling this press briefing, Dyantyi took charge of her story in the public domain and was able to use her own voice, speak up and fight back against what she calls a wider trend by universities aimed at pushing out and thereby silencing young student leaders who dare to challenge "patriarchy, capitalism (commodification of higher education) and ultimately, the calling of decolonized institutional spaces" (December 15, 2017).

Notably, Dyantyi's ability to do this is a privilege that many sexual violence survivors are not afforded. There is a sense she has access to other discourses other than feminism that allow her to validate her story, legitimize her authority to speak and to be believed. Her situation demonstrates access to respectability as mentioned in the previous section. Because for the majority of Black womxn without access to education, and by extension respectability, their lives are "valueless" and considered unimportant (Armstrong, 1994, p. 36). This was also evident in Floretta Boonzaier's analysis of media representations of Anene Booysen – a young, colored woman who was raped and killed in 2013 – whose story captured the nation's attention. According to Boonzaier (2017), "When one reads the media reports about the rape and murder of Anene Booysen, one is left with a profound sense of invisibilisation – about a life that did not matter even after it was ended" (p. 477). However, a shift is occurring whereby specific Black women's lives seem to matter more than others. In the last few years alone, there have been numerous victims of rape and femicide reported in the news, and yet only a few of these cases have gone viral on social media and these were of young, Black middle-class women who are viewed as attractive and/or educated. They are positioned as worthy of protection in the same way that some White women were during the colonial period. This is what Boonzaier (2017, p. 476) also found in her analysis:

> Some victims of crime are more readily accorded an 'ideal' victim status, whereas others are considered 'undeserving'. These notions of worthiness are inevitably shaped by racialised, gendered, classed discourses – such that 'idealised depictions of heterosexual, able-bodied, middle-class, attractive white women have become the metaphor for "innocence".'

It should be noted, however, that this protection is only in public discourse and not necessarily in practice on the ground because, in the same way that although White women were "protected" from the Black rapist out there, they remained vulnerable to experiences of rape that involved their husbands and the larger White community. More importantly, these incidents were not prosecuted because of a "narrow, racialized definition of the 'real'" (Black) rapist, leaving White men's (read: any men in a powerful position) power and domination over women's bodies unchallenged. What this illustrates is that women's (whether White or Black) access to respectability does not protect them from sexual violence. Hence the need to pay attention to these power dynamics between diverse groups of womxn.

As the face of the #RhodesWar campaign, Dyantyi was not the only activist engaging actively on social media. Naledi Chirwa, an Economic Freedom Front (EFF) member of parliament and one of the activists who participated in the #RememberKhwezi protest, was actively tweeting and using her platform to galvanize support. As a well-known SGBV activist, she has amassed a large following on Twitter whereby what she tweets about SGBV is taken seriously. Chirwa's history of speaking out against SGBV has carved a space for her to belong to what Serisier (2018, p. 114) calls a "genre of collective narrative authorized through hashtags" in which stories of sexual violence and social injustice are viewed as acceptable and therefore believed. As Serisier explains further, "the politics of 'speaking out' has produced a genre of experiential rape narratives" (2018, p. 44). The existence of this genre encourages and enables stories, providing them with a cultural location that allows them to be heard and understood. It also connects individual speech or writing acts to a collective practice of narrative in a way that can produce political effects (Serisier, 2018, p. 44). A remarkable example is a tweet where she shares a screenshot sent to her by another activist who has been excluded but did not make the news. She states,

> Another Black Womxn who was purged by Rhodes University for being a student activist. For particularly #RUReferenceList. Asked to be anonymous. There's a war at Rhodes against Womxn…Against Black Womxn. We can't keep quiet. {3 broken hearts emojis} #RhodesWar.
>
> *(December 11, 2017)*

In sharing this story, she is contributing to a particular genre that is distinctive of the #RhodesWar hashtag and that is the exclusion or purging of those who dared to protest and speak out against rape. Even though the stories involve sexual violence, the focus is on the silencing mechanism deployed by RU and other institutions of higher education. The #RhodesWar campaign, like all the other feminist hashtag campaigns we have witnessed over the years in South Africa, is different because of who is being targeted. For instance, the hashtag #JusticeforLulu focused on the justice system and its failure to provide justice for all victims, and not just those who are deemed worthy of protection. The collection of personal stories that are shared also pointed to the hypocrisy displayed by the university through their decision in that as highlighted in this tweet, "A rapist (Jason) WHO WAS FOUND GUILTY OF SEXUAL ASSAULT GRADU-ATED AT RHODES. Black Womxn who protested against rape DID NOT GRADUATE. NOR CAN THEY CONTINUE THEIR STUDIES ANY-WHERE ELSE. This is war. RhodesWar" (Dec 11, 2017). Even though the rapist here is named, it is not the rape that is in question but how he managed to graduate while those who protested rape are excluded.

Some also shared their first-hand experience of rape, recounting as much as they could in the 140 characters that were allowed on Twitter at the time. As shown here:

> Raped at Rhodes University 4th of August, 2017.
>   Reported my case and applied for extended Leave of Absence (and had to deregister) bcs I couldnt cope. They said they can only investigate once I reregister as a student in 2018.
>   I'm not going back. Forget it RhodesWar.
> *(December 12, 2017)*

> RhodesWar
>   I was gang raped on Rhodes university campus on April 7th, 2017
>   A whole entire counseling center manager wanted evidence
>   I have given up on the case, I mean, if a rapist gets a 10year ban and activists a life ban, what am I bound to get as a victim???
> *(December 12, 2017)*

What is interesting in these narratives of rape is not just the personal recounting of what happened but how their cases were handled by the respective members of the institution. The stories all point to their vulnerability as victims and the treatment they face as sexual violence survivors at the hands of management. Remarkably, and this might speak to the collective narrative of speaking out with regards to sexual violence in the country, what is at stake here is not whether they were raped or not, but how the institutions fail them as survivors of sexual violence. Serisier argues that feminist anti-rape politics is guided by the belief that "producing and disseminating a genre of personal experiential narratives can end sexual violence" (2018, p. 4). Interestingly, the hashtag #RhodesWar and its collection of stories does indicate that although speaking out has not ended sexual violence yet, it has shifted the discourse to where womxn can share their personal stories without still asking for their experiences of rape to be believed. This is not to argue that narratives of denial and disbelief have completely disappeared, but it is more that the digital activists rely on a recognizable narrative of rape whose parameters have shifted from just sharing stories of "asking to be believed" to also including stories of rape as a "matter of fact."

Conclusion

> I've been fighting for my right to have been given a free and fair trial by the university in 2017. I continue to fight for my right to justice because I refuse to be silenced and to have my story tainted and disregarded because the Vice-chancellor and his colleagues think they have the power to do so (well, they did have the power and I too have my power to fight back).
>
> *(Dyantyi, 2022)*

This quote is taken from a recent essay titled, "Remaining Relentless; Reclaiming my Voice against Violence" penned by Dyantyi in February 2022 and published on the website African Feminism (AF), a pan-African feminist online platform aimed at creating a space for collaborative writing between African authors/writers. Five years on, this essay is one of the avenues used by Dyantyi to engage in various forms of digital labor in an effort to publicize and garner support for her case that was to be heard in the Supreme Court of Appeal on 21 February 2022. As of writing (March, 29 2022), she has won her appeal in the Supreme Court of Appeal and her lifetime expulsion has been overturned (Chabalala, 2022). Through this verdict, Dyantyi's relentless fight against RU has not only vindicated her but has also kept the hashtag #RhodesWar active on the various social media platforms and mainstream media, revealing not only the importance of having a figurehead attached to a hashtag but also that these young feminist activists see the significance of the need to "riot" and "write" at the same time as outlined by Dlakavu et al. This fighting back occurs on social media platforms where activists can control their own stories and, Dyantyi argues, refuse their stories to be "tainted and disregarded" by those in power. This was also evident in Mfocwa's activism on Twitter and her subsequent media interview. Further, their speaking out as a form of "writing" relies on a particular genre of experiential rape narratives that can be prescriptive and yet in the case of the #RhodesWar hashtag, a shift has occurred in the way that the womxn share their stories of rape. Instead of womxn's personal recounting of their rape online as those in need of being believed, the focus here is on talking about their rape as self-evident, with attention directed at the university's silencing tactics. These ideas are based on the knowledge that the past and present reflects a society that doesn't value its womxn, especially Black womxn but it is also understood that Black womxn who "riot" but do not "write" run the risk of being erased out of public discourse or even worse, being rendered visible only through the body, which is what RU has attempted to do by representing the activists as criminal and violent.

Centering the voices of the activists, it became evident that social media affords activists the space to contest the narratives being set out by those in power. More importantly, it allows the telling of diverse stories in mainstream reporting, featuring voices that would have otherwise been excluded because through the sharing of their stories on social media, the activists themselves become easily accessible. These contestations occur in the form of "writing" which has always been the domain of those who are educated or had access to formal jobs and thus highlighting two important elements. Firstly, that activists like Dyantyi, Chirwa and Mfocwa, can "write" and be heard by the wider public because they are tapping into the politics of respectability that are primarily associated with middle-class Whiteness via their access to education. This has resulted in a shift where certain Black womxn are deemed worthy of protection while others such as those in the margins like Anene Booysen are regarded as undeserving of our sympathy. Secondly, it is also at the university – a space that offers them the privilege to speak and be heard (to "write") – that certain parameters as to who can/cannot stay in this space of respectability are enacted by policing and punishing those who are deemed to be engaging in transgressive behavior such as "rioting" i.e. #RUReferencelist and the naked protests of 2016.

Notes

1 Womxn is a term adopted by the university feminist activists who participated in the Fallist movements and is predominately used in feminist hashtags against gender based violence in South Africa. See Mbalenhle Matandela (2017), pp. 11–12.
2 Fallist is a term used to describe the #RhodesMustFall and FeesMustFall movements that took place at South African universities in 2015. See Alude Mahali and Noxolo Matete (2022), p. 132.

References

Allen, M. (2017). *The sage encyclopedia of communication research methods* (Vols. 1–4). Thousand Oaks, CA: SAGE Publications, Inc. http://doi.org/10.4135/9781483381411

Armstrong, S. (1994). Rape in South Africa: An invisible part of apartheid's legacy. *Gender &Development, 2*(2), 35–39. http://doi.org/10.1080/09682869308520009

Boonzaier, F. (2017). The Life and death of Anene Booysen: Colonial discourse, gender-based violence and media representations. *South African Journal of Psychology, 47*(4), 470–481. http://doi.org/10.1177/008124631777916

Britton, H. (2006). Organising against gender violence in South Africa. *Journal of Southern African Studies, 32*(1), 145–163. https://doi.org/10.1080/03057070500493852

Chabalala, J. (2022, March 29). Victory for banned-for-life student Yolanda Dyantyi as SCA refers matter back to Rhodes University. *News24.* https://www.news24.com/news24/southafrica/news/victory-for-banned-for-life-student-yolanda-dyantyi-as-sca-refers-matter-back-to-rhodes-university-20220329

Chengeta, G. (2017, November 3). A recollection of the #RUreferencelist protests. *WordPress.* https://goratachengeta.wordpress.com/2017/11/03/a-recollection-of-the-rureferencelist-protests/

Chiumbu, S. (2016). Media, race and capital: A decolonial analysis of representation of miners' strikes in South Africa. *African Studies, 75*(3), 417–435. https://doi.org/10.108 0/00020184.2016.1193377

Dixon, K. (2014). Feminist online identity: Analyzing the presence of hashtag feminism. *Journal of Arts and Humanities, 3*(7), 34–39.

Dlakavu, S., Ndelu, S., & Matandela, M. (2017). Writing and rioting: Black womxn in the time of fallism. *Agenda, 31*(3–4), 105–109. https://doi.org/10.1080/10130950.201 7.1392163

Dyantyi, Y. (2022, February). Remaining relentless; Reclaiming my voice against violence. *African Feminism*. https://africanfeminism.com/remaining-relentless-reclaiming-my-voice-against-violence/

Etherington, N. (1988). Natal's black rape scare of the 1870s. *Journal of Southern African Studies, 15*(1), 36–53. https://doi.org/10.1080/03057078808708190

Gqola, P. D. (2001). In search of female s/staffriders: Authority, gender and audience, 1978–1982. *Current Writing: Text and Reception in Southern Africa, 13*(2), 31–41. https://doi.org/10.1080/1013929X.2001.9678103

Helman, R. (2018). Mapping the unrapeability of white and black womxn, *Agenda, 32*(4), 10–21. https://doi.org/10.1080/10130950.2018.1533302

Honwana, A. (2019). Youth struggles: From the Arab spring to black lives matter & beyond. *African Studies Review, 62*(1), 18–21.

Maduna, M. (2017, December 12). #RhodesWar: University stands by decision to expel rape activists. *Power98.7*. https://www.power987.co.za/news/rhodeswar-university-stands-by-decision-to-expel-rape-activists/

Mahali, A., & Matete, N. (2022). #MbokodoLeadUs: The gendered politics of black womxn leading campus-based activism in South Africa's recent university student movements. *Journal of Contemporary African Studies 40*(1), 132–146. https://www.tandfonline.com/doi/full/10.1080/02589001.2021.1946490

Maldonado-Torres, N. (2007). On the coloniality of being: Contributions to the development of a concept. *Cultural studies, 21*(2–3), 240–270. https://doi.org/10.1080/09502380601162548

Maluleke, G., & Moyer, E. (2020). "We have to ask for permission to become": Young women's voices, violence, and mediated space in South Africa. *Signs: Journal of Women in Culture and Society, 45*(4), 871–902. https://doi.org/10.1086/707799

Matandela, M. (2017). Redefining black consciousness and resistance: The intersection of black consciousness and black feminist thought. *Agenda, 31*(3–4), 10–28.

Matshili, R. (2017, December 13). #RhodesWar as two students are expelled for life. *IOL*. https://www.iol.co.za/pretoria-news/rhodeswar-as-two-students-are-expelled-for-life-12401839

Mendes, K., Ringrose, J., & Keller, J. (2018). #MeToo and the promise and pitfalls of challenging rape culture through digital feminist activism. *European Journal of Women's Studies, 25*(2), 236–246. https://doi.org/10.1177/1350506818765318

Moffett, H. (2006).'These women, they force us to rape them': Rape as narrative of social control in post-apartheid South Africa. *Journal of Southern African Studies, 32*(1), 129–144. https://doi.org/10.1080/03057070500493845

Motsemme, N. (2004). The mute always speak: On women's silences at the truth and reconciliation commission. *Current Sociology, 52*(5), 909–932. https://doi.org/10.1177/0011392104045377

Nakamura, L. (2015). The unwanted labour of social media: Women of colour call out culture as venture community management. *New Formations, 86*(86), 106–112.

Pather, R., & Smit, S. (2017, December 15). RhodesWar students battle revealed in internal disciplinary documents. *Mail & Guardian*. https://mg.co.za/article/2017-12-14-rhodeswar-students-battle-revealed-in-internal-disciplinary-documents/

Qukula, Q. (2018, August 27). 'My future career has been taken away'- anti-rape activist expelled from Rhodes. *CapeTalk567AM*. https://www.capetalk.co.za/articles/316935/my-future-career-has-been-taken-away-anti-rape-activist-expelled-from-rhodes

Rapp, L., Button, D. M., Fleury-Steiner, B., & Fleury-Steiner, R. (2010). The internet as a tool for black feminist activism: Lessons from an online antirape protest. *Feminist Criminology, 5*(3), 244–262. https://doi.org/10.1177/1557085110371634

Reddy, T. (2006). Higher education and social transformation in South Africa since the fall of apartheid. *Cahiers de la Recherché Sur L'education et les Saviors, 5*, 121–145.

Rhodes University (2017, November 13). *Rhodes exclusions a result of criminality, no student disciplined for protesting* [Press Release]. https://www.ru.ac.za/latestnews/archives/2017/rhodesexclusionsaresultofcriminalitynostudentdisciplinedforprotesting.html

Scully, P. (1995). Rape, race, and colonial culture: The sexual politics of identity in the nineteenth-century Cape Colony, South Africa. *The American Historical Review, 100*(2), 335–359.

Seddon, D. (2016, June 01). 'We will not be silenced': Rape culture, #RUReferencelist, and the university currently known as Rhodes. *Daily Maverick*. https://www.dailymaverick.co.za/opinionista/2016-06-01-we-will-not-be-silenced-rape-culture-rureferencelist-and-the-university-currently-known-as-rhodes/

Serisier, T. (2018). *Speaking out: Feminism, rape and narrative politics*. Springer. https://doi.org/10.1007/978-3-319-98669-2

Solomon, M. (2017, December 16). Why Rhodes' heavy handed action against student activists is misplaced. *City Press*. https://www.news24.com/citypress/voices/why-rhodes-heavy-handed-action-against-student-activists-is-misplaced-20171216

Staff Reporter (2016, April 20). Interdict brought against Rhodes students. *Mail & Guardian*. https://mg.co.za/article/2016-04-20-interdict-brought-against-rhodes-students/

Thornberry, E. (2016). Rape, race, and respectability in a South African port city: East London, 1870–1927. *Journal of Urban History, 42*(5), 863–880. https://doi.org/10.1177/0096144216665307

Thornberry, E. (2019). *Colonizing consent: Rape and governance in South Africa's Eastern Cape* (Vols. 141). Cambridge University Press.

Yang, G. (2016). Narrative agency in hashtag activism: The case of #BlackLivesMatter. *Media and communication, 4*(4), 13–17. https://doi.org/10.17645/mac.v4i4.692

9

RECTIFYING GENDER VIOLENCE WITHIN RELIGIOUS COMMUNITIES THROUGH HASHTAG ACTIVISM

Kristin M. Peterson

Introduction

As the activism work around #MeToo gained momentum in the fall of 2017, smaller subgroups emerged that addressed gender-based violence and sexual harassment in various institutional and cultural spaces. Two prominent movements to address sexual abuse within religious communities coalesced around the hashtags #ChurchToo and #MosqueMeToo. By focusing on abuse within Christian Churches and Islamic holy sites, these Twitter discussions illustrated how religious teachings can be weaponized to justify abuse and shame victims. At the same time, Twitter hashtags can be deployed by marginalized groups to claim power (Clark-Parsons, 2021).

This chapter analyzes a sample of #ChurchToo and #MosqueMeToo Tweets to understand how these textual spaces allow victims to reclaim power away from the perpetrators, specifically through appeals to religious language and teachings. While perpetrators and their enablers may justify religious abuse by referencing scripture and religious teachings, these Tweets often point out the hypocrisies of their justifications and the deep pain caused by appealing to religious language. Having experienced this double-harm of both sexual abuse and the religious justification for the abuse, the victims engage with Twitter hashtags to critically address these hypocrisies, to share the trauma perpetuated by this religious abuse, and to offer support for victims. Through a comparative analysis of these campaigns from Muslims and Christians, I assert that these two hashtag movements allow participants to effectively reverse harmful religious teachings, which protect abusers and blame victims, by instead using religious language to reclaim the value of individuals who have been victimized and shamed.

DOI: 10.4324/9781003260851-12

Hashtag Activism

Both #ChurchToo and #MosqueMeToo are subsets of the larger #MeToo movement, which initially was created by Tarana Burke in 2006 as a supportive community for women of color who had experienced sexual violence. The #MeToo
movement expanded into widespread social discussions in October 2017 when
allegations of sexual abuse against producer Harvey Weinstein became public
and actor Alyssa Milano encouraged women specifically to write #MeToo if
they had experienced sexual harassment and/or assault (Clark-Parsons, 2021).
The movement evolved to sharing more detailed discussions of abuse, calling out
perpetrators, and addressing abuse within specific institutions, such as the media,
the military, and religions.

Hashtag activism has been criticized for promoting endless circulation of content and granting everyone a voice, while little significant political change comes
from increased visibility (Couldry, 2010; Dean, 2009; Fuchs, 2017; Marwick,
2013). However, research centering on marginalized communities often finds
that hashtags provide a significant initial step of claiming power and speaking
back. Rather than empty circulation, Clark-Parsons (2021) asserts, "hashtag
feminism engages in a performative politics of visibility, in which one person's
narrative, when shared and connected with many others, makes power visible so
that it might be deconstructed and challenged" (p. 369). There is significance in
connecting individual stories of abuse with a larger collective struggle to address
systemic forms of oppression.

Similarly, Jackson et al. (2020) see #MeToo as a space of "solidarity and an
insistence that stories about the personal are systemic and political" (p. 26). Twitter hashtags can be a space of support where those on the margins are able to have
their experiences and perspectives valued. Specifically, the authors assert that
marginalized groups develop counterpublics and use Twitter to speak against the
dominant public and "to push the mainstream public sphere on issues of social
progress in ways more powerful and visible than possibly ever before" (p. xxvii).
Marginalized voices may not be heard in mainstream media spaces, but hashtags
bring forward these perspectives within supportive communities and advocate
for progressive change (p. xxviii). Hashtags can be a space to counteract dominant stereotypes and reclaim narratives. For example, Masullo Chen et al. (2018)
examine how Donald Trump's use of the term "nasty woman" in a debate with
Hillary Clinton was taken up by women on Twitter in order to assert political
power by changing the negative meaning of that term and focusing on disman-
tling the patriarchy.

The networks on Twitter also allowed women to "challenge patriarchal ideas,
bolstered by the intimate publics that form through the site" (Masullo Chen
et al., 2018, p. 379). The intimate connections of Twitter hashtags may curate
supportive spaces for victims of gender-based violence. The #MeToo movement
specifically addresses traumatic experiences, and the highly emotional nature

of these stories can potentially enable others to feel themselves into these affective experiences (Papacharissi, 2015). Therefore, Suk et al. (2021) assert that #MeToo "enabled a network of acknowledgment, where people found a space to provide public testimony about their trauma, share experiences, and receive acknowledgment" (p. 15). Particularly for victims who have experienced shame or gaslighting in response to their trauma, the community around a hashtag can acknowledge the significance of this trauma and offer empathetic support.

#ChurchToo and #MosqueMeToo

In the midst of online conversations around #MeToo in the fall and winter of 2017–2018, smaller discussions sprang up around gender-based violence and sexual harassment in niche communities. #ChurchToo emerged in November 2017 when Emily Joy Allison shared her story on Twitter of being groomed at age 16 by an adult youth pastor into starting an unhealthy and abusive relationship (Allison, 2017). Sensing that this story had struck a chord with others who had been raised in Evangelical Christian communities, Allison and her friend, Hannah Paasch, created the #ChurchToo hashtag to share stories of abuse, misogyny, and homophobia in Christian churches (Colwell & Johnson, 2020; Paasch, 2017; River, 2017). As Allison told me about #ChurchToo and other Twitter activist projects, there is power in saying "me too" and connecting over a "really niche experience that other people don't understand" (E. J. Allison, personal communication, October 26, 2019).

The "specificity" of the #ChurchToo hashtag provided an opportunity "for the subset of survivors who experienced sexual victimization in a religious context to connect and be heard" (Bogen et al., 2020, p. 20). For young people raised in these niche Evangelical communities, Herrmann (2021) explains that #ChurchToo "provides hope, counseling, a reckoning, and most importantly a voice to the women and men who have been sexually, physically, and psychologically abused in fundamental evangelical circles" (p. 423). In addition to offering support for victims, the hashtag campaign created an environment in which victims felt encouragement to name perpetrators of abuse, either through the #ChurchToo hashtag, blogs, or news articles. In the months after #ChurchToo was launched, numerous stories were shared online and several religious leaders have been forced to resign over allegations of sexual misconduct (Bruinius, 2018). For instance, Bill Hybels stepped down as pastor of Willow Creek Community Church, the suburban Illinois megachurch that he co-founded, after several allegations of inappropriate sexual behavior with female church members and employees (Pashman & Coen, 2018). In this case, victims shared stories through online blogs (Dyer, 2018) and news articles (Goodstein, 2018), which were then circulated and amplified through the #ChurchToo hashtag. In another prominent case, Andy Savage, the pastor of a megachurch in Memphis, Tennessee, stood in front of his congregation and admitted to having an inappropriate sexual relationship with a 17-year-old girl when he was 22. The congregation gave him a standing ovation, and he remained in his position. In response to a video of the apology, the victim shared her story of sexual assault through a blog (Smith, 2018) and an online video (Woodson, 2018). #ChurchToo supporters spread the victim's story of abuse through Twitter, eventually leading to Savage's resignation from his post (Johnson, 2018).

#ChurchToo Tweets reflect an institutional culture that often excuses abuse and harassment by blaming female victims while at the same time forgiving male leaders who confess to their indiscretions. As Wilder (2019) explains, the repentant perpetrators are "immediately forgiven without any systemic reflection on what kind of religious structure sets up abusers to cause harm again and again" (p. 159). A significant aspect of this culture of abuse is the prominence of purity teachings, which promote sexual abstinence until one is in a heterosexual marriage. Significantly, the pressure to maintain this purity often falls on the women, and men are more easily forgiven when they are "tempted" by women who fail to meet the purity standards. This purity culture has been criticized for promoting feelings of shame around normal sexual desires, placing blame on women for any sexual indiscretion, and devaluing those who fall outside of the narrow purity norms—namely Black women and queer individuals (Emba, 2018; Graham 2016; Klein 2018; Stankorb, 2019; Valenti, 2009). Following her experience in co-launching the #ChurchToo movement, Allison (2021) wrote a book that addresses how the stories of abuse documented in #ChurchToo are the consequence of an institutional culture of misogyny, homophobia, and racism. In addition, other young people raised in Evangelical churches have launched projects like the Exvangelical movement (Chastain, 2021; Onishi, 2019) and the Empty the Pews (Marz, 2020) project both to address the problematic aspects of Evangelical institutions and to offer support to those leaving Evangelical Christianity.

Alongside these efforts to publicly shame and remove abusive Christian leaders is a tamer project centered on the #SilenceIsNotSpiritual statement that was released in December 2017, which called on church organizations and leaders to take more tangible actions to stop gender-based violence. Signed by several thousand people, the statement said,

> We call our pastors, our elders, and our parishioners who have been silent to speak up and stand up for all who experience abuse. There is no institution with greater capacity to create protected spaces for healing and restoration for survivors, as well as confession, repentance and rehabilitation for perpetrators.
>
> *(Quoted in Shellnutt, 2017)*

This statement was an effort to get church leaders to stop ignoring and silencing women when they come forward with stories of sexual abuse, harassment, or domestic violence. Not only are pastors often unaware of how to give pastoral care to women dealing with gender-based violence, but they also may push women to stay in violent relationships out of a belief that wives must obey their husbands (Griswold, 2018).

Within Islam, related but distinct projects have also arisen to tackle misogyny and gender-based violence. Inspired by the story of a young Pakistani woman named Sabica Khan who was sexually harassed during the hajj to Mecca, the feminist activist Mona Eltahawy shared her own experiences of sexual assault while on the hajj and launched #MosqueMeToo in February 2018 (Amidi, 2018; Barron, 2018; Kaur, 2018). The online discussion around this hashtag allowed other Muslims to share experiences of being assaulted or harassed in Islamic holy sites. Eltahawy (2018b) explains in an article the deep shame and conflicted feelings of being groped while on pilgrimage: "That such a violation was happening to me as we performed the fifth pillar of our religion at Islam's holiest site traumatized and shamed me, even though I had obviously done nothing to be ashamed of" (para. 4).

Eltahawy's experiences illustrate similar trends within Islam and Christianity, as religious teachings are used to hide the sinful actions of men in power while at the same time making women and girls feel responsible for these terrible acts. Muslim women may feel a sense of betrayal for experiencing abuse during their pilgrimage along with a deep shame. As Boles (2019) explains, the female victims "felt that because this was a place where such things are not supposed to happen, the harassment or assault they experienced must have been their fault" (p. 80). Similar to how #ChurchToo provides support and a space to counteract Evangelical cultures of abuse and shame, #MosqueMeToo allows victims to celebrate rather than shame their sexualities. "MosqueMeToo's mission is to teach women that they do not have to be ashamed of their bodies nor their voices" (Boles, 2019, p. 80).

The #MosqueMeToo hashtag not only addresses particular issues within Islam but also connects them to wider issues of misogyny and gender-based violence. Like #ChurchToo, the #MeToo movement within Islam also brought to light sexual misdeeds of prominent leaders. Before the emergence of #MeToo, Nouman Ali Khan, a popular preacher among young Muslims, was accused of sending inappropriate text messages to persuade young women into having sexual relationships. The allegations against Khan were shared in a Facebook post and circulated on social media in September 2017 (Allam, 2017). In the midst of the #MeToo movement in October 2017, another prominent Islamic intellectual Tariq Ramadan was accused of rape in a Facebook post written by the female victim (Chrisafis, 2017), and other allegations were shared on Twitter through #MeToo and the French language version, #balancetonporc (*denounce your pig*). These cases opened up online conversations about how popular Muslim leaders often misuse the trust of their followers and harm the wider Muslim community by their actions (Baig, 2017). Along with this work to address the abuse of power from prominent Muslim leaders, more organizations and resources have emerged to address sexual abuse within Muslim communities. For example, the prominent Canadian Muslim scholar Ingrid Mattson founded the Hurma Project to provide resources to end violence and abuse in Islamic spaces. Facing Abuse in Community Environments (FACE) was created to share resources and take direct action against religious leaders who are abusing their power. There is no institutional structure in American Islam for reporting misconduct, but FACE provides an online form where people can report abuse or financial misconduct by Muslim leaders or organizations. Just as Allison and others in the #ChurchToo movement use the collective power of social media and digital tools, organizations like FACE work collaboratively to bring to light abuses in Muslim communities and hold these leaders accountable for their actions.

Methods

In order to study how Twitter hashtags can be a space of community for victims of religious abuse, I focused on the initial Tweets that spread around both #ChurchToo and #MosqueMeToo. For both hashtags, I selected every third Tweet until I reached 150 Tweets for each hashtag and 300 in total. I did not collect Tweets that were simply sharing a news article about the hashtag trend. I examined Tweets from #ChurchToo, starting on November 21, 2017, and finishing on November 22, 2017. For #MosqueMeToo, I began selecting Tweets on February 6, 2018, when the hashtag launched. It took a few more days for the hashtag to take off, so I collected Tweets until February 9, 2018. Notably, #MosqueMeToo quickly attracted trolling and critical responses both from those writing against Islam and from male Muslims defending Islam. Some of the Tweets expressed anti-Islam racism and misogyny.

In analyzing the content of these Tweets, I used a grounded theory approach, rooted in feminist methodology, to build on the themes that emerged in the hashtag discussions. Rather than approach these Twitter discussions with preconceptions, grounded theory allows the concepts and theories within the data to rise to the surface (Glaser & Strauss, 1967). In addition, by bringing together grounded theory and feminist methodology, researchers are able "to privilege our respondents' voices and modify received theory when it cannot fully account for new empirical discoveries" (Avishai et al., 2013, pp. 418–419). When examining a topic like gender violence and harassment, it is relevant to center on the voices of those who have been victimized and silenced.

At the same time, I am cognizant of the ethical concerns when studying a space like Twitter discussions, in which people contribute their voices to a wider public discussion but do not necessarily intend for these comments to be circulated widely or analyzed in an academic context. I follow the Association of Internet Researchers' ethical guidelines in considering the vulnerability of the participants and their expectations of privacy when they post to digital spaces (Markham & Buchanan, 2012, p. 6). Excluding the Tweets by the founders of this movement (Allison, Paasch, & Eltahawy), all of the Tweets in this chapter have been amended to protect the privacy of the posters. I slightly changed the wording and do not include the user names.[1] Since these posters are sharing traumatic experiences of assault, abuse, and emotional harm, it is important to bring an ethics of care and compassion to this research.

Findings

First, I will present the initial findings of the themes that emerged in these Twitter discussions, and then, the following sections will analyze how these Tweets address the institutional abuse in religious spaces while providing support for other victims. Of the 300 Tweets that were analyzed (150 for #ChurchToo and 150 for #MosqueMeToo), three main thematic categories emerged: expressing anger at the hypocrisies of religious spaces that enable abuse (42%), sharing personal stories of religious abuse (23%), and expressing solidarity and support for victims (20%). The data also included a small number of Tweets that were naming specific perpetrators of abuse, as well as a few trolling Tweets and criticisms from outside the movement.

Several relevant differences were found between the #ChurchToo and #MosqueMeToo posts. #ChurchToo posts were almost all in English, but #MosqueMeToo posts were written in a variety of languages (Persian, Arabic, French, Spanish, Indonesian, German, Swedish, Finnish, and Turkish), which I used the imbedded tool on Twitter to translate. While #ChurchToo Tweets addressed various types of sexual abuse, harassment, and domestic violence, the #MosqueMeToo discussion focused on stories of assault in religious sites, namely while on hajj. There were more than twice the number of stories of gender-based violence from Christian participants than the Muslim contributors, who focused more on addressing the hypocrisies in religious institutions and offering support for victims.

The Christian Tweets named specific perpetrators in a few of the posts, but none of these were high-profile Christian leaders. Some of the posts linked to Twitter profiles of abusers, who have since closed their accounts, or they made references to people at particular churches, so the details cannot be confirmed. Among the #MosqueMeToo posts, the Swiss Muslim academic Tariq Ramadan was mentioned a couple times because of his allegations and later convictions for sexual assault. The early posts under #MosqueMeToo featured personal stories of abuse and harassment, but the hashtag quickly coalesced around critiques, statements of support, and circulating news articles. #ChurchToo was able to maintain an internal discussion centered on sharing stories and offering support, whereas #MosqueMeToo attracted highly critical comments, misogynistic attacks on Eltahawy and other women, and racist posts against Islam. These distinctions might be reflective of the pressure on Muslim women who, Eltahawy (2018b) explains, are often trapped between a "rock and a hard place." Muslim women are often portrayed by Western media as victims of violent, irrational Muslim men, but when Muslim women address abuse and misogyny in Islam, they are silenced so as not to paint this already maligned religion in a negative light. While some Muslim women face backlash for speaking out, it is impossible to know how many women are afraid to voice these concerns in a public forum like Twitter. Additionally, the Tweets from women about sexual abuse and harassment can also be used by Islamophobes to justify arguments about the inferior nature of Islam.

Discussion

Sharing Stories of Abuse

Along the same lines as #MeToo, the primary purpose of the #ChurchToo and #MosqueMeToo hashtags is to share personal stories of abuse—stories that are often silenced by those in power. In the case of religious abuse and spiritual trauma, the Tweets often address the deep pain of being abused in religious spaces that are meant to provide people comfort and meaning. Some of the stories also share the compounding harm caused when religious leaders blame victims for their abuse and absolve perpetrators. Of the total Tweets analyzed, 23% were primarily sharing personal stories of abuse and harassment that intersected in some way with religious institutions. Under the #ChurchToo hashtag, countless stories were shared about religious abuse by figures in churches, such as church camp counselors, youth group leaders, pastors, and fellow church members. The abuse ranged from sending explicit emails and uncomfortable touches from youth ministers to sexual assault and groping.

Several of the participants shared stories of being young and not knowing how to address sexual harassment from older church leaders. For instance, one participant wrote, "I was around 9 or 10 when the respected deacon would always greet me with a kiss on the lips and called me 'baby'." Another writer shared a similar story of having to learn as a teenager to avoid an older greeter at church who would hug and grope women. One person posted, "A middle age man would chase girls in the youth group around church and would hug, flirt and tease them to see their discomfort." Other people shared stories of inappropriate activities in youth groups, like being forced to hug or kiss each other.

Outside of the abuse by members of the church, other participants discussed how when they experienced gender-based violence outside of church (such as domestic violence or sexual assault), the church leaders provided little support and often made the problem worse. Some people discussed how the church leaders supported the perpetrators (often husbands and fathers) over the victims. One person wrote, "When I was in middle school, I told my pastor that I was being physically and sexually abused at home. I wanted his help, but instead he trusted my parents and did not report my story." Another individual shared that because the church leaders thought their father was a "good guy," no one at church suspected abuse. Other people explained that youth pastors are often not trained in how to respond to stories of abuse. When one person reported her experiences of sexual assault as a pre-teen and teenager to a youth minister, the minister spoke of the need for the victim to repent, but the minister never reported the incident.

These stories of abuse in the church and retraumatizing language around sexual violence are further reflected by misogynistic and abusive language within church communities. People wrote about experiences that might seem harmless but indicate a larger culture of abuse, such as church leaders making jokes about domestic violence and hyper-sexualizing women's bodies. One woman wrote about how when she was 17, the youth pastor's wife wrote her a letter, telling the young woman to dress more modestly to not cause the pastor to sin. Another individual posted about a misogynistic joke that compared women to dogs. Not only are women and girls made uncomfortable in church settings with unwelcome touches and offensive language about their bodies, but if they experience sexual assault and harassment, these Tweets illustrate how the church can further victimize them by siding with the perpetrator and blaming the victims.

While #ChurchToo Tweets address various ways that the culture of abuse and misogyny has infiltrated Christian church communities, the #MosqueMeToo discussion centers around, as Eltahawy (2018a) writes in one of her first Tweets, the "experience of sexual harassment/abuse during Hajj/Umra or in sacred spaces." Many people discuss related stories of being verbally harassed or physically assaulted while in the crowded spaces of the pilgrimage in Saudi Arabia— either the annual hajj or the lesser umrah. In a variety of languages, women post related stories of being groped in the chest, slapped in the butt, or having a penis press up against them. For instance, participants tweeted, "I was shoved around, felt up, groped, but must remain quiet since this was a 'holy space'" and "While on umrah with my family, I was inappropriately touched twice while circling the Kabah and groped while waiting to kiss the black stone." Some people discussed how they thought the touching was accidental since people are crowded together or that this was a rare experience. After sharing stories with other women, they expressed a realization that these experiences are unfortunately common among a larger group of women.

The women also discussed being sexually harassed while on pilgrimage. One person tweeted, "I observed Saudi police forcefully pushing women around while on umrah. The aggression was greater for women not from the Gulf and Arab countries. This is racism and misogyny. I also saw sexual harassment of women." Another person discussed how she noticed a woman in their pilgrimage group who started to wear the niqab face veil because she was tired of being harassed and followed by men if she was only wearing the hijab.

Along with sharing personal stories of abuse in religious settings, a small number (eight total) of the #ChurchToo Tweets either encouraged people to name and shame perpetrators of sexual violence or included specific names of abusers. These Tweets often exhibit rage and seek retribution for traumatic abuse. One person encouraged, "don't be afraid of naming names to get these monsters out of church leadership. We need to bring this darkness into the light if we seek to move forward and heal." Another poster called on victims to share the names of pastors, parents, teachers, and all of those "who did not believe us when we shared our stories." One person even used the language of religious rituals to call for retribution: "Proclaim their names. Hold them responsible. Empty the pews. Lord, have mercy; Christ, have mercy. This is our form of worship and liturgy." This author engages with religious language to call for divine justice on behalf of those who have been abused in religious settings. While these Tweets primarily share personal stories of abuse and misogynistic language, the Tweets in the next section address how misogyny and patriarchal interpretations of religion promote an abusive culture in Islam and Christianity.

Hypocrisies of Religious Institutions

As offshoots of the #MeToo movement, #ChurchToo and #MosqueMeToo provide important spaces for victims to call out the sexual abuse that they experienced and to hold those in power to account for perpetrating and condoning this abuse. Through analyzing these two Twitter conversations, a distinction emerged in how these Tweets addressed the religious layer of this abuse. The largest percentage (42%) of these Tweets expressed disgust, anger, and sadness that this abuse happened within religious institutions and that religious teachings were used to justify misogyny and racism. These participants often point to the hypocrisies of religious figures employing religious teachings and scripture to excuse abuse and harassment. In a study of #ChurchToo Tweets, Bogen et al. (2020) found that discussions of "institutional harm" were common, as participants mentioned elements like "male privilege, the power of church leadership, and the use of hierarchy and status to intimidate critics within the church" (p. 10). The power of the religious institutions enables leaders to cover up and downplay abuse, while shifting the blame from perpetrators to victims. The following series of Tweets demonstrates how participants refute the harmful religious teachings about sexuality and gender norms. In turn, these participants are able to both provide an incisive critique of the hypocrisies of religious institutions and reclaim the value of their lives.

Some of the participants in the #ChurchToo discussion engage with religious language that was often used to denigrate women in order to celebrate and support the victims who are sharing their stories. Paasch, one of the creators of the #ChurchToo tag, posted a Bible passage: "'Shout it aloud, do not hold back. Raise your voice like a trumpet. Declare to my people their rebellion and to the descendants of Jacob their sins.' Isaiah 58:1 As @emilyjoypoetry puts it, a day of reckoning is coming for the church, as it is with Washington & Hollywood" (River, 2017). In this Tweet, Paasch deploys biblical language—often used to condemn those who stray from the straight path of purity culture—in order to encourage victims to share their stories and call on perpetrators to account for their sins. Another participant refused the biblical language that is often used to position women as submissive victims: "I will no longer be your forgiving and sweet and passive Jesus. I bring fire and war, burn it down." Twitter becomes a space not only to share stories but for a reckoning that will bring perpetrators to justice and comfort the victims.

Several of the Tweets addressed the deep roots of misogyny and abuse in religious teachings, especially around sexual purity and modesty. Among Evangelical Christians, women are portrayed as both pure virgins in need of protection and sexual temptresses, causing men to sin. A woman's definition as virgin or temptress is irrelevant because female victims of abuse are often to blame no matter how modest they appear and behave. One person referenced the biblical story of Adam and Eve as they wrote, "Women are set up for abuse when the church teaches that women brought sin into the world and that women must submit to men." Other participants wrote about how religious institutions often push forward these misogynistic teachings that women are inferior and inherently sinful, while religious leaders downplay how abuse might be a consequence of these teachings. For instance, one person stated, "To those who want to simply call out the abusers but ignore the larger theology and culture that perpetuates that abuse: no, you can't do that." Another writer pointed to the connections between #ChurchToo and patriarchal terms for God: "When you deify masculinity, this produces an atmosphere where abusive and predatory behavior among men can hide and women's concerns are silenced." Evangelical Christian men are raised in a culture that provides religious justification for abusing women. In the #MosqueMeToo conversation, a participant discussed a similar concern about how Muslim men are taught that women's bodies are there for their own pleasure: "Sexual assault and groping of women is horrible. Men's feelings that they are entitled and possess women's bodies is the cause." All of these Tweets point to the hypocrisy of using religious teachings, which are intended to promote justice and equality for all people, to justify abusive behavior toward women and other marginalized individuals.

Within the #MosqueMeToo discussion, participants often addressed how religious directives for modest dress and behavior among men and women are often used to police the way that women appear and behave in public, but are rarely sufficient to protect women from assault and harassment. The Tweets often discuss this regular hypocrisy: No matter what a woman wears, she still faces misogynistic attacks in daily life, and the woman is often framed as the cause of these attacks. A participant stated, "#MosqueMeToo is a clear example of the intentional delusion of people who blame women and their clothing for sexual assault and harassment." Other people shared similar ideas that what a woman wears or doesn't wear is not an excuse for being assaulted and harassed. Another person tweeted, "It was good to see Muslim women realize that an apparent sacred piece of fabric on their heads does not provide protection against physical abuse, even during the hajj." While the headscarf may be presented as a way to protect women's modesty, it offers little coverage from the larger misogynistic culture that frames women as objects of male sexual desire.

Furthermore, the Tweets from Muslims address the blatant hypocrisy of Muslim men harassing and assaulting women in holy spaces. A lot of these Tweets engage with humor and sarcasm to call out this duplicitous behavior. For instance, one person wrote, "If you can't hold back your sin even in this holy place, you are pathetic. And all women are covered so there's no BS about dressing appropriately. What is your excuse?" Another participant discussed, "men who have one hand on their heart and eyes raised up to pray" while they have their other hand "on the buttocks of women." Other people expressed shock, anger, and sadness when they hear about stories of sexual assault in Mecca, a space that is meant to be, as one person wrote, "the safest, holiest place on Earth."

Another repeated theme in these Tweets is the hypocrisy of blaming women for sexual abuse and harassment while dismissing men's sexual sins as insignificant. One person explained, "Have girls and women ever been valued, protected, or heard in the church? I know many women who were sexually assaulted or harassed and then forced to confess and repent for their impurity." Another person discussed being called "damaged" after being raped by a pastor who was later charged with sexually abusing an underage boy. Another participant shared that in a meeting with a youth pastor, she was told that she was dirty for kissing a boy at church, but the boy was told to avoid such temptresses. The message behind these stories is that women are sinful temptresses who threaten male holiness. As one participant tweeted, "The dehumanizing and revolting message that is communicated to victims is that these terrible crimes of clergy abuse are not nearly as significant as protecting the careers and honorable reputations of the beloved church leaders." These Tweets reflected the dichotomous experiences of male perpetrators and female victims. If men confess to sexual indiscretion, one participant on Twitter wrote, they are "praised for their bravery and holiness." Another person shared that the perpetrators are often "protected while the victims are left in an exposed, perilous, and traumatized position."

While the conversations in #ChurchToo focus on the hypocrisy of protecting male abusers, the discussions in #MosqueMeToo address how shedding light on abusive cultures is often seen as a threat to the entire religion. One person explained the pressure to not speak poorly about Islam, "Like all women, Muslim women face harassment but when it happens in the context of religion they are told to remain silent for a larger cause." Other writers expressed that revealing this abuse does not harm the religion but actually can help the religion by rooting out this misogyny and violence. For example, one person explained, "This reveals a rotten culture, and good Muslims need to address this issue and redeem this beautiful image. Silence is worse than what Twitter is able to do." Another person responded to the argument that #MosqueMeToo is meant to "smear Islam" with the rhetorical question, "How would the act of denouncing sexual assault be anti-Islam?" These writers argue that revealing that abuse and harassment take place at Islamic holy sites is not meant to harm Islam but is a way to rescue the faith from the perpetrators who cause harm.

Support, Solidarity, and Healing

Another large portion (20%) of the Tweets under #ChurchToo and #MosqueMeToo express solidarity and support for the victims. These positive affirmations signal a path forward for victims by using collaborative networks like Twitter as a beginning step toward healing. Paasch explained the strength that can come from sharing these experiences on Twitter:

> What I do believe is that there is power in numbers. A cord of three strands is not easily broken. In exposing the harm and abuse covered up by the church, I hope that the devout, the secular & those of us who exist in these liminal ex-vangelical spaces can all find healing. In keeping with the good traditions I was raised with, I am here to bear your burdens. Not to take them or carry them, but to hold space for them.
>
> *(River, 2017)*

The collective nature of the hashtag can be a powerful space not only to take down those in power but also to support each other and create a space to hold these traumatic experiences.

Many of the Tweets shared under both #ChurchToo and #MosqueMeToo expressed similar sentiments, such as "I stand with you," "I believe you," "We share your pain," or "Let's heal together." The language in the Tweets exhibited deep emotions of empathy with phrases like "breaks my heart," "heavy heart," "crushing," "painful stories," "stirs my heart," "I'm in tears," and "I've got chills." People who have not personally experienced religious abuse offered their support for others, often by proclaiming that victims are brave and strong. One person wrote under #ChurchToo, "you are very brave for sharing your story. And if you cannot share your story or don't want to, you are also brave. It takes unbelievable strength to live through this." Another poster shared that victims should not feel shame,

> It wasn't your fault if you were abused. You are worthy of respect and have freedom over your own body. You can tell your own stories, form your own opinions and make your own choices. Do not be ashamed of who you are.

Similar expression of praise and support appear under #MosqueMeToo, such as "I'm impressed by Muslim women who have the courage to assemble around #MoqueMeToo," "I am proud of Muslim women who explicitly break the silence and courageously discuss sexual harassment during the Hajj," and "Expressing solidarity with my Muslim sisters who are posting under #MosqueMeToo. Their voices are significant and they must be heard." These individuals may not have experienced harassment and abuse in Islamic spaces, but they engage with the hashtag conversations to show solidarity with fellow Muslim women who are brave to share these experiences. While victims of abuse are often shamed and retraumatized in religious spaces, these Twitter discussions provide a supportive community to reinforce that these victims should not feel ashamed since they have profound and immutable value.

Trolling and Defensive Critiques

One final category of Tweets that had some prominence is the trend of either trolling comments on #MosqueMeToo that express anti-Islam critiques from outside the religion or defensive critiques, mainly about Islam, from those within the religion. Of the total 300 Tweets, 8.3% were these trolling or critical Tweets and notably all but one (i.e., 24 out of 25) fell under #MosqueMeToo, meaning that 16% of the #MosqueMeToo Tweets were trolling or critical. As I mentioned before, #ChurchToo in the first two days maintained much more of an internal discussion among victims and those who support them. The one defensive Tweet under #ChurchToo encouraged people not to let this tag, "keep you from God's people." Among Muslim commentators, some criticized #MosqueMeToo for putting the whole religion of Islam in a bad light. One person stated that they support the victims but that "the media is using this platform to give all Muslim men a bad name. There are some idiots who do these things and they should be dealt with appropriately." Another person called the Tweets propaganda against Islam, and one person wrote that the hashtag is a new form of Islamophobia.

Other people acknowledge that there might be problems in Islam, but they do not see Twitter as a space to air this dirty laundry or to address these issues. One individual criticized the movement for "westernizing Islam" by engaging with social media rather than report these incidents of abuse to Islamic authorities. Another person posted, "The #MosqueMeToo discussion violates Islam and projects a negative image of our beautiful religion. How do you think Twitter will help?" These comments position hashtags as Western tools that are not particularly effective at solving these problems in Islam. One writer interrogated the victims by asking for proof of these allegations of assault, and another person dismissed these claims as insignificant because of the crowding and close body contact that inevitably occurs on the hajj. Finally, one poster argued, "The religion is not responsible for this, but this depends on a person's morals and ethics. If you really want to disparage a religion for sexual abuse, then disparage Christianity since incidents of rape are highest in Christian countries." This small section of the Tweets defended Islam against critiques that the religion has been corrupted by misogynist men. These defensive Tweets often used the claim of a few bad apples that are responsible instead of addressing systemic abuse. Along with the Tweets from Muslims, defending the religion, a few other Tweets under #MosqueMeToo repeated blatant anti-Islam rhetoric, reinforcing stereotypes of Islam and Muslims as backward, primitive, irrational, and violent.

Conclusion

Through an examination of the #ChurchToo and #MosqueMeToo conversations that emerged in November 2017 and February 2018, respectively, we can observe how these discussions around gender-based violence in religious spaces are distinct from the general #MeToo movement in several ways. While these two hashtags were started to share stories of abuse and give voice to the victims, in the same manner as #MeToo, the Tweets address the particular trauma of religious abuse. Participants discuss the ways that their pain was compounded when leaders used religious language and scripture to justify the abuse. Twitter provides a space for victims not only to share their stories and to call out their abusers, but also to point to the hypocrisies of religious leaders who protect perpetrators and shame victims. After years of being silenced and forced to deal with abuse and unwanted touches, these victims engage with Twitter to reverse the harmful religious teachings used to justify abuse, to shame the perpetrators and those who enable the abuse, and to cultivate supportive spaces to celebrate the inherent value of victims.

In some cases, the Twitter hashtags provided a site for victims to share stories of abuse and to name specific perpetrators, which hopefully would lead to these abusers being removed from leadership positions in religious communities or even facing legal consequences for their abuse. At the same time, the larger conversations around #MeToo, #ChurchToo, and #MosqueMeToo developed an environment where victims were less afraid to share their stories, whether this be through Twitter and other social media platforms, blogs, news articles, or even by telling those in positions of religious authority. Twitter was not the only site where these stories were being shared, but it was a space that employed collective strength to shift the conversation and reinforce that these cultures of abuse need to be brought to light and reformed.

Note

1 By slightly changing the wording of the Tweets, this makes it difficult to search for the original phrasing in the Tweet and reveal the identity of the user. Because of the sophisticated searching programs on social media platforms like Twitter, it is not sufficient to protect a user's identity by not sharing their user name.

References

Allam, H. (2017, December 21). Payoffs, threats, and secret marriages: How an accused preacher is fighting to save his empire. *BuzzFeed News*. https://www.buzzfeednews.com/article/hannahallam/payoffs-threats-and-sham-marriages-women-say-a-celebrity

Allison, E. J. [@emilyjoypoetry] (2017, November 20). *Hey so. This is me being brave.* [Tweet]. Twitter. https://twitter.com/emilyjoypoetry/status/932789409551929345

Allison, E. J. (2021). *#ChurchToo: How purity culture upholds abuse and how to find healing.* Broadleaf Books.

Amidi, F. (2018, February 9). 100 women: Muslim women rally round #MosqueMeToo. *BBC*. https://www.bbc.com/news/world-43006952

Avishai, O., Gerber, L., & Randles, J. (2013, August). The feminist ethnographer's dilemma: Reconciling progressive research agendas with fieldwork realities. *Journal of Contemporary Ethnography, 42*(4), 394–426. https://doi.org/10.1177/0891241612458955

Baig, J. (2017, December 21). The perils of #MeToo as a Muslim. *Atlantic*. https://www.theatlantic.com/international/archive/2017/12/tariq-ramadan-metoo/548642/

Barron, L. (2018, March 7). "A revolutionary moment." Activist Mona Eltahawy talks sexual assault, self-defense and #MosqueMeToo. *Time*. https://time.com/5170236/mona-eltahawy-mosquemetoo/

Bogen, K. W., Haikalis, M., Meza Lopez, R. J., López, G., & Orchowski, L. M. (2020). It happens in #ChurchToo: Twitter discourse regarding sexual victimization within religious communities. *Journal of Interpersonal Violence, 37*(3–4), 1–29. https://doi.org/10.1177/0886260520922365

Boles, K. (2019). On #MosqueMeToo: Lessons for nuancing and better implementing the goals of #MeToo. In R. Graybill, M. Minister, & B. Lawrence (Eds.), *Rape culture and religious studies: Critical and pedagogical engagements* (pp. 73–92). Lexington Books.

Bruinius, H. (2018, April 20). Churches struggle with their #MeToo moment. *Christian Science Monitor*. https://www.csmonitor.com/USA/Politics/2018/0420/Churches-struggle-with-their-MeToo-moment.

Chastain, B. (2021). *#Exvangelical podcast*. https://www.exvangelicalpodcast.com/

Chrisafis, A. (2017, October 22). Feminist campaigner accuses Oxford professor of rape. *Guardian*. https://www.theguardian.com/world/2017/oct/22/feminist-campaigner-accuses-oxford-professor-tariq-ramadan

Clark-Parsons, R. (2021). "I see you, I believe you, I stand with you": #MeToo and the performance of networked feminist visibility. *Feminist Media Studies, 21*(3), 362–380. https://doi.org/10.1080/14680777.2019.1628797

Colwell, K., & Johnson, S. (2020). #MeToo and #ChurchToo: Putting the movements in context. *Review & Expositor, 117*(2), 183–198. https://doi.org/10.1177/0034637320924053

Couldry, N. (2010). *Why voice matters: Culture and politics after neoliberalism*. SAGE.

Dean, J. (2009). *Democracy and other neoliberal fantasies: Communicative capitalism and left politics*. Duke University Press.

Dyer, V. (2018, April 8). Vonda Dyer's statement re: Chicago Tribune and Bill Hybels. *VondalDyer.com*. https://vondadyer.weebly.com/blog/vonda-dyers-statement-re-chicago-tribune-and-bill-hybels

Eltahawy, M. [@monaeltahawy] (2018a, Feburary 5). *I have shared my experience of being sexually assaulted during Haj in 1982*. [Tweet] Twitter. https://twitter.com/monaeltahawy/status/960701491328712706

Eltahawy, M. (2018b, February 15). #MosqueMeToo: What happened when I was sexually assaulted during the Hajj. *Washington Post*. https://www.washingtonpost.com/news/global-opinions/wp/2018/02/15/mosquemetoo-what-happened-when-i-was-sexually-assaulted-during-the-hajj/

Emba, C. (2018, November 14). The dramatic implosion of 'I kissed dating goodbye' is a lesson—and a warning. *Washington Post*. https://www.washingtonpost.com/opinions/the-dramatic-implosion-of-i-kissed-dating-goodbye-is-a-lesson--and-a-warning/2018/11/14/eeecd65c-e850-11e8-bbdb-72fdbf9d4fed_story.html.

Fuchs, C. (2017). *Social media: A critical introduction* (2nd ed.). SAGE.

Glaser, B. G., & Strauss, A. L. (1967). *The discovery of grounded theory: Strategies for qualitative research*. Aldine.

Goodstein, L. (2018, August 5). He's a superstar pastor. She worked for him and says he groped her repeatedly. *New York Times*. https://www.nytimes.com/2018/08/05/us/bill-hybels-willow-creek-pat-baranowski.html

Graham, R. (2016, August 26). Hello goodbye. *Slate*. https://slate.com/human-interest/2016/08/i-kissed-dating-goodbye-author-is-maybe-kind-of-sorry.html

Griswold, E. (2018, June 15). Silence is not spiritual: The Evangelical #MeToo movement. *New Yorker*. https://www.newyorker.com/news/on-religion/silence-is-not-spiritual-the-evangelical-metoo-movement.

Herrmann, A. F. (2021). Purity, nationalism, and whiteness: The fracturing of fundamentalist Evangelicalism. *International Review of Qualitative Research, 13*(4), 414–432. https://doi.org/10.1177/1940844720937813

Jackson, S. J., Bailey, M., & Foucault Welles, B. (2020). *#HashtagActivism: Networks of race and gender justice*. The MIT Press.

Johnson, A. (2018, March 20). Tennessee pastor Andy Savage resigns weeks after admitting "sexual incident" with minor. *NBC News*. https://www.nbcnews.com/storyline/sexual-misconduct/tennessee-pastor-andy-savage-resigns-weeks-after-admitting-sexual-incident-n858541

Kaur, C. (2018, February 12). #MosqueMeToo: Women call out sexual harassment at holy places. *The Quint*. https://www.thequint.com/neon/social-buzz/mosquemetoo-sexual-harassment-during-hajj-holy-places

Klein, L. K. (2018). *Pure: Inside the Evangelical movement that shamed a generation of young women and how I broke free*. Touchstone.

Markham, A., & Buchanan, E. (2012). Ethical decision-making and internet research: Recommendations from the AoIR ethics working committee (Version 2.0). *AOIR*. http://www.aoir.org/reports/ethics2.pdf

Marwick, A. E. (2013). *Status update: Celebrity, publicity, and branding in the social media age*. Yale University Press.

Marz, M. (2020, January 16). Personal stories of the exodus from Christianity. *Washington Post*. https://www.washingtonpost.com/outlook/personal-stories-of-the-exodus-from-christianity/2020/01/16/7594a8f8-1472-11ea-a659-7d69641c6ff7_story.html.

Masullo Chen, G., Pain, P., & Zhang, J. (2018). #NastyWomen: Reclaiming the Twitterverse from misogyny. In J. R. Vickery, & T. Everbach (Eds.), *Mediating misogyny: Gender, technology, and harassment* (pp. 371–388). Palgrave Macmillan.

Onishi, B. (2019, April 9). The rise of #Exvangelical. *Religion and Politics*. https://religionandpolitics.org/2019/04/09/the-rise-of-exvangelical/.

Paasch, H. (2017, December 5). Sexual abuse happens in #ChurchToo—We're living proof. *Huffington Post*. https://www.huffpost.com/entry/sexual-abuse-churchtoo_n_5a205b30e4b03350e0b53131

Papacharissi, Z. (2015). Affective publics and structures of storytelling: Sentiment, events and mediality. *Information, Communication & Society, 19*(3), 307–324. https://doi.org/10.1080/1369118X.2015.1109697.

Pashman, M. B., & Coen, J. (2018, March 23). After years of inquiries, Willow Creek pastor denies allegations. *Chicago Tribune*. https://www.chicagotribune.com/news/breaking/ct-met-willow-creek-pastor-20171220-story.html

River [@riverpaasch] (2017, November 21). *As @emilyjoypoetry puts it, a day of reckoning.* [Tweet]. Twitter. https://twitter.com/riverpaasch/status/932858367868944384

Shellnutt, K. (2017, December 20). Women speak up in #SilenceIsNotSpiritual campaign. *Christianity Today*. https://www.christianitytoday.com/ct/2017/december-web-only/women-speak-up-in-silenceisnotspiritual-campaign.html.

Smith, A. (2018, January 5). Silent no more: A survivor of sexual assault by prominent Memphis pastor Andy Savage shares her story #metoo #churchtoo #silenceisnotspiritual. *WATCHKEEP*. https://watchkeep.org/2018/01/silent-no-more-a-survivor-of-sexual-assault-by-prominent-memphis-pastor-andy-savage-shares-her-story-metoo-churchtoo-silenceisnotspiritual/

Stankorb, S. (2019, February 5). Inside the scam of the 'purity' movement. *Cosmopolitan*. https://www.cosmopolitan.com/politics/a26026217/sexual-abstinence-joshua-harris-purity-movement-scam/

Suk, J., Abhishek, A., Zhang, Y., Ahn, S. Y., Correa, T., Garlough, C., & Shah, D. V. (2021). #MeToo, networked acknowledgment, and connective action: How "empowerment through empathy" launched a social movement. *Social Science Computer Review*, *39*(2), 276–294. https://doi.org/10.1177/0894439319864882

Valenti, J. (2009). *The purity myth: How America's obsession with virginity is hurting young women*. Seal Press.

Wilder, C. (2019 Spring). Revelation and testimony in the age of #MeToo and #ChurchToo. *Word & World*, *39*(2), 157–165.

Woodson, J. (2018, March 9). I was assaulted. He was applauded. [Video]. *New York Times*. https://www.nytimes.com/2018/03/09/opinion/jules-woodson-andy-savage-assault.html

10

"YOU CAN START A MOVEMENT WITH A HASHTAG"

An Exploration of Student-led Social Media Activism

Candace Parrish, Rowena Briones Winkler, Avina Ross, Tremayne Robertson and Alyssa Glace Maryn

According to a report released by the Bureau of Justice Statistics (2014, 2015), nine out of every ten victims of rape are female, and women enrolled in college are three times more likely to be victimized than all women, including physical abuse from partners. In addition, male college-aged students (18–24) are 78% more likely than nonstudents of the same age to be victims of rape or sexual assault (Bureau of Justice Statistics, 2015). With these statistics in mind, determining the most effective ways to spark open dialogue and disseminate information about sexual assault/intimate partner violence (SA/IPV) issues among this age group is essential to protect vulnerable populations and slow the rates of sexual and intimate partner violence.

Research by Lee, Caruso, Goins and Southerland (2003) highlighted that as far back as 1987, sexual assault has been a long-standing problematic area of university campus interest. In recent years, this issue of sexual assault has become increasingly imperative to address and prevent as it has become one of the most prevalent crimes on college campuses nationally (Krebs et al., 2007; RAINN, 2017). According to RAINN (2017), a national sexual assault organization, there are "five reported robberies for every four sexual assaults." Over the past 30 years, various efforts have sought to address sexual safety on college campuses and empower students to prevent sexual assault via educational programs. In 1990, the Crime and Awareness Security Act (Campus Security Act) was endorsed by the Bush administration to amend and advance the Title IV portion of the Higher Education Act of 1965 to enforce special strategies toward safety on college campuses (Lee, Caruso, Goins and Southerland, 2003).

Several years after sexual assault was labeled a *constitutional threat* to students' campus learning experiences, the Obama administration placed special emphasis on addressing the issue and advocated for prevention (Eilperin, 2016). Despite many political and social efforts, sexual assault and misconduct reports on college

DOI: 10.4324/9781003260851-13

campuses are still on the rise (Eilperin, 2016). The era of social media usage has only illuminated the issue of IPV/SA, as students increasingly use social media to communicate and share personal experiences about the matter (Carlson, 1999; Fass et al., 2008; Gulliam, 2012). As a result, there is an urgent need to explore social media used for activism, education, and prevention around IPV/SA.

Further examining the issue, IPV/SA researchers and prevention advocates are assessing whether social media are potentially effective platforms to facilitate positive communication about these issues among the college student population. According to Christensson (2013), social media is a "collection of Internet-based communities that allow users to interact with each other online" (p. 1). The Pew Research Center has noted that more than 90% of young adults aged 18–29 use social media (Perrin, 2015). Given these large numbers, researchers and prevention advocates can potentially use social media to act as effective communication platforms through which it might be possible to quickly spread helpful and factually accurate information about pressing issues such as SA/IPV across college campuses. Several campuses, such as the University of North Carolina at Chapel Hill and the University of New Hampshire, among others, have already been working on leading this charge. In the past years, grassroots campaigns such as Know Your IX (www.knowyourix.org) and End Rape On Campus (www.endrapeoncampus.org) have emboldened the national conversation on both the startlingly high incidence of IPV/SA on college campuses, and the institutional response, or lack thereof, of such cases. Many of these student-led activist organizations use websites and social media platforms as a means of social support for activists and survivors.

The aim of this study was to examine social media and its use surrounding IPV/SA communication among the college student population. The researchers sought to understand (1) how students use social media as a way to find information about these issues and (2) how to use these channels as a platform to speak out about them. Furthermore, this study examines any unique challenges and opportunities that might be faced by college students attempting to use social media as a communication tool in relation to these important issues. The findings of this study provide valuable insight to social media communicators on college campuses, along with student groups interested in using these channels for digital activism (pertaining to sexual assault and dating violence) in order to move institutions to more realistic, actionable strategies to engage and mobilize campuses from merely actors to change agents.

Summary

According to the United States Department of Justice (2015), students enrolled in college face higher percentages of potential encounters with IPV/SA. As many college-aged students use social media as a means of communication and idea transmission, researchers and prevention advocates are assessing social media platforms as potential methods of disseminating IPV/SA prevention campaigns/materials.

Many campuses and university organizations have begun to use social media to communicate prevention information and strategies, as well as to provide survivors with national support communities. To further this body of research, the researchers of this study examined social media and its use surrounding SA/IPV communication among the college student population to improve the future of social-mediated approaches to IPV/SA prevention among college-aged students.

Literature Review

In order to highlight the opportunities and disadvantages of using social media as a platform for social awareness and activism among college students concerning IPV/SA, an examination of extant literature was conducted to explicate the ways in which college students interact and engage with social media. An overview of college students' overall use of social media, along with a discussion of work surrounding digital activism and the complex relationship between IPV/SA and social media, will be detailed further below.

College Students and Social Media

Research examining motivations and methods of social media use for college students shows that students receive emotional, cognitive, and social support from engaging on social networking sites (Gray et al., 2012; Pempek et al., 2009; Zheng et al., 2012). Students have also been found to use these platforms for school-related tasks. Furthermore, there has been a rise in the use of social media for scholastic endeavors despite earlier recognition that college students prefer utilizing search engines, such as Google, for information retrieval for academic research (O'Connor & Lundstrom, 2011).

The adaptation of digital and social media uses for academic purposes can be seen in early research on college students and Internet engagement. A Pew Internet Project conducted in the early 2000s highlighted that university students were positively impacted by Internet transactions (e.g., email and instant messaging) that allowed for easier communication with peers, professors, and university staff (Gray et al., 2012; Jones, 2002). Nearly two decades later, research is still being conducted on new and improved social media platforms (such as Facebook and Twitter) that further allow students to continue to connect with peers about university activities and work. Studies have found that social media channels have been useful for predicting outcomes in the classroom, such as stronger critical thinking skills, quicker information-processing skills, and more nuanced dialogue with instructors and classmates (Gray et al., 2012; Lampe et al., 2011; Moody, 2010).

In addition to academic purposes, college students also utilize Social Network Services (SNS), such as Facebook, to combat "friendsickness"—despair deriving from missing high school or hometown friends (Gray et al., 2012;

Lampe et al., 2007; Paul & Brier, 2001). During the transition from high school to college, students have been known use social media as a key information source for both college resources and peer social support (Gray et al., 2012; Pempek et al., 2009). Supporting this notion, survey research on college students using social media found that many used SNSs to maintain existing friendships rather than for cultivating new ones (Pempek et al., 2009). As research shows that college student development now includes a number of outcomes correlated to social media use, such as emotional, cognitive, and social support (Gray et al., 2012; Pempek et al., 2009; Zheng et al., 2012), empirical research should be conducted to explore how students use social media in the context of social issues. As college campuses have traditionally been spaces reflective of the political and social grievances of the nation overall, students have an opportunity to impact social change (Barnhardt, 2016).

In particular, in response to the campus climate surrounding IPV/SA that prompted the Office for Civil Rights of the Department of Education to send colleges and universities a "Dear Colleague" letter reinforcing that the requirements of Title IX include sexual violence and emphasizing that colleges and universities have a responsibility to take immediate and effective steps to respond to sexual violence (Ali, 2011), more exploration is warranted for campus communicators to determine how to effectively produce social media campaigns for social awareness of these issues. Although there are a number of initiatives on college campuses that address this need (e.g., The Red Flag Campaign, www.theredflag-campaign.org/), study researchers noticed a lack of empirical research on how college students retrieve or perceive information about IPV/SA on social media. In 2017, new government administration announced intentions of rescinding "Obama-era" IPV/SA and Title IX efforts on college campuses (Camera, 2017). The change incited public dissatisfaction from sexual assault activists, campus administrators, and survivors as they felt the decision to rescind current efforts to prevent IPV/SA occurrences on college campuses would be detrimental in providing protection of IPV/SA survivors and guidance for campus investigation of incidences (Camera, 2017). However, the Biden administration announced early on that it would review and consider a rollback of the Trump administration rule (Chalfant, 2021; Rogers & Green, 2021). The new Biden administration rules are expected to provide additional protection for LGBTQ+ students (Attridge et al., 2021).

Digital Activism

As SNSs allow individuals to engage and maintain new and existing friendships and connections, it makes sense that these social media platforms would also be used to exchange ideas and content surrounding social and political movements (Kim & Khang, 2014). This type of online socially charged engagement is often coined "digital activism"—a combination of real-time activism coupled with social media movements for more widespread participation (Kelley, 2013).

Digital activism movements can highlight a variety of social injustice causes and be jumpstarted by "street-level" individuals or organizations (Kelley, 2013). For young adults in particular, due to feelings of neglect and misapprehension from traditional sources of civic engagement (Bennett, 2008), online channels are seen as particularly attractive spaces to share ideas and opinions. Individuals lacking confidence to participate offline may feel capable of discussions on social media (Velasquez & LaRose, 2015). These online engagements not only allow students to draw direct, clear lines between causes they feel strongly about and how they can help, but also they can initiate a process where students can begin to negotiate their identities as activists through building online connections and feeling a part of a collective that can expand to a global level (Svensson et al., 2015).

Along with digital activism, additional terms have been created that criticize the practice—including "slacktivism" and "clicktivism"—that allude to a generation of less motivated and engaged activism participants with limited physical calls-to-action involved (Gladwell, 2010; Peuchaud, 2014; Vie, 2014). However, research describing the potential positive implications of digital activism tends to highlight the various digital tools—such as SNSs—utilized in unique and affordable ways to generate greater momentum and engagement (Earl & Kimport, 2011; Joyce, 2010). Recently, digital activism is gaining momentum on college campuses as college students may find it easier to get involved considering their high usage of social media. Several studies have indeed focused on specific incidences of college student involvement in digital activism, such as campaign engagement during the election of Barack Obama, or civic engagement with the community related to issues such as homelessness or sex trafficking (e.g., Biddix, 2010; Kim & Khang, 2014).

Pertaining to IPV/SA, a gap exists in empirical research examining how social media is used as means to promote awareness of this issue via digital activism. Through recent research, perspectives of the intersections of IPV/SA and social media address areas including opportunities for social support, such as the #WhyIStayed campaign that emerged as a result of the online conversations surrounding Baltimore Ravens player Ray Rice assaulting his then-fiancée, now-wife Janay Palmer (Bahadur, 2014). Additional social media campaigns discuss the ramifications of publicizing the alleged perpetrators as well as case study accounts—such as digital sexual assault activism in Egypt (Madavanhu & Radloff, 2013; Peuchaud, 2014; Salter, 2013). In addition, more anecdotal evidence of IPV/SA and digital activism movements have been identified, such as student-run Facebook pages Know Your IX, which provides a support system for victims, and IX Network, which provides assistance to student activists and those who want to file federal complaints (Sandra, 2013).

IPV/SA and Social Media

Over the past several decades, research surrounding adolescents and college student experiences with IPV/SA has revealed the need for prevention and awareness campaigns that help frame and exemplify healthy relationships among the age group (Carlson, 1999; Fass et al., 2008; Gulliam, 2012). Previous work on the issue has highlighted that aggressive behaviors in dating culture among young adults and adolescents have not always been effectively addressed in public discussion (Carlson, 1999; Gulliam, 2012; Miller, 2011). As research has found that increasingly high numbers of college students are involved in intimate partner violence (Miller, 2011), and high amounts of college students utilize social media for information-seeking purposes (Gray et al., 2012; Lampe et al., 2007; Pempek et al., 2009; Zheng et al., 2012), more research must be conducted to examine the intersection for future intervention purposes.

In recent years, social media has been seen as a catalyst for both good and bad movements and experiences concerning IPV/SA. On the more tragic side, there have been instances where teens have committed suicide in the aftermath of their traumatic cases going viral. Both Rehtaeh Parsons and Audrie Pott endured cyberbullying and digital harassment after photos of their assaults were spread through email and social media, which investigators believe was the basis of their suicides (Fuchs et al., 2013). In the case of highly publicized Steubenville, Ohio, a young girl found out she had been sexually assaulted via YouTube and Instagram posts. After the case was made public, she received a tremendous amount of backlash on social media (Fuchs et al., 2013; Robinson, 2013). Social media also offer support for perpetrators, demonstrating that the discussions online have been complex and multifaceted, and not entirely from victims' points of view. For example, a case in Torrington, Connecticut, that involved two teen males being arrested for assault of minors, had nontraditional social media reactions, as the hashtag "#FreeEdgar" was spread to support the freedom of one of the perpetrators (Robinson, 2013).

On a more hopeful note, however, not all social media uses surrounding IPV/SA are negative. Several movements capitalize on social media use to disseminate awareness messages and motivate individuals to act against IPV/SA. On Twitter, hashtag movements such as #YesAllWomen and #RapeHasNoUniform were created and used to provide both a space for positive discussion surrounding SA and rape and an opportunity for victims to share their experiences and grievances (Medina, 2014). Another popular hashtag, #WhyIDidntReport, allowed victims of IPV/SA to speak out about the reasons they kept silent after being assaulted (Giorgis, 2014).

During both the good and bad occurrences surrounding IPV/SA on social media, the notion and role of the social media bystanders is a rising topic of discussion. From the discovery of the bystander effect in the 1960s, it was proposed that the higher number of people present during an afflicting event, the less likely it will be that someone intervenes (Darley & Latane, 1968). Presently, and from a more digital perspective, many victims feel this same notion relates, as many viewers are aware of (and perhaps even share), IPV/SA-related posts, yet few people speak out for fear of the backlash turning on themselves (Gills, 2013). However, these tragic and oftentimes complex occurrences are the premise for this research study—to add to the existing literature by developing strategies on empowering college students to join in on the cause of preventing IPV/SA both on- and off-campus.

Summary

College-aged students use social media and various Internet functions (such as search engines) for a variety of uses—from social to educational purposes. Regarding social purposes, college students use social media to maintain communicative transactions with long-distance friends and communities. Students also use social media to connect with and share insight on various social and cultural issues. Recently, "digital activism" has been a term used to define activism that occurs on social online platforms. Several social media campaigns and discussions have occurred publicly addressing matters of IPV/SA—examples are the social-mediated discussion of #WhyIDidntReport and #YesAllWomen. Incidences of cyberbullying have also increased among this study's population (paralleling the rise in use of social media). More research needs to be conducted on how to harness social media for fostering of positive conversation on IPV/SA prevention as well as to combat cyberbullying situations involving these issues.

Research Questions

Based on the review of the literature on social media, digital activism, and IPV/SA, the following two research questions were asked:

> **RQ1:** How, if at all, do college students use social media as a source for obtaining information that leads to social awareness and action for dating violence and sexual assault?
>
> **RQ2:** What are the challenges and opportunities associated with using social media for activism associated with dating violence and sexual assault?

Method

Study researchers used the qualitative method of focus groups, as this method is appropriate for observing topics that are not well defined in extant literature (Stalmeijer et al., 2014). Use of focus groups allowed the researchers to learn about the "conscious, semiconscious, and unconscious psychological and sociocultural characteristics and processes among various groups" (Berg, 2009, p. 158) through the use of dialogue. The primary purpose of this method is to create dynamic interactions among participants that can stimulate discussion made by one another's comments (Berg, 2009). In addition, focus groups can offer participants a greater role in formulating the data collected, granting them more power and control and creating a more egalitarian research environment (Reinharz, 1992). For this study, this power shift can be particularly useful in enhancing self-empowerment and consciousness-raising among students for IPV/SA issues. Researchers specifically sought to gain insight on the study population's cultural processes and beliefs for future improvement of targeted IPV/SA social-mediated messaging campaigns. The focus group methodology is widely used as a method of gaining these types of insights from desired/target populations (Stalmeijer et al., 2014).

Sample

Both male and female undergraduate students were recruited for this study from a large urban public university located in the southeastern part of the United States. The five focus groups with a total of 29 participants were included in the study (for a listing of demographic characteristics, see Table 10.1). The focus groups averaged five participants in each group.

Data Collection

Purposive sampling techniques were used to recruit participants for this study (Rubin & Rubin, 2005). Researchers obtained participants via a recruitment email to a large online communication course, where students were eligible

TABLE 10.1 *Demographics of Study Participants*

Characteristic	Number of Participants
Sex	
Male	8
Female	21
Race	
White	7
Black	15
Hispanic	3
Asian	2
Middle Eastern	2
Age	
18–20	14
21–25	11
25+	4
Sexual orientation	
Heterosexual	25
Homosexual	3
Bisexual	1
Relationship status	
Single	23
In a relationship	6

to receive extra credit for their participation in research activities. The focus groups took place in a conference room located on campus and lasted on average 60 minutes. Two researchers alternated moderating the focus groups and taking notes. After consent was obtained from all participants, a semi-structured interview guide was used to structure the discussion and answer the study's research questions. The guide was comprised of three major parts: (1) general social media usage; (2) awareness of current IPV/SA social media campaigns or messages; and (3) suggestions for developing social media strategy related to IPV/SA. Sample questions asked during the focus groups include "What does being a bystander mean to you?" and "If you could design your own online bystander intervention education campaign, what would it look like?"

Data Analysis

All of the data were transcribed verbatim by hired research assistants, who fully retained the speech style of the moderators and the participants. Study researchers analyzed focus group transcriptions using techniques derived from the grounded theory approach (Charmaz, 2000; Charmaz, 2008; Corbin & Strauss, 2008), using a constant comparative method to allow for themes to emerge from the data toward answering the proposed research questions. First, researchers used open-coding procedures to examine the transcripts line-by-line to locate initial themes and potential categories. Study researchers then used axial coding to explore how data can fit into the categorical themes identified in the first step, along with finding data that explicates the concepts presented in the literature review (Charmaz, 1998). According to Lindlof and Taylor (2010), axial coding is a part of the integration process of the grounded theory approach that narrows down the number of categories by finding similarities across data in order to make the data clearer and more understandable. However, though single statements were combined to create various concepts, stand-alone statements that were unique or exceptional were also coded in an effort to avoid too much coherency in the data (van Zoonen, 1994). Furthermore, other methodological approaches were used to enhance the rigor of this study (Creswell, 2013; Greckhamer & Cilesiz, 2014). Peer review was used during the design and analysis of the study to enhance validity and reliability. The research team also engaged in reflexive processes and provided rich data reporting (Creswell, 2013). Additionally, the study's emergent design nurtured the team's flexibility (Creswell, 2013), while the research questions were informed by the literature and study data to establish a recommended balance of systematic analysis (Greckhamer & Cilesiz, 2014).

Summary

Qualitative research is frequently used by researchers to explore areas and phenomena that are not well defined in extant literature. More specifically, focus groups are used in qualitative research studies to gain insight on behaviors and beliefs of specific populations. Thus, the researchers in this study chose the focus group method to explore social media use in digital IPV/SA prevention messaging to propose cohesive and strategic methods to harness positive social media use in future campaigns directed toward this study's target population. Male and female undergraduate students were recruited from a large urban public university. A total of five focus groups were conducted, which resulted in a total of 29 study participants. After consent to participate was obtained, a focus group guide was constructed and administered, including questions revolving (1) general social media usage; (2) awareness of current IPV/SA social media campaigns or messages; and (3) suggestions for developing social media strategy related to IPV/SA. After focus groups were transcribed, study researchers analyzed the data using the grounded theory approach—a method of data analysis that allows themes to be identified from the data as opposed to prior speculation.

RQ1: Social Media as a Source for Information that Leads to Social Awareness and Action

The student participants in this study used social media as an information source in a variety of ways regarding dating and sexual violence, including (1) *bystander intervention strategies*; (2) *developing and promoting awareness, action, and change*; (3) *providing supplemental education*; and (4) *recognizing platform limitations*. These emergent themes will be discussed in further detail below.

Bystander intervention strategies: Bystander intervention through specifically helping someone experiencing violence was referenced as a tool for social media. Multiple students shared sentiments that suggested social media could be used to combat IPV/SA versus being a passive bystander. One participant created a Reddit page to share information and challenge victim blaming:

> ...One of the first posts that I did was about [how] this girl was roofied and raped essentially, and the victim blaming was out of control, and disgusting...I'm gonna stop this victim blaming on reddit now. That's like my goal.

Other instances of active bystanding via social media included reporting verbally abusive language about friends or celebrities via Instagram. As one participant shared, "On Instagram...one of the things that I've done is if I'm on a star's picture, or just anyone's picture, if too many negative comments people are saying things, I usually report them and [Instagram will] take [the comments] off." However, being an online bystander does come with its limitations for those who aren't ready to take action. For instance, one participant stated, "...I couldn't really do anything about it; as a bystander, you're just watching it." The majority of student participants reported feeling like inactive bystanders who could become proactive activists against IPV/SA if given education on prevention/intervention strategies.

Developing and promoting awareness, action, and change: Awareness sharing about IPV/SA was apparent given the consistent mentioning of national stories such as the reports about Ray Rice and the *Rolling Stone* article about fraternity culture at the University of Virginia (UVA). These stories appeared on all forms of social media and fueled the imagination of students. Participants mentioned using social media—Facebook, Twitter, Instagram, and Tumblr—to receive and share news around IPV/SA issues and resources for help. Creating social media groups, promoting events addressing social issues, and developing and employing hashtags were discussed as helpful mechanisms for raising social awareness. As one participant contended, "I see people forming groups and talking about issues on social media, but a lot of what I see is people creating events for everyone to go to." Two other participants reported on the usefulness of social media: "I honestly haven't seen or been to any of those events, but it definitely is a great way to promote and really raise social awareness. As far as the hashtags … people really do follow those hashtags" and "[Social media] is just such a great resource and then, you know, you have more in-depth things to talk about … like, real issues going on in the world." Many student participants expressed the belief that social media is an excellent way to disseminate IPV/SA information and evoke meaningful discussions with millennials around the matter.

Participants also suggested that social media is a beneficial utility to promote social action and change. For example, a participant shared a sense of increased social agency:

> Another pro [of social media] is, I think, we have more control of our world now. [In the past you] just look at the news and that was it; you receive it. But now, you interact with it. We can, you know, affect change…

Another participant revealed, "You can start a movement with a hashtag," to which many of the participants within that particular group agreed.

Providing supplemental education: Other students intentionally educated community members and friends from a place of care and concern. The latter is illustrated by a student when assessing the positives of social media campaigns: "…links to resources and just anything like that I would retweet those or, you know share them on Facebook with people who I care about so that they can have those resources too because it's a very real thing." Dating and relationship violence is indeed a reality that this student felt necessary to share with friends to ensure safety. In addition, a participant emphasized that prevention materials addressing males and females as survivors were important to frame IPV/SA. As one student posited in agreement with that participant, "I do like how [the campaign] includes both male and females. It shows that it's not just women who are victims."

Recognizing platform limitations: During the discussions on the constructive use of social media for social awareness, action, and/or change, a few disclosed social media limitations related to using these channels for this purpose. Some felt that social media was only useful for generating social awareness, but others reported it less useful in other ways as well. The major limitation posed by the participants stemmed from the slacktivism point of view that it creates merely awareness and not much action afterward. As stated by one participant:

> ...social media is definitely good at [sic] disseminating information, but it kind of stops there...So I think when it comes to informing people about things, I think that's its greatest power. But I don't think I have been able to see it do much past that.

Similarly, another student stated: "...It's just so easy to make a Facebook page like we, one of my classes, one of our assignments was to like do a service project and almost everyone made a Facebook page..." The critique suggested that this medium by itself was not action-oriented enough to warrant merit of service to a cause. Yet another participant made this valid point regarding social media's capacity for publicity versus education:

> Maybe the only thing that social media can help solve...[regarding] social problems is maybe bringing it to light, you know? Actually publicizing it so we can actually have a conversation about it because I think the problem with social media is that a lot of people have opinions, but not everybody is educated on that subject.

Regarding IPV/SA in particular, one participant discussed how dealing with issues via social media can be particularly challenging due to how deeply rooted the problem is in our society:

> Well I think the problems are real deep, like its gonna be awhile, and beyond technology. So, misogyny, it's kind of ingrained in society in general. And so I think it'd be hard to put that weight on social media you know, but I feel like you could still spread awareness.

In addition, while many participants cited social media as a favorable tool to promote social awareness, action, and/or change (with varied limitations), only a few participants actually spoke of personal attempts at using social media as a vehicle for social action. One participant reported, "I use [social media] to post a lot of political awareness articles." Another reached out and provided support to two friends after reading their social media posts disclosing experiences of sexual assault. Although further expounded in the discussion section, students can be empowered to prevent and intervene against social media IPV/SA incidences if given training and education on specific strategies to implement when an incident arises—such as having a campus or digital university liaison in which to report these occurrences.

Results

RQ2: Challenges and Opportunities for Social Media Activism

In response to the second research question, the following themes pertaining to challenges and opportunities of using social media for activism emerged, including: (1) *lack of bystander education;* (2) *recognizing IPV/SA online;* (3) *dealing with misinformation/rumors;* and (4) *harnessing social media's untapped potential.* These themes will be discussed further in the sections below.

Lack of bystander education: Although participants are aware of bystander intervention strategies as was discussed in RQ1, many of the students had conflicting perceptions of what it actually means to put these strategies into practice, which at times can be seen as counterproductive. This confusion pertained to how they personally defined the bystander role as well. When asked what being a bystander means to them, one participant replied: "To me personally, what I believe a bystander is, someone that's at the situation observing and just not doing anything, just chilling there..."

Through the discussion, it also became evident that the participants' counterproductive knowledge surrounding being a bystander affected how they would address IPV/SA situations on social media. Many participants agreed that they would not intervene or report an incident because of feeling like they would be invading the victim's privacy or jumping to conclusions without knowing the full story. In spite of ambiguity or confusion over the specific term "bystander," a few participants felt they would indeed intervene with IPV/SA occurrences online if they felt that circumstances were bad enough or if they personally knew the victim and would reach out to them in real life. One participant shared:

> I think the only time I would interact with that person is if I felt like in real life I would've done the same thing. Like if I have that personal connection or even if we're really good friends on social media. But if it's someone that I just follow, that I don't really have any ties to them or I've never really talked to them and I just see them posting stuff, I probably wouldn't. Unless I felt really moved by what they said.

When participants shared that they may have witnessed IPV/SA occurrences from online acquaintance in more distant social circles, they expressed reluctance to intervene because of a lack of information on exactly what to do. When sharing an experience of watching an IPV/SA and dating violence victim express suicidal thoughts online, one participant stated:

> ...it was really sad, just, seeing somebody in that state of mind, and just reading the comments, I don't know, it's just. I'm not above it, but like that fact that I couldn't really do anything about it as a bystander you're just watching it. You know, I couldn't really, be like you know you can talk to somebody. Or you know, things like that.

<u>Recognizing IPV/SA online</u>: During the discussion of IPV/SA prevention, many participants expressed that either themselves or their peers are not completely familiar with how to recognize these issues on social media. More specifically, they expressed uncertainty surrounding being able to differentiate the extent of normal, healthy relationships versus abuse. As one participant said:

> Yeah I feel like women feel like it's the norm for them, like that's just how a relationship is, like we argue, we fight, and then the next day we make up. That's just the norm, and it's not healthy, and I feel like it doesn't click for people, especially when they're in a long-term relationship. They're so used to it. I was in a relationship like that too, where he was verbally abusive, but I didn't realize it, I was just like 'oh this is normal.'

In addition, there seemed to be confusion pertaining to the most effective method when it came to IPV/SA. Some participants felt that efforts should focus on perpetrators, while others argued that efforts should be focused on educating victims. Unfortunately, some of ideas presented took a victim-blaming point of view, such as this comment from one participant:

> It's just like where are we gonna take the steps to tell girls well maybe you shouldn't go upstairs with somebody you don't know. Where were your friends? You know what I mean? Like there's this whole thing that when you put stuff, you're posting it but then you're forgetting about these other facts so stop putting general things out there. To use it as a way to educate, to do better.

Dealing with misinformation/rumors: Affirming the importance of the presence of information-sharing regarding IPV/SA on social media, it was also discussed that rumors and noncredible sources are being shared as credible sources, at least until further dispelled. This signifies that disseminating positive and credible information on social media could potentially combat the noncredible, biased information that promotes and perpetuates negative thinking and actions toward IPV/SA occurrences. While sharing personal experiences of encounters with biased and noncredible information, one participant said, "People just lose focus on the real issue and it's just like oh I heard this, I heard this talk about it, kind of thing. Like it's a gossip piece." Students also mentioned that messages could be misinterpreted over Facebook, controversial messages should be avoided on social media, and the use of celebrities to promote healthy relationships was trivial because they were not authentic or real.

Harnessing social media's untapped potential: In spite of the many previously mentioned challenges, participants still felt that the sharing of information on social media could help spread positive information. Aligning with this notion, a participant conveyed:

> I mean I think it definitely made more people aware, more people were talking about it, you know, people know it's an issue. And I saw my fair

share of and like retweeted or posted on Facebook you know every, I don't want to say positive, because you can't really get a positive from a situation like that, but you know like resources, links to resources and just anything like that I would retweet those or, you know share them on Facebook with people who I care about so that they can have those resources too because it's a very real thing.

In a similar vein, potential strategies and platforms in terms of how IPV/SA information could be shared were also discussed, as was relayed by this participant:

I think maybe through social media and YouTube, have videos that give information like what do you do in this situation or how do you avoid a certain situation. Like having conversations and dealing with it more than feel(ing) bad for what happened and what didn't happen. Have more stuff like that socially.

Thus, although some students addressed apprehensions about the extent to which social media could help in IPV/SA prevention, many agreed that focusing on awareness initiatives, in addition to other campaign strategies that use social media, could lead to potential positive outcomes.

Discussion

This research explored how participants of five undergraduate focus groups use social media regarding IPV/SA. Issues related to what it means to be a bystander, information-sharing, education, and awareness are a few themes that students referenced consistently. As college-aged students are one of the largest populations of social media users (Smith et al., 2011), it was no surprise that every student participating in the focus groups engaged with social media to some extent. Whether on Facebook or Snapchat, many students expressed utilizing social media for social support and relationship-building, as was also found in existing literature (Gray et al., 2012; Lampe et al., 2011; Pempek et al., 2009; Smith et al., 2011).

Furthermore, conversation during the focus groups indeed uncovered the nature of how this particular demographic uses social media for dating and relationship advice and encounters. Although most mentioned that they casually read and entertained articles and hashtags—such as #RelationshipGoals—they often agreed that those types of informative and interactive methods do not suffice as credible content and were seen more as satirical representations of their interactions. However, during discussion of controversial social issues such as the Ray Rice case, Rolling Stone's article about fraternity culture at UVA, as well as the conversation surrounding Ferguson, there were heavily mediated IPV/SA and dating violence issues and occurrences discussed in the focus groups as being widely promoted via social media posts, retweets, and pages/groups.

In completing the analysis, there was an identifiable disconnect between the participants' belief that social media was useful to promote social action and change and the actual explicit use of social media by participants to incite action and change, which was seemingly very minimal. Optimistically, however, the participants have been using social media to receive and send information on social issues, which indicate that social media can be a relevant and fruitful space to promote social issues, in spite of hesitancy on the part of students to participate in more explicit digital activism (Gills, 2013). This hesitation may stem from confusion regarding what it means to be a bystander in the first place. There were major points of misunderstanding among the participants in terms of what it actually takes to intervene with IPV/SA situations that arise in the realm of social media. For communicators on college campuses in particular, this disconnect between engagement and action through social media can present a potential opportunity for more thoughtful dialogue with students on what it means to be a digital activist (Biddix, 2010) and how it can increase IPV/SA awareness among college students. For example, student participants expressed they would like to have a specific method of reporting an incidence of IPV/SA or bullying on social media to campus administrators or IPV/SA educators/communicators. In their current experiences, without having a specific action or method of reporting, some did not feel like there was much they could do to prevent or intervene in witnessed IPV/SA social media occurrences. Strategies for effective outreach to the college population could include a strong message component to empower students toward positively intervening (i.e., reporting online incidences, providing social support) and overcoming potential negative self-perceptions as being unable to actually make a difference in this particular arena.

An example of how to use social media to empower/educate students and increase their sense of ownership in social-mediated IPV/SA prevention and awareness is the "Chicago Says No More" campaign (CSNM, 2017). The campaign includes a portion titled, "Social Media Toolkit for College Students," which seeks to raise awareness about IPV/SA on Chicago college campuses, through having students after their own photos with tailored messages of IPV/SA misconceptions (CSNM, 2017).

Another way to address this issue is to provide more comprehensive education as several students voiced concerns such as dealing with uninformed peers without substantive information and understanding complex issues such as IPV/SA enough to feel confident in sharing their opinions. More specifically, these educational dialogues with students should include effective bystander intervention information (including barriers and strategies), components of healthy/unhealthy relationships, signs of dating violence, and resources for survivors and allies. In addition, it became apparent through the focus group sessions that many misconceptions of good/bad or acceptable/unacceptable behaviors within relationships among college students are in dire need of being addressed (Carlson, 1999; Fass et al., 2008; Miller, 2011). Educational information geared toward college students concerning IPV/SA should aim to inform students about the implications of victim blaming, and how the communication choices they make via social media can further perpetuate the very rape culture they may be attempting to eliminate. These conversations can touch on related subjects associated with online-based communication, such as online verbal harassment and cyberbullying. IPV/SA-focused campaigns geared for college students should work to address these narrow assumptions by highlighting these key educational indicators to give students a more nuanced perspective on this issue, and do not necessarily have to be disseminated solely online. Therefore, social media as a single, stand-alone resource to promote social issues should not be considered in a vacuum, and should be treated as platforms through which information can be shared quickly and more cost-effectively to reach as many people as possible.

The Red Flag Campaign, a national sexual assault and domestic violence prevention campaign with special emphasis on college campuses, has created initiatives that not only raise awareness but also educate students on the issue and its importance since 2005 (O'Malley, 2012). Although the bystander intervention program uses several methods and strategies to education and promote awareness, perhaps the most widely known activity is the placing of up to 100 red flags on a campus lawn during sexual assault and domestic violence awareness weeks on campuses (O'Malley, 2012; "Red Flag Campaign," 2021). The red flags are a symbolization of the "red flags" that may arise in IPV/SA incidences (RFC, 2015). This strategy of red flag displays is usually accompanied by several online and campus discussion activities (RFC, 2015; "Red Flag Campaign," 2021).

Summary

Students involved in the focus groups validated prior literature (to various extents) that they use social media for social support and relationship-building. Regarding IPV/SA, students expressed that they may not seriously entertain all social-mediated articles of hashtag movements for relationship advice. However, students acknowledged how social media allowed for vast discussion and sharing of IPV/SA information online after serious social incidents occurred. While students may not have been clear on how to use social media to ignite change in IPV/SA prevention, they did express how they use social media to receive and share information on political and social justice issues. Potential methods to decrease online bystander behavior and increase positive actions toward IPV/SA prevention among college-aged students include proper education on (1) what it means to be a bystander, (2) specific details and explanations on what IPV/SA is and looks like on college campuses and digital platforms, and (3) how to intervene when witnessing IPV/SA circumstances. Ultimately, social media should not be viewed as a total solution, but as a powerful tool used along with various other IPV/SA prevention efforts—both online and offline.

Limitations and Future Research

In terms of using social media for IPV/SA education, awareness, and prevention, conducting a series of focus groups with college students created a unique opportunity for many meaningful findings to surface, such as how social media can be used as helpful information sources when it comes to education, awareness, and intervention strategies related to dating and sexual violence, as well as the possible benefits and challenges associated with using social media for activism purposes. With this said, however, the research team was faced with a number of limitations throughout the process. First, the lack of empirical research on perceptions surrounding IPV/SA for this specific demographic served as both a challenge and an opportunity for this study. Moving forward, the study findings can be used as a guide toward future exploration in this realm that is more outcomes-based versus purely perceptions-based. Secondly, using a purposive sample of college students may not reflect perceptions of the general population in terms of IPV/SA. As a result, future research could be conducted on a number of different populations (i.e., sexual minorities) to gain even more unique perspectives and experiences with using social media for IPV/SA for more tailored intervention and campaign strategies. Finally, some of the participants may have felt more comfortable, and as a result would have been more transparent, during one-on-one interviews than in a focus-group setting. For this reason, future research could explore this topic area even further through the qualitative in-depth interview method to more extensively identify the most effective prevention models of using social media to promote awareness, action, and social change related to social issues.

Conclusion

As IPV/SA are areas in need of continuous exploration concerning its relationship with social media in terms of its capacity as a communication tool, promising opportunities of this intersection as digital technologies can be used to harness awareness and prevention efforts, especially among college students. With the click of a button or a tap on a screen, conversations, photos, and videos can be shared with people completely outside of users' immediate geographic locations. For college students, social media has already been proven an essential part of their learning and relationship-building experiences. As focus on IPV/SA has increased, in terms of creating awareness and prevention strategies via social media, college students have the potential to be informed and empowered to know the red flags on social media and effectively act in ways that discourage negative behavior while promoting positive social change. The findings of this are the start of exemplifying the importance of more deeply assessing college student perceptions involving IPV/SA and social media. Not only can this help extend already-existing scholarly research in this area, but it can also be utilized from a more applied standpoint to cultivate more effective campaign strategies and tactics that can help prevent future IPV/SA cases and to ensure that communication tools are used as a way to eliminate violence, not perpetuate the trend.

References

Ali, R. (2011). *Dear Colleague letter.* Washington, DC: United States Department of Civil Rights. Retrieved from http://www2.ed.gov/about/offices/list/ocr/letters/colleague-201104.html

Attridge, M., Rosier, J. & Motamedi, A. (2021, March 3). *Biden administration preps new rules covering sexual misconduct at schools, colleges.* Retrieved on April 4, 2022 from https://www.stardem.com/news/national/biden-administration-preps-new-rules-covering-sexual-misconduct-at-schools-colleges/article_6d7723c5-de05-55b1-9218-20f7ad0cfdd8.html

Bahadur, N. (2014). *#WhyIstayed stories reveal why domestic violence survivors can't 'just leave.'* Huffington Post. Retrieved from http://www.huffingtonpost.com/2014/09/09/whyistayed-twitter-domestic-violence_n_5790320.html

Barnhardt, C. (2016, March 2). *Embracing student activism.* Retrieved from https://www.higheredtoday.org/2016/03/02/embracing-student-activism/

Bennett, W. L. (2008). Changing citizenship in the digital age. In W. L. Bennett (Ed.), *Civic life online: Learning how digital media can engage youth* (pp. 1–24). Cambridge, MA: The MIT Press.

Berg, B. L. (2009). *Qualitative research methods for the social sciences* (7th ed.). Boston, MA: Pearson Education, Inc.

Biddix, J. P. (2010). Technology uses in campus activism from 2000 to 2008: Implications for civic learning. *Journal of College Student Development, 51*(6), 679–693.

Camera, L. (2017), September 22). *Administration rescinds Obama-era campus sexual assault guidance.* Retrieved December 13, 2017, from https://usnews.com/news/education-news/articles/2017-09-22/trump-administration-rescinds-obama-era-campus-sexual-assault-guidance.

Carlson, B. E. (1999). Student judgments about dating violence: A factorial vignette analysis. *Research in Higher Education, 40*(2), 201–220.

Chalfant, M. (2021, 3 March). *Biden orders review of Trump era rule on campus sexual misconduct.* Retrieved April 4, 2022 from https://thehill.com/homenews/administration/542146-biden-orders-review-of-trump-era-rule-on-campus-sexual-misconduct/

Charmaz, K. (1998). Grounded theory. In J. A. Smith, R. Harre & L. V. Langenhove (Eds.), *Rethinking methods in psychology* (pp. 27–49). Thousand Oaks, CA: Sage.

Charmaz, K.(2000). Grounded theory: Objectivist and constructivist methods. In N. Denzin & Y. S. Lincoln (Eds.), *Handbook of qualitative research* (2nd ed., pp. 509–535). Thousand Oaks, CA: Sage.

Charmaz, K. (2008). Grounded theory as an emergent method. In S. N. Hessebiber & P. Leavy (Eds.), *Handbook of emergent methods* (pp.155–170). New York and London: The Guilford Press.

Christensson, P. (2013, August 7). *Social media definition.* Retrieved 2017, Jun 11, from https://techterms.com

Corbin, J. M., & Strauss, A. C. (2008). *Basics of qualitative research, 3rd edition.* Thousand Oaks, CA: Sage.

Creswell, J. W. (2013). *Qualitative inquiry & research design: Choosing among five approaches.* Los Angeles, CA: Sage.

CSNM (2017). *Social media Toolkit for college students.* Retrieved December 15, 2017, from http://chicagosaysnomore.org/college-campus-social-media-campaign/

Darley, J. M., & Latane, B. (1968). Bystander Intervention in emergencies: Diffusion of responsibility. *Journal of Personality and Social Psychology, 8*(4), 377–383.

Earl, J., & Kimport, K. (2011). *Digitally enabled social change: Activism in the Internet age.* Cambridge, MA: MIT Press.

Eilperin, J. (2016, July 03). *Biden and Obama rewrite the rulebook on college sexual assaults.* Retrieved December 15, 2017, from https://www.washingtonpost.com/politics/biden-and-obama-rewrite-the-rulebook-on-college-sexual-assaults/2016/07/03/0773302e-3654-11e6-a254-2b336e293a3c_story.html?utm_term=.35498fc13a50

Fass, D. F., Beson, R. I., & Legget, D. G. (2008). Assessing prevalence and awareness of violent behaviors in the intimate partner relationships of college students using internet sampling. *Journal of College Student Psychotherapy, 22*(4), 66–74.

Fuchs, E., Kelley, M. B., & Lubin, G. (2013). Social media makes teen rape more traumatic than ever. *Web Log Post.* Retrieved from http://www.businessinsider.com/the-impact-of-social-media-on-rape-2013-4- ixzz3VmBpvDoB

Gills, C. (2013). A deafening silence. *Maclean's, 126*(16), 1.

Giorgis, H. (2014). My body is more than a crime scene: #WhyIDidntReport and what I learned from talking about it. *Web Log Post.* Retrieved from http://youngist.org/why-I-didnt-report/ -.VRf1YlZ5B6k

Gladwell, M. (2010). *Small change: Why the revolution will not be tweeted 2015.* Retrieved from http://www.newyorker.com/reporting/2010/10/04/101004fa _fact_gladwell?currentpage=all

Gray, R., Vitak, J., Easton, E. W., & Ellison, N. B. (2012). Examining social adjustment to college in the age of social media: Factors influencing successful transitions and persistence. *Computers & Education, 67,* 193–207.

Greckhamer, T., & Cilesiz, S. (2014). Rigor, transparency, evidence, and representation in discourse analysis: Challenges and recommendations. *International Journal of Qualitative Methods, 13,* 422–443.

Gulliam, T. L. (2012). "There's so much at stake": Sexual minority youth discuss dating violence. *Violence Against Women, 18*(7), 725–745.

Jones, S. (2002). *The Internet goes to college.* Retrieved from http://www.pewinternet.org/files /oldmedia/Files/Reports/2002/PIP_College_Report.pdf

Joyce, M. (2010). *Digital activism decoded: The new mechanics of change.* New York: International Debate Education Association.

Kelley, P. (2013). *Study shines light on what makes digital activism effective.* Retrieved from http://www.washington.edu/news

Kim, Y., & Khang, H. (2014). Revisiting civic voluntarism predictions of college students' political participation in the context of social media. *Computers in Human Behavior, 36,* 114–121.

Krebs, C. P., Lindquist, C., Warner, T., Fisher, B., & Martin, S. (2007). *The campus sexual assault (CSA) study.* Retrieved from https://www.ncjrs.gov/ pdffiles1/nij/grants/221153.pdf

Lampe, C., Ellison, N., & Steinfield, C. (2007). *A familiar Face(book): Profile elements as signals in an online social network.* Paper presented at the Conference on human factors in computing systems, New York.

Lampe, C., Wohn, D. Y., Vitak, J., Ellison, N., & Wash, R. (2011). Student use of Facebook for organizing collaborative classroom activities. *International Journal of Computer-supported Collaborative Learning, 6*(3), 329–347.

Lee, R. W., Caruso, M. E., Goins, S. E., & Southerland, J. P. (2003). Addressing sexual assault on college campuses: Guidelines for a prevention/awareness week. *Journal of College Counseling, 6*(1), 14–24. doi:10.1002/j.2161-1882.2003.tb00223.x

Lindlof, T. R., & Taylor, B. C. (2010). *Qualitative communication research methods.* Thousand Oaks, CA: Sage.

Madavanhu, S., & Radloff, J. (2013). Taking feminist activism online: Reflections on the 'Keep Saartjie Baartman Centre open'e-campaign. *Gender & Development, 21*(2), 327–341.

Medina, J. (2014). *Campus Killings set off anguish conversation.* Retrieved from http://www.nytimes.com/2014/05/27/us/campus-killings-set-off-anguished-conversation-about-the-treatment-of-women.html?_r=0

Miller, L. M. (2011). Physical abuse in a college setting: A study of perceptions and participation in abusive dating relationships. *Journal of Family Violence, 26*(1), 71–80.

Moody, M. (2010). Teaching Twitter and beyond: Tips for incorporating social media in traditional courses. *Journal of Magazine & New Media Research, 11*(2), 1–10.

O'Connor, L., & Lundstrom, K. (2011). The impact of social marketing strategies on the information seeking behaviors of college students. *Reference & User Quarterly, 50*(4), 351–356.

O'Malley, G. (2012, August 29). *The red flag campaign on campus.* Retrieved December 15, 2017, from https://obamawhitehouse.archives.gov/blog/2012/08/29/red-flag-campaign-campus

Paul, E. L., & Brier, S. (2001). FriendSickness in the transition to college: Precollege predictors and college adjustment correlates. *Journal of Counseling and Development, 79*(1), 77–89.

Pempek, T. A., Yermolayeva, Y. A., & Calvert, S. L. (2009). College students' social networking experiences on Facebook. *Journal of Applied Developmental Psychology, 30*(3), 227–238.

Perrin, A. (2015, October 8). *Social media usage: 2005–2015.* Retrieved from http://www.pewinternet.org/2015/10/08/social-networking-usage-2005-2015/

Peuchaud, S. (2014). *Social media activism and Egyptians' use of social media to combat sexual violence: An HiAP case study.* Paper presented at The Eighth Global Conference on Health Promotion, Helsinki, Finland.

RAINN (2017). *Campus sexual violence: Statistics.* Retrieved December 15, 2017, from https://www.rainn.org/statistics/campus-sexual-violence

Red flag campaign brings domestic violence awareness to GCC. Gateway Community College. Retrieved April 4, 2022 from https://gatewayct.edu/Offices-Departments/Public-Affairs/News/News-Items/Red-Flag-Campaign-Brings-Domestic-Violence-Awarene

Reinharz, S. (1992). *Feminist methods in social research.* New York: Oxford University Press.

RFC (2015). *Overview.* Retrieved December 15, 2017, from http://www.theredflagcampaign.org/welcome/

Rogers, K., & Green, E. L. (2021, 16 June). Biden will revisit Trump rules on campus sexual assault. *New York Times.* Retrieved on April 4, 2022 from https://www.nytimes.com/2021/03/08/us/politics/joe-biden-title-ix.html

Robinson, K. (2013). *Social media shaming: When sexual assault goes "viral".* Retrieved from http://www.thehotline.org/2013/05/social-media-shaming-when-sexual-assault-goes-viral/

Rubin, H. J., & Rubin, I. S. (2005). *Qualitative interviewing: The art of hearing data* (2nd ed.). Thousand Oaks, CA: Sage.

Salter, M. (2013). Justice and revenge in online counter-publics: Emerging responses to sexual violence in the age of social media. *Crime Media Culture, 9*, 225–242.

Sandra, L. (2013). Quiet no longer, rape survivors put pressure on colleges. *Chronicle of Higher Education, 59*, A20–A22.

Smith, A., Rainie, L., & Zickuhr, K. (2011, July 19). *College students and technology.* Pew Research Center: Internet, Science & Technology. Retrieved April 11, 2022, from https://www.pewresearch.org/internet/2011/07/19/college-students-and-technology/

Svensson, J., Neumayer, C., Banfield-Mumb, A., & Schossbock, J. (2015). Identity negotiation in activist participation. *Communication, Culture & Critique, 8*, 144–162.

Stalmeijer, R. E., Mcnaughton, N., & Van Mook, W. N. K. A. (2014). Using focus groups in medical education research: AMEE Guide No. 91. *Medical Teacher, 36*(11), 923–939.

Bureau of Justice Statistics. (2014). *Nonfatal domestic violence, (2014).* Bureau of Justice Statistics. Retrieved from https://bjs.ojp.gov/library/publications/nonfatal-domestic-violence-2003-2012

Bureau of Justice Statistics. (2015). *National Crime Victimization Survey (NCVS).* Bureau of Justice Statistics. Retrieved from https://bjs.ojp.gov/data-collection/ncvs

van Zoonen, L. (1994). *Feminist media studies.* Thousand Oaks, CA: Sage.

Velasquez, A., & LaRose, R. (2015). Social media for social change: Social media political efficacy and activism in student activism groups. *Journal of Broadcasting & Electronic Media, 59*(3), 456–474.

Vie, S. (2014). In defense of "slacktivism": The human rights campaign Facebook logo as digital activism. *First Monday, 19*, 4–7.

Zheng, W., Tchernev, J. M., & Solloway, T. (2012). A dynamic longitudinal examination of social media use, needs, and gratifications among college students. *Computers and Human Behavior, 28*(5), 1829–1839.

11
USING SOCIAL MEDIA TOOLS TO CONTRIBUTE TO AND CHALLENGE GENDERED VIOLENCE

Victoria Carty

Introduction

New information and communication technologies (ICTs) and social media tools, including social, mobile, and interactive media, have had a great impact on how individuals communicate, interact, and relate to each other. Gender relations have not been immune to these technological advancements. However, ICTs can be used as a source of online harassment, cyberbullying, and sexual violence to sabotage, embarrass, threaten, and bully those being preyed on, and now at an accelerated speed and volume through the availability of cheap and easy means to widely distribute images and comments. Sexual violence involving social media goes beyond physical violence and includes emotional, psychological, and verbal abuse through communication and is a form of cyberbullying. Cases of virtual sexual harassment, threats, and bullying can exceed those in the material world. For example, according to a 2014 Pew Research Center survey, 25% of women aged 18–24 reported being sexually harassed online, while 23% say they have been physically threatened (Duggan, 2014). Research interviewing women who had left or were attempting to leave abusive relationships found that electronic communications played a significant role in 90% of domestic violence situations (Dimond et al., 2011).

On the other hand, ICTs can also be used as a form of resistance to challenge and prosecute those who engage in forms of online harassment and gendered violence. In some situations, the digital traces left behind by the perpetrators of the sexual violence or online harassment provide evidence for the authorities to prosecute them. They can also serve as a platform to embrace social justice and feminist agendas against sexual assault and other forms of gender discrimination against women. In many instances, individuals and groups coordinate online through weak ties to protests against gendered violence. Sometimes this leads to

DOI: 10.4324/9781003260851-14

the "spillover" effect—meaning that online organizing morphs into protest on the streets as part of a social movement.

This chapter examines issues related to how new technologies can serve as a platform for sexual harassment and violence as well as a forum in which to challenge bullying and violent behaviors by exploring a number of brief case studies that took place from 2012 to 2017. The first part provides an overview of social movement theory but only as it pertains to the digital revolution, and how this has impacted contentious politics regarding social justice issues. I then address issues of sexting and bullying as it affects both teenage females and members of the LGBTQ community. These issues also shed light on how digital traces left in cyberspace and digital phones can help track down perpetrators of crimes related to gendered violence. The next section discusses examples of the spillover effect as online campaigns often turn into local and international protests in public spaces, illustrating the effectiveness of hybrid forms of activism. The chapter ends with examples of tactics used by activists to challenge a range of forms of misogyny.

Social Movement Organizing and New Technology

Theorists have long noted that social networks, relational ties, and friendships are invaluable resources in serving as a conduit of information and as a channel through which to recruit people to a cause, and especially for high-risk protest movement actions (Verba et al., 1995). Other research has found that an invitation through a personal (preexisting) tie is one of the strongest predictors of individuals' engagement in activism (Gould, 1991), which in turn fosters collective identity. ICTs expand the potential of these networks to develop and mutate exponentially, and especially through weak ties across diffuse networks and among individuals who might not receive this information through any other communicative format (Giungi, 1998). Contrary to what some theorists feared, that the advent of digital information communication technologies would replace collective identity and weaken the capacity for collective behavior in real communities (for example see Hindman, 2008; Jordan, 2001), mediated forms of communication often *complement* those based on face-to-face interaction and have a positive effect on political participation (Boulianne, 2009; Carty, 2015). The instantaneous peer-to-peer sharing also allows technologically enabled networks to serve as hybrids in that they do not result in mere "clicktivism" but rather encourage viewers of information to engage in contentious politics. New media technologies also substantially shift the way that activists can create, distribute, and consume information. This broadens the public sphere of communication by allowing organizers to quickly and cheaply reach a critical mass, in contrast to the one-to-many flow of information through mainstream media (Kahn & Kellner, 2003).

Additionally, Tufekci (2012) argues that new digital technology and social media also facilitate the development of community in spite of physical distance, creating virtual public spheres and encourage new organizational structures of social movements. This new media ecology, and its virtual infrastructure, helps to build networks of coordinated action that are loosely articulated, decentralized, egalitarian, and pluralistic. We will see how this has assisted a new kind of cyber feminism when it comes to violence against women as activists establish new forms of collective identity online that leads to protest on the streets. First, however, I will explore the darker side of how new digital technologies and social media enable gendered violence.

Cyberbullying and Sexting

Cyberbullying consists of often, but not always, anonymous forms of harassment that are threatening toward an individual. Females are the targets more so than males, but the LGBTQ community is also at high risk, especially when it comes to bullying and shaming LGBTQ teens (Fairbairn et al., 2013). Additionally, cyberbullying can take on the form of recording and distributing incidents of sexual assault through social media. Thus, bystanders sometimes become part of the bulling process when they share photographs or other information of the targets of the violence. In some circumstances, this has resulted in acts of suicide by those who were the subjects of the bullying.

The tragic case of Audrie Pott is an example of this. She was a 15-year-old high school student in California who was sexually assaulted at a party by three boys and was later subject to further bullying and revictimization after pictures of the assault were posted online. The pictures showed her naked and passed out with pen marks all over her body (Sulek, 2015). Pott hanged herself days after the assault. Her death was a tragedy and a result of sexting of images of her assault among other teenagers. She received dozens of Facebook messages from classmates and friends berating and making fun of her about the rape (Burleigh, 2013). The night after the attack she sent messages via Facebook to her male "friends." In one post, she stated, "I swear to god if u still have those pictures ill kill u." In another exchange, one of the males at the party Facebooked "lol that shit gets around haha everyone knows mostly everything hahaah." Audrie replied "oh my god…I fucking hate people." In yet another, she wrote on Facebook to another boy, "My life is over….I ruined my life and I don't even remember how" (Burleigh, 2013). In 2014, California Governor Jerry Brown signed Audrie's Law. The bill added penalties for cyberbullying and decreased privacy protections for teens convicted of sex acts on someone who was not conscious or responsive due to their intoxication or being under the influence of drugs, and could therefore not give consent to sexual activity.

After Audrie's suicide, there was an investigation into the case. Police removed one of suspects from class on September 14th and cited him with a misdemeanor. They then interviewed the other two boys and cited them as well. Digital traces of the assault were critical in the prosecution of the boys, but there was also an attempt to obstruct the investigation once students became aware of the seriousness of the case. By the time the police interviewed students, word had spread about who was being called into the school authorities' offices and why. One of Audrie's friends was overheard telling a student, "Shut down your Facebook, cops are looking" (Burleigh, 2013). After police received a search warrant to check the phones for each of the suspects, on September 21st, one of the boy's phones was broken and the other was lost. On April 11th, seven months later, the Santa Clara County sheriff arrested the three boys on charges of misdemeanor sexual battery, felony possession of child pornography, and felony sexual penetration. The police confiscated the new phones that their parents had purchased for them and found pictures of other nude teen girls, so they added new charges in July. Two of the boys admitted being guilty of the extra felonies of possessing or controlling sexual photographs of girls under 18 (Burleigh, 2013). However, the punishment of 30 and 45 days, critics protested, was too light a sentence and calls into question how seriously the courts took the rape and sexual cyberbullying.

Typical of many rape cases, the victim was in part on trial herself and excuses were made for the victimizers. Attorneys portrayed Pott as troubled and emphasized that the boys had never committed other crimes. Saratoga school officials also balked at taking responsibility and denied that her suicide had anything to do with what occurred at the school (the bullying). Students, teachers, and the overall community were divided. Some viewed the incident and aftermath as an innocent prank, and the boys as deserving of sympathy because they did not think it was a crime. Others wanted the boys severely punished for the engagement in sexual violence and sexting which led to endless online harassment. Teachers also came under scrutiny as one of Pott's friends stated that the teachers knew about the bullying but did nothing to stop it (Burleigh, 2013). This incident, therefore, highlights some of the difficulties in prosecuting those accused of cyberbullying and the underlying sexism within the criminal justice system.

In another instance, displaying the harmful effects of sexting and gendered online harassment, in April of 2013, 17-year-old Canadian Rehtaeh Parsons hanged herself following the online distribution of photographs of four boys raping her. The assault occurred 17 months prior to her suicide. She had very little memory of the assault as she was intoxicated at the time. The photographs were shared among members of the community and her classmates, some of whom called her a "slut." She also received text and Facebook messages from people wanting to have sex with her (Fuchs, 2013). The two 18-year-old boys and the two minors were charged with disseminating child pornography. In September 2014, one who had turned 20 pleaded guilty to a charge of making child pornography, and in November of that same year, another was sentenced to a conditional discharge and mandated to serve probation for 12 months. Also in November another pleaded guilty to the distribution of child pornography and was sentenced to a year of probation (Dissell, 2013).

On a Facebook page called Angel Rehtaeh, which she created in a memorial to her daughter, Parsons' mother blamed the four boys who raped and released images of her. She was also very critical of the subsequent constant bullying and harassment, as well as the failure of the Canadian justice system to handle the case appropriately. For example, the boys were not immediately questioned and their phones were not reviewed for the photographs of the rape. Instead, the police called it a "he said, she said" case. The blog of Rehtaeh's father also went viral. On it he stated, "The two boys involved in taking and posing for the photograph stated Rehtaeh was throwing up when they had sex with her. That is not called consensual sex. That is called rape" (Fuchs, 2013). The story drew international attention and sparked outrage on the Internet, with CBC reporting on the case, and the phrase "Nova Scotia" trended globally for weeks. Ultimately, in response to Parsons' suicide, Nova Scotia enacted a law in August 2013 allowing victims to seek protection from cyberbullying and to sue the perpetrator. Unfortunately, and similar to the Audie's Law, this was too little too late for the victims and demonstrates a lack of institutional support for rape victims until there are challenges to the system, in these cases after a tragic suicide due to sexting and bullying in cyberspace.

Another case, this one concerning an LGBTQ victim, also drew national prominence when Rutgers University student, Tyler Clementi committed suicide by jumping off the George Washington Bridge in 2012. His roommate, Dharun Ravi, after agreeing to allow Clementi to have their shared dorm room to himself for the night, used a webcam to spy on him and his male date (McGeehan, 2016). After recoding the sexual activity between the two, Ravi encouraged others to view the encounter. He tweeted, "Roommate asked for the room till midnight. I went into Molly's room and turned on my webcam. I saw him making out with a dude. Yah!" (Pilkington, 2010). Clementi committed suicide not long after he learned that he had been spied on and that images of his sexual encounter had been circulating online and through social media. Though Ravi was not charged with murder, he pleaded guilty to attempted invasion of privacy. The appeals court judge overturned the conviction but censured his actions by declaring;

> The social environment that transformed a private act of sexual intimacy into a grotesque voyeuristic spectacle must be unequivocally condemned in the strongest possible way. The fact that this occurred in a university dormitory, housing first-year college students, only exacerbates our collective sense of disbelief and disorientation.
>
> *(McGeehan, 2016)*

In response to Parson's suicide, in August 2013, Nova Scotia enacted a law that allows victims of cyberbullying to sue the individuals or the parents in the case of minors (CBC News, 2013).

Each of these cases demonstrates the dangers, and literally matters of life and death, related to the nature of sexting and cyberbullying. The combination of the millennial generation having grown up with digital media and new ICTs, and the culture on many college and high school campuses in which administrators and other authority figures turn a blind eye, or downplay the seriousness of

sexual violence and sexual cyberbullying against young women, is further analyzed in the next two cases. One helpful sign is that political officials and other
authorities are enacting new laws that take sexting and online forms of bullying
more seriously and distribute harsher punishments.

Stanford University Assault: Male Class and Privilege vs. Justice for the Victim

In January of 2015 a 23-year-old woman, who had been visiting Stanford University and attended a fraternity party, was informed by news reports that witnesses
found her, missing much of her clothing, behind a dumpster being assaulted by
a male Stanford student, Brock Turner. Turner was attending the university on
a swimming scholarship (Stack, 2016). The witnesses stopped the assault and
detained Turner until the police arrived. The victim was unconscious at the time
and later had no memory of the assault. Turner faced up to 14 years in state prison
but was ultimately sentenced to only six months in jail and three years' probation
for three felony counts of sexual assault. What ensued was a recall effort against
the Santa Clara judge, Aaron Persky, who concluded that, "A prison sentence
would have a severe impact on him. I think he will not be a danger to others"
(Hunt, 2016). Groups and individuals rallied to the victim's support, questioning
the legal process and sentencing. The main contention was that this was an obvious case of class and male privilege. Turner's defense attorney also brought up
the victim's attire the evening of the assault, exploiting the sexist argument that
women should dress a certain way to avoid rape, thus re-victimizing the victim.

During the trial, the victim read an approximately 7,000-word statement
about the role of privilege in the trial. She stated:

> The probation officer weighed the fact that he has surrendered a hard-
> earned swimming scholarship. How fast Brock swims does not lessen the
> severity of what happened to me, and should not lessen the severity of his
> punishment. If a first-time offender from an underprivileged background
> was accused of their felonies and displayed no accountability for his actions
> other than drinking, what would his sentence be? The fact that Brock was
> an athlete at a private university should not be seen as entitlement to leni-
> ency, but as an opportunity to send a message that sexual assault is against
> the law regardless of social class.
>
> *(Stack, 2016)*

Her statement was published by BuzzFeed, an internet news media site, the next
day, and then went viral (Stack, 2016). It was eventually viewed over 5 million
times on the BuzzFeed site. That same day one of the anchors for CNN, Ashleigh
Banfield, recited the entire statement on the air supporting her argument that
the court was more concerned with Turner's athletic career and academic future
than the victim's well-being (Stack, 2016). Looking at the broader picture, in an
editorial, the *San Jose Mercury News* referred to the sentencing of Brock as a "slap

on the wrist" and an "utter failure to seriously address the issue of campus rape" (Kaplan, 2016). In a similar vein, the Santa Clara, California district attorney, Jeff Rosen said in a formal statement that the sentence "did not fit the crime. Campus rape is no different than off-campus rape. Rape is rape" (Kaplan, 2016).

The lack of awareness of the seriousness of the crime, and of the emotional and physical toll this had on the victim was perhaps most clearly displayed through statements made by Turner's father that he read in court and spoke about to the media. He opined in the media that his son's life was ruined for "twenty minutes of action," and that his only real mistake was that he was drinking (Stack, 2016). He further stated that his son should not do jail time for the sexual assault, which he referred to as "the events" that were not violent. He also lamented that his son suffered from depression and anxiety in the wake of the trial and argued that having to register as a sex offender and the loss of his appetite for food he once enjoyed was punishment enough. He further elaborated,

> I was always excited to buy him a big rib-eye steak to grill or to get his favorite snack for him. Now he barely consumes any food and eats only to exist. These verdicts have broken and shattered him and our family in so many ways.
>
> *(Stack, 2016)*

Michele Dauber, a law professor and sociologist at Stanford University, helped to organize the recall challenge of Judge Persky (Murphy, 2016). She asserted that the judge had misapplied the law by granting Turner probation and by taking his age, academic achievement and alcohol consumption into consideration. She clarified "If you're going to declare that a high-achieving perpetrator is an unusual case, then you're saying to women on college campuses that they don't deserve the full protection of the law in the state of California." She also posted the statement on Twitter that was read to the court by the defendant's father. Following Professor Dauber's criticism of the judge, the next day, organizers used Change.org to send out a petition calling for the judge's removal and collected over 400,000 signatures of support (Jackson, 2016). Social media users also asked online why Turner's mug shot had not been released. The coverage only used his yearbook photograph with no connection to being a convicted sex offender. With the huge backing of Twitter users and others, a few media outlets did track down the mug shot, which then circulated widely online. The recall effort failed and Turner's light sentence remained, but online challenges to the ruling increased the awareness of the how rape on college campuses is often not handled appropriately by the courts.

Steubenville: Using ICTs to Catch and Prosecute Sexual Predators

In the Turner case, there were no recordings or distribution of images of the assault in cyberspace. While the lack of such evidence may have impacted the outcome of that trial, the Steubenville example specifically highlights that while sexual violence and intimidation can be distributed in the virtual sphere through new technology devices, these tools can also be used to catch and prosecute the assailants. In March of 2013, two Steubenville High School football stars of the "Big Red" football program (which is famous for winning several state championships), at a house party in Steubenville, OH were found guilty of gang-raping a 16-year-old girl (Oppel, 2013). One was sentenced to serve at least two years in the state juvenile system and the other player at least one year. The one who served an additional year was convicted of child pornography because he had sent out photographs of a minor in a sex act. Additionally, witnesses of the attack circulated dozens of text messages, videos, and cell-phone pictures to classmates of the victim naked and passed out. This played a major role in the initial prosecution of the suspects and later fed into the ensuing fury over the assault among citizens and groups across the United States (Oppel 2013).

Because the victim had passed out and therefore had no memory of the events, she was unable to testify on her own behalf. The facts of the case were therefore put together initially through the trail left by those at the party on digital media. The parents of the young woman, in fact, brought a flash drive to the authorities that was full of social media postings about the flagrant assault, and this initiated the investigation (Zirin, 2013). One Instagram message, for instance, included a picture of the unconscious girl accompanied by tweets that read "rape" and "drunk girl" (Zirin, 2013). The police then sought out the assailants, confiscated over a dozen cellphones and analyzed hundreds of text messages to find more evidence of the attack as well as the public sharing of the assault to create a re-enactment of the crime.

Yet, the damage of revictimization had already set in. Classmates and friends, people in the community and even the victim's family saw in full detail her sexual abuse. The group Anonymous' (an online and loosely organized group of individuals who advocate for various social justice issues) release of a video that one of the students involved in the assault recorded during and after one of the rapes helped to increase the awareness of the case both nationally and internationally (Welsh-Huggins, 2013). One of the rapes occurred in a car going to a party and the other in the basement of a house where the party was held (Welsh-Huggins, 2013). In mid-December, Anonymous sent out a "partial dox," which include a list of names and addresses of those allegedly involved in the rape. This was accompanied by a threat of further leaks if the alleged perpetrators failed to apologize by January 1st. When there was no apology, the group released the entire 12-minute video, which circulated online and further incriminated the two youths charged with rape, also embarrassing those present during the incident who chose to film, rather than stop the attack (Zirin, 2013).

The public became even more outraged with the discovery of an attempted cover-up by Steubenvile High School and its Big Red football program. Once again, it was the digital sphere that provided the evidence. For example, quarterback Trent Mays (one of the two who was later convicted) sent a text to one of his friends regarding a conversation with his coach saying, "I got Reno. He took care of it and shit ain't gonna happen, even if they did take it to court. Like he was joking about it. I'm not worried" (Grieco & McCarthy, 2013). This put the football program and the high school under even more scrutiny. The alleged criminals later realized the gravity of the situation, and Mays sent another text message to a friend asking him to stop the distribution of the video. He advised him, "Just say she came to our house and passed out" (Grieco & McCarthy, 2013). However, this would prove to be a futile attempt at damage control as the story had gained much traction both in cyberspace and in the mainstream media. In response to the growing accusations and outrage, town authorities launched a website of their own called "Steubenville Facts" in an attempt to defend themselves against the accusations of the cover-up.

Additionally, at an individual level, in an attempt to control the situation, and again demonstrating little understanding of the gendered violence that he had committed, in a text message to the victim Mays admitted that he sent the picture of her and spread it across social media. However, he claimed that it was consensual sex and that he was protecting her since she was drunk. He also asked her, through texts, not to press charges against him because it would harm his football aspirations. In one of his texts, he specifically stated: "This is the most pointless thing. I'm going to get in trouble for something I should be getting thanked for taking care of you." The reply from the victim was, "It's on YouTube. I'm not stupid. Stop texting me" (Macur & Schweber, 2012).

As tension in the community grew amidst the incoming evidence of both the incident and the cover-up, and in an effort to protect the school authorities and coaching staff against the mounting bad publicity and fear of physical violence, the school superintendent requested that armed guards be posted on the premises of the district schools (Grieco & McCarthy, 2013). This was after individuals, who were upset with the case procedure, posted threats made on Facebook. More than 1,000 protesters congregated outside of the county courthouse calling for an additional and more stringent case against the alleged rapists (Grieco & McCarthy, 2013). This shows how forms of hybrid activism can build strength through an interplay between the different forms of resistance and protest. Similar to the Turner case, one of the main grievances expressed initially in the virtual world was the reluctance of authorities to jeopardize athletic opportunities and compromise the futures of the criminals with little regard for the physical, psychological, and emotional damage done to the victim. In this case, the strong presence outside of the courthouse after reaching a critical mass via digital tools, also helped to garner attention from mainstream media, which then even furthered the cause as it came to more people's awareness and put pressure on the authorities to punish the boys. Thus, old and new social movement tactics to organize and protest complemented one another, resulting in the spillover effect in which a primarily online campaign against official procedures and policies evolved into protests in physical public spaces.

The protests against the handling of the Turner and Steubenville cases under-score the expression of outrage at the individual level regarding the assailants committing gendered violence. However, they also incriminate the structural conditions at the institutional level that enable perpetrators to get off with light sentences without concern for the traumatization of the victim.

Protests against Authorities' Response to Blaming the Victim: The SlutWalks Campaign

The SlutWalk protests are another example of how activism often starts out as an online campaign but later results in the spillover effect that embraces contentious politics in public spaces, in this case challenging the perception that women are at least partially responsible for being raped. The campaign began when, in January of 2011 a police officer in Toronto, while speaking to University students, made a callous remark that "women should avoid dressing like sluts in order to not be victims by rape" (Pilkington, 2011). In response to his comments, femi-nist activists organized protests in more than 75 cities across the world. The first march was held in Toronto, Ontario on April 2, 2011 and over 3,000 people gathered– over 2,000 more than organizers anticipated (Valenti, 2011). During the rally several people gave personal accounts, as rape victims of being victim-ized for their appearance or behavior. The protests spread globally, from Canada, the United States, Europe, Australia, and South Africa. Most of the organizing and awareness of the event was done through Facebook groups and other social media tools.

The group's Facebook page explained

> When we began SlutWalk, it was in our city as a response to a specific dynamic in Toronto and we had a very specific goal in mind: to demand better from protective services and institutions in our city of Toronto: we wanted to loudly and fiercely fight victim-blaming and slut-shaming men-talities and ideas that persistently circulate around sexual assault in our city.
> *(Gilmore, 2011)*

In essence, the protests are a resistance to excusing rape by referring to the vic-tim's appearance, including dress, or level of intoxication. Some women attended the demonstrations scantily dressed, wearing fishnets, and stilettos in an attempt to get a "shock" response that would attract media attention—it worked.

These protests and marches diverged greatly from mainstream, well-funded, and long-term planned types of organizing and activities employed by more established feminist groups. The SlutWalks protests are more spontaneous and connoted a new way for feminists to organize (Valenti, 2014). Online emotional outrage and sharing can originate in cyberspace and morph into demonstrations on the streets, which in turn reaches the global community online, where activ-ist begin their own local forms of protest. This is another great example of the spillover effect and the complementary role that new interactive digital tools can have on contentious politics that theorists of social movements speak to, but on a global level. It is also indicative of the evolving structure of many contemporary social movements, which tend to be leaderless and more flexible. Furthermore, in previous types of organizing, momentum and rage often ceased when a large demonstration came to an end. With new technological tools, it is much easier, faster and cheaper to keep that momentum alive in the virtual world as activists organize themselves using online interactive ICTs, until the next wave of protest action occurs in public spaces.

There are, however, some critics of the SlutWalks campaign, and especially its framing. Some feminists who have been working on gender issues for a long time view the term slut as "irredeemable" rather than a sense of empowerment by reclaiming it (Valenti, 2014). They also contend that the new and younger activists are not cognizant of class and race issues that have haunted the feminist movement for decades. Clarifying this concern, Harsha Walia wrote on the Canadian site Rabble, "I personally don't feel the whole 'reclaim slut' thing. I find that the term disproportionally impacts women of color and poor women to reinforce their status as inherently dirty and second-class" (Valenti, 2014). Gail Dines, an anti-pornography activist argues that the SlutWalks activists are playing into the hands of patriarchal attitudes; celebrating the word slut, and dressing in risqué clothing at demonstrations is an embrasure of what she refers to as a "pornified consumer mentality" (Valenti, 2014). There are other instances of sexual inequality that are both promoted and resisted in cyberspace, though not necessarily related to physical sexual abuse. Below I focus on issues related to misogyny and the degradation of women, and challenges to these dynamics.

Misogyny and Irresponsible Marketing: Other Types of Violence against Women

The Victoria's Secret Marketing Controversy

The upscale lingerie retail store, Victoria's Secret is no stranger to protest as feminist groups have, over the years, aggressively decried the body image that the company promotes. Many claim that the unrealistic body types they use in their marketing strategies contribute to eating disorders, unnecessary plastic surgery, and low self-esteem among females. One of the biggest protests occurred when the company ran its new PINK line of underwear that is marketed under the tagline "Bright Young Things" (Alexander, 2013). Some of the imprints on the undergarments read: "sure thing," "call me," and "feeling lucky." The main objections to the line were that the product trivializes rape and demeans women by insinuating that they are open to sex without being asked (Radley, 2013). Another strongly held grievance is that this marketing campaign sexualizes girls at an early age and gives confusing messages as some of the panties read "yes," "no," "maybe." Many of the challenges against the campaign originated online.

A pastor in Huston TX, who posted an open letter on his blog regarding the "Bright Young Things" line stated, "I don't want my daughter to ever think her self-worth and acceptance by others is based on the choice of her undergarments. In less than a week the blog was visited 3.5 million times (Radley, 2013).

A feminist group called FORCE: Upsetting Rape Culture electronically organized protests against the PINK line in conjunction with the national parental organization called Mommy Lobby. They mobilized supporters to organize outside of Victoria's Secret stores to shame the company. Attendees wore underwear that read, "no means no" and "ask first." This framed the message in a way that declares it is a woman's decision whether or not to have sex, and that it is not a given. They also held consent-theme parties and marches to raise awareness about rape and framed their events in a way that sought to emphasize the distinction between rape and consensual sex. At one event FORCE "consent enthusiasts" hosted Operation Panty Drop to satirize the line of underwear by leaving consent-themed panties in more than a dozen of Victoria's Secret stores across the United States (Arnowitz, 2013). FORCE also created an antirape website of Victoria's Secret called pinklove.com which led viewers to believe the company was re-releasing a new line of "flirty-sexy" underwear with "powerful statements" for its PINK lingerie line (Radley, 2013). This was a hoax, as there was no such product, but it went viral and spread rapidly over the Internet and social media platforms.

In an effort to stop the damage to its reputation Victoria's Secret contacted some of the companies that were hosting FORCE's and Mommy Lobby's information online, such as Facebook and Pinterest, to try to convince them to deny service to the challenging groups (Stampler, 2011). The company also tried to defend itself from the growing criticism electronically in another way. On its website Victoria's Secret claimed that the line of underwear and the advertising campaign was aimed at 18 to 21-year-olds. However, the CEO of the company, behind closed doors at conferences, was recorded admitting the truth of the marketing strategy. He stated: "When somebody's 15 or 16 years old, what do they want to be? They want to be older, and they want to be cool like the girl in college, and that's part of the magic power of PINK (Arnowitz, 2013).

A Change.org petition requesting that Victoria's Secret apologize and change the campaign garnered over 27,000 signatures (Stampler, 2011). It stated:

> Every day women are bombarded with advertisements aimed at making them feel insecure about their bodies in the hope that they will spend money on products that will supposedly make them happier and more beautiful. All this does is perpetuate low self-esteem among women who are made to feel that their bodies are inadequate and unattractive because they do not fit into a narrow standard of beauty. It contributes to a culture that encourages serious health problems such as negative body image and eating disorders.
>
> *(Stampler, 2011)*

After the pushback from customers and critics Victoria's Secret changed its website slogan to read: "a body for every body."

Misogyny, Other Forms of Women's Degradation, and Feminist Reactions

Many authors have written about the ways in which misogyny contributes to violence against women in both physical and virtual spaces. One clear instance involving both forms is the case of 22-year-old Elliot Roger, who had written about his anger toward women online in many YouTube posts, and subsequently shot and killed six college students and wounded 13 others in Santa Barbara, CA before committing suicide (Nagourney et al., 2014). In one particular YouTube video he promised revenge against the women who he said forced him to live "an existence of loneliness, rejection and unfulfilled desires." After the rampage the hashtag #YesAllWomen trended for weeks. Through Twitter thousands of women shared their stories about sexism and violence against women. The framing of the hashtag message was influential in the rebuke to the common response among men that "not all men" commit rape, or are misogynist, or are sexist. This framing of the message emphasizes that, though these statements may be true, the reality is that all women are impacted by those men who are (Valenti, 2014). Through these Twitter exchanges victims of misogynist behavior were able to forge a sense of collective identity without necessarily having face-to-face interaction, and also had a sense of connectivity and empowerment through interactive ICTs.

The troubling video of the professional football player, Ray Rice, punching his fiancé in the face in an elevator and knocking her unconscious, provoked a similar response. There were public inquiries in the mainstream media as to why his fiancé, Janay Rice stayed with him and later married him. Thousands of women used the hashtag #WhyIStayed posting their own personal stories of domestic violence on Twitter. (Dockterman, 2014). This is another instance where victims of abuse are able to establish connections that foster a sense of collective identity and verify their accounts and feelings, that in turn can then inform others who may have little understanding about the complexity of the issues, even if only online.

The 2016 presidential election also raised concerns about the degradation of women. Donald Trump's recorded statement stating that he could get away with grabbing women "by the pussy" was one of many examples of his disrespect for women (Kramer, 2017). Shannon Coulter, one of the founders of the #GrabYourWallet campaign, a movement to boycott supporting the financial growth of anything Trump-related, advocated that women use their purchasing power as a form of activism (Taylor, 2017). The group pressured major retailers such as Nordstrom, Amazon, T.J. Maxx and Macey's to stop carrying products related to the Trump family. The website listed about 50 companies to boycott, with the assumption that since Trump was a businessman, and ultimately about the bottom line, an impact on his profits would cause a disruption. They also addressed a broader plan in terms of tactics. For example, retailer L.L. Bean did not sell Trump merchandise but was targeted on the basis that the granddaughter of the company's founder donated $60,000 to a PAC that supported Trump (Taylor, 2017). The organization called for a boycott demanding that the granddaughter, Linda Bean, be removed from the board. The website also encouraged consumers to not shop at stores that carry the Ivanka brand. Petitions also included putting pressure on Gucci, Nike and Starbucks to reconsider their business strategy of selling products in Trump owned space.

Issues of degrading women also came to notoriety at the Fox News network. After several years of scandal regarding sexual harassment in the workplace including the resignation of Roger Ailes after the publication of Gretchen Carlson's book, the company fired popular host Bill O'Reilly. Over 20 women reported "degrading conduct" at the headquarters workplace (Acevedo, 2017) by O'Reilly and others. O'Reilly and the network were also complicit in a settlement of almost $13 million dollars that included five women making accusations of sexual harassment. In April 2017 an online group called UltraViolet, with an agenda to fight sexism and advance women's' rights, organized a protest in New York City outside of Fox News headquarters to put pressure on the network to fire O'Reilly (Acevedo, 2017). Hundreds protested holding signs that read, "Danger: Sexual Predator Works Here" and "Shame on Fox." UltraViolet also had a plane fly over Manhattan reading "FOX:#DROPOREILLY, THE SEXUAL PREDATOR. Additionally, it posted flyers around headquarters asking, "Have you also been sexually harassed by Bill? (Acevedo, 2017) and created an online petition requesting that advertisers pull their ads from the "O'Reilly Factor" broadcast, which over 360,000 people signed (McLaughlin, 2017). Colorofchange.org placed advertisements on Facebook and Google promoting the campaign, and also placed ads on the job-placement websites that targeted Fox News employees, offering financial and legal help to women who had been, or believed they were, subject to sexual harassment by O'Reilly. When over 50 companies pulled their advertisements from his show Fox eventually did fire O'Reilly.

These last two cases demonstrate the complementary and hybrid forms of social movement activity and resistance to gendered violence, either physical or verbal or both, that social media and interactive communication technologies afford. These hybrid forms are essential to how activist networks develop and mutate, and coordinate groups who might not otherwise receive information about a cause that is important to them or be moved to participate in contentious politics in physical public spaces. Technology in these cases has facilitated distribution of information and organization of individuals in protest against instances of harassment and assault.

Conclusion

As these cases illustrate, ICTs have greatly impacted how individuals interact, share information, and relate to each other. In terms of gender relations, there is great cause for concern given the climate of cyberbullying and online harassment. Revictimization is now a common occurrence as sexual assault can be recorded and shared widely, cheaply, and quickly. This has a devastating effect on victims of assault and as this chapter explores, can lead to desperation and even suicide. Institutions, from schools to the police to the courts, have been slow to respond to the concerns of victims and their families.

Yet, traces left in cyberspace by assailants have aided victims and their families' members to seek justice. Online tools also assist social justice and feminist agendas against various forms of sexual assault and discrimination against women. Weak ties and a form of collective identity forged through new interactive technology often lead to the development of hybrid forms of protest through a "spillover effect" whereby contentious politics in the streets is the outcome of online organizing and mobilizing. Thus, the digital revolution can be utilized as way to challenge sexting, cyberbullying, and other forms of gendered violence that are demeaning to their targets. This issue is of crucial importance because of the widespread ramifications of gendered violence that individuals can monitor, amplify, and distribute through social media. The case studies in this chapter illustrate the limitations and affordances of communication in virtual spaces to perpetrate misogyny, violence, and homophobia, but also to facilitate response and resistance to gendered violence.

References

Acevedo, Y. (2017, April 17). Bill O'Reilly: Women's group to fly plane banner over New York calling him a 'sexual predator'. *Indiewire*. http://www.indiewire.com/2017/04/bill-oreilly-sexual-harassment-claims-protest-fox-news-womens-group-ultraviolet-1201806415.

Alexander, E. (2013, March 26). *Victoria's secret criticized over bright young things campaign*. https://www.vogue.co.uk/article/victorias-secret-criticised-over-bright-young-things-campaign.

Arnowitz, L. (2013, March 29). Victoria's Secret nationwide protest planned by parenting organization boasting 50,00 members. *Fox News*. http://www.foxnews.com/entertainment/2013/03/29/victorias-secret-bright-young-things-protest.html.

Boulianne, S. (2009). Does Internet use affect engagement: A Meta-analysis of research. *Political Communication 26*(2), 193–211.

Burleigh, N. (2013). Sexting, shame and suicide. *Rolling Stone*. http://www.rollingstone.com/culture/news/sexting-shame-and-suicide-20130917.

Carty, V. (2015). *Social movements and new technology*. Boulder, CO: Westview Press.

CBC News (2013, August 7). Nova Scotia cyberbullying legislation allows victims to sue. *CBC News*. http://www.cbc.ca/news/canada/nova-scotia/n-s-cyberbullying-legislation-allows-victims-to-sue-1.1307338.

Dimond, J., Fielser, C., and Bruckman, A. (2011). Domestic violence and information communication technologies. *Interacting with Computers, 23*, 413–421.

Dissell, R. (2013, August 7). Two Steubenville football players are sentenced to youth prison for raping 16-year-old girl. *CBC News*. http://www.cbc.ca/news/canada/nova-scotia/n-s-cyberbullying-legislation-allows-victims-to-sue-1.1307338.

Dockterman, E. (2014, September 9). Why women stay: The Paradox of abusive relationships. *Time*. http://time.com/3309687/why-women-stay-in-abusive-relationships/.

Duggan, M. (2014, October 22). Online harassment. *PEW Research Center*. http://www.pewinternet.org/2014/10/22/online-harassment.

Fairbairn J., Bivens, R., and Dawson, M. (2013). Sexual violence and social media: Building a framework for prevention. *Report of OCTEVAW & Crime Prevention*, Ottawa, Canada. https://www.crimepreventionottawa.ca/wp-content/uploads/2019/02/Sexual-Violence-and-Social-Media-building-a-framework-to-prevention-full-report.pdf.

Fuchs, E. (2013, April 11). A Canadian teen hanged herself after everybody at school saw pictures of her alleged rape. *Business Insider*. http://www.businessinsider.com/rehtaeh-parsons-hangs-herself-2013-4.

Gilmore, S. (2011, Fall). Marcha de las putas: Slutwalking crosses global divides. *OnTheIssues*. http://www.ontheissuesmagazine.com/2011fall/2011fall_gilmore.php.

Giungi, M. (1998). Was it worth the effort? The Outcomes and consequences of social movements. *Annual Review of Sociology, 24*, 371–393.

Gould, R. (1991). Multiple networks and mobilization in Paris commune, 1871. *American Sociological Review 56*, 716–729.

Grieco, L., and McCarthy, M. (2013, January 16). *Social media under fire in Ohio rape case*. http://www.morrisherald-news.com/2013/01/16/social-media-under-fire-in-ohio-rape-case/auepthz.

Hindman, M. (2008). *The myth of digital democracy*. Princeton, NJ: Princeton University Press.

Hunt, E. (2016, June 26). 20 Minutes of action': Father defends Stanford student son convicted of sexual assault. *The Guardian*. https://www.theguardian.com/us-news/2016/jun/06/father-stanford-university-student-brock-turner-sexual-assault-statement.

Jackson, A. (2016, June 7). Over 400,000 people are calling for the removal of the judge who gave the ex-Stanford swimmer a 'lenient' sentence. *Business Insider*. http://www.businessinsider.com/brock-turner-petition-to-remove-judge-2016-6.

Jordan, T. (2001). Measuring the Internet: Host counts versus business plans. *Information Communication and Society (4)*1, 34–53.

Kahn, R., and Kellner, D. (2003). Internet subcultures and oppositional politics. In *The post-subcultures reader*, Muggleton, D. (Ed.). London: Berg, pp. 299–304.

Kaplan, T. (2016, June 14). Brock Turner: DA gets judge kicked off new sex case. *San Jose Mercury News*. http://www.mercurynews.com/2016/06/14/brock-turner-da-gets-judge-kicked-off-new-sex-case.

Kramer, M. (2017). Could a 'boycott Trump' movement change his policies? *Alernet*. http://www.gopdebates.org/tag/could-a-boycott-trump-movement-change-his-policies.

Macur, J., and Schweber, N. (2012, December 17). Rape case unfolds on web and splits case. *New York Times*. htttp://www.nytimes.com/2012/12/17/sports/high-school-football-rape-case-unfolds-online-and-divides-steubenville-ohio.html.

McGeehan, P. (2016, September 10). Conviction thrown out for ex-Rutgers student in Tyler Clementi case. *New York Times*. https://www.nytimes.com/2016/09/10/nyregion/conviction-thrown-out-for-rutgers-student-in-tyler-clementi-case.html.

McLaughlin, M. (2017, April 29). Petition demands Fox News fire Bill O'Reilly over harassment claims. *Huffington post*. http://www.huffingtonpost.com/entry/petition-fox-news-bill-oreilly_us_57c470b6e4b0664f13c9b2f2.

Murphy, K. (2016, June 9). Stanford Professor Michele Dauber leads effort to recall judge. *Santa Cruz Sentinel*. http://www.santacruzsentinel.com/article/NE/20160609/NEWS/160609736.

Nagourney, A., Cieply, M., and Feur, A and Lovett, I. (2014, June 2). Before brief, deadly spree, trouble since age 8 Elliot O. Rodger's killings in California followed years of withdrawal. *New York Times*. https://www.nytimes.com/2014/06/02/us/elliot-rodger-killings-in-california-followed-years-of-withdrawal.html.

Oppel, R. (2013, March 18). Ohio teenagers guilty in rape that social media brought to light. *The New York Times*. http://www.nytimes.com/2013/03/18/us/teenagers-found-guilty-in-rape-in-steubenville-ohio.html.

Pilkington, E. (2010, September 30). Tyler Clementi, student outed as gay on internet, jumps to his death. *The Guardian*. https://www.theguardian.com/world/2010/sep/30/tyler-clementi-gay-student-suicide.

Pilkington, E. (2011, May 6). Slutwalking gets rolling after cop's loose talk about provocative clothing. *The Guardian*. https://www.theguardian.com/world/2011/may/06/slutwalking-policeman-talk-clothing

Radley, W. (2013, March 28). *Houston pastor's protest against Victoria's Secret "Bright Young Things" lingerie ad goes viral*. http://houston.culturemap.com/news/fashion/03-28-13-houston-pastors-protest-against-victorias-secret-bright-young-things-lingerie-ad-goes-viral/.

Stack, L. (2016, June 9). In Stanford rape case, Brock Turner blamed drinking and promiscuity. *The New York Times*. https://www.nytimes.com/2016/06/09/us/brock-turner-blamed-drinking-and-promiscuity-in-sexual-assault-at-stanford.html.

Stampler, L. (2011). SlutWalks sweep the nation. *Huffington Post*. http://www.bing.com/search?q=Stampler, +Laura.

Sulek, J. (2015, April 1). Audrie Pott trial: Lawyers battle over moving trial out of San Jose and naming defendants. *San Jose Mercury News*. http://www.mercurynews.com/2015/04/01/audrie-pott-trial-lawyers-battle-over-moving-trial-out-of-san-jose-and-naming-defendants.

Taylor, K. (2017). An anti-Trump movement is calling for the boycott of 51 companies. *Business Insider*. http://www.businessinsider.com/author/kate-taylor.

Tufekci, Z. (2012, August 30). New media and the people-powered uprisings. *MIT Technology Review*. https://www.technologyreview.com/2011/08/30/191614/new-media-and-the-people-powered-uprisings/

Valenti, J. (2011, June 3). Slut Walks and the future of feminism. *Washington Post*. https://fourc.ca/wp-content/uploads/2011/11/SlutWalks-and-the-future-of-feminism.pdf

Valenti, J. (2014, May 24). Elliot Rodger's California spree: Further proof that misogyny kills. *The Guardian*. https://www.theguardian.com/commentisfree/2014/may/24/elliot-rodgers-california-shooting-mental-health-misogyny.

Verba, S., Schlozman, K. L., and Brady, H. (1995). *Voice and Equality*. Cambridge MA: Harvard University Press.

Welsh-Huggins, A. (2013, March 17). Online threats complicate Ohio school rape case. http://www.timesunion.com/news/article/Ohio-football-players-found-guilty-in-4361355.php.

Zirin, D. (2013). Why did Steubenville renew the football coach's contract? *The Nation*. https://www.thenation.com/article/dave-zirin-why-did-steubenville-renew-football-coachs-contract.

INDEX

Note: Page numbers followed by "n" denote endnotes.

For Product Safety Concerns and Information please contact our EU
representative GPSR@taylorandfrancis.com
Taylor & Francis Verlag GmbH, Kaufingerstraße 24, 80331 München, Germany

www.ingramcontent.com/pod-product-compliance
Lightning Source LLC
Chambersburg PA
CBHW070326270326
41926CB00017B/3772

9 7 8 1 0 3 2 1 9 7 9 1 3